TEARS FOR A TINKER

JESSIE'S JOURNEY CONCLUDES

JESS SMITH

mercatpress
www.mercatpress.com

First published in 2005 by Mercat Press Ltd
10 Coates Crescent, Edinburgh EH3 7AL
www.mercatpress.com

ISBN: 184183 078X

Cover photograph courtesy of Barrie Law

Set in Bembo and Adobe Jenson at Mercat Press

Printed and bound in Great Britain by Bell & Bain Ltd

CONTENTS

ILLUSTRATIONS

Between pages 56 and 57:

Coronation of the Gypsy King, Charles Faa Blythe
Camp of Highland travellers at Pitlochry
Isabella Macdonald, tinsmith
Nineteenth-century travellers at the berry-picking
Strathdon tinkers
A camp high in the hills
Tinkers' cave, Wick

Between pages 152 and 153:

Jess's father during the Second World War
Jess's mother and father in 1942
Jess's children—Barbara, Stephen and Johnnie
Jess's husband, Dave
Jess with Johnnie and Stephen in 1983
Jess today

Acknowledgements

Once more, to the army of workers who shouted at me, prodded and hugged me, and phoned my ears into oblivion: thanks forever.

To my family—well, what can I say?

To Mamie, for allowing me to share her father Keith's poem.

To Douglas Petrie from Pitlochry for his river poems.

To Martha Stewart for all her help, and her belief in Scotland's travelling people.

To cousin Alan for the Glen Lyon tale.

To Bob Dawson, my radji gadji, who never sleeps.

To Robbie Shepherd and his team for giving me a louder voice.

To Caroline Boxer of the *Strathearn Herald*, a wee worker.

To Alan Smith and family from Foggy.

To John Gilbert for allowing me to use his grandfather's poem.

To the late Violet Jacob.

Special thanks to Charlotte Munro (sister Shirley), for always being there regardless—'Ye cannae sleep us away'.

To Jenny and George—gone, but never forgotten.

To Tom, Seán, Caroline, Vikki.

Finally, thanks to the travelling people; my tinkers of the roads; the roots wherein I cleave.

> *Come all you tramps and hawker lads,*
> *Come listen one and a',*
> *An' I'll tell tae ye a roving tale o' sichts that I hae seen,*
> *Far up and to the snowy north and doon by Gretna Green.*

—all gone now.

I dedicate this book to my wee Mammy,
who dedicated her life to her eight daughters

INTRODUCTION

Something niggled in my mind after I finished *Tales from the Tent*. It nagged and bothered me. I put on the kettle, poured a cup of tea and slumped down in that old tattered armchair of mine that refuses to die. Heidi, my cat of twenty or so years, curled into a ball of ginger and white fluff, licked her old, weak paw, yawned and settled for sleep. Then, as if a veil had lifted from my eyes, I saw in my mind what it was that so annoyed me. Remembering how brittle Heidi's frame was, I gathered her into my skirt and darted back to the computer screen. Two tiny words leapt from the last page of my manuscript—'The End'.

How could it be?! I hadn't shared the stories of my parents' childhood with you, nor some whoppers about Dave and my earlier wanderings. What about Glen Lyon, and Daisy thinking the Germans during the last war would steal the washing off the dyke, so she kept it in? What did she know of Europe? To her Germany was somewhere north of Inverness! And those fearsome ghost stories? How many times did I laugh at my father's tall tales, I did so want to tell you about them. Och, nae way could we part, you and I, after all this time, without telling you of my nit-infested wild man who drove Mammy mental whenever we saw him on the road. The story of the row of turnips I pretended to some towny bairns was a row of rabbits just had to be shared, and so many more happy days. No, it certainly wasn't 'the end'.

Anyway how could I part from you? You'd become my good friends, fellow dog-walkers and tea-suppers.

So, gently uncurling the half-dead fluff ball from the threads of my skirt and laying her on a fleecy blanket beneath the radiator, I finished my now cold tea.

If you fancy another journey with me, settle back with your favoured beverage and let's take once more to the road in: *Tears for a Tinker.*

The reason for the title is a story in itself.

My oldest son Johnny, then aged six, was not a happy chappie. You see, his wee pal Horace had died. This little pet, a goldfish his dad had spent loads of money trying to win at a fair, was our lad's nearest and dearest in the entire world. He shared all his sorrows with that fish for the best part of a year, when one morning his heart broke at finding it tail-fin up at the top of its bowl. To take his mind off this tragedy we took the bus to Perth, the nearest town with toy-shops. Christmas being round the corner, Perth was crowded and draped in sparkly lights. In the centre outside Woolworth's, Johnny saw a poor travelling woman with four bairns round her coat hem. All the wee ones were in tears. Poor gentle-hearted Johnny said to me, 'Mammy, what is wrong with them bairns?'

'I'll tell you when we get home,' I told him, adding, 'now stop staring at people.'

That night after supper, with Horace laid to rest in a matchbox buried underneath a soft patch on the washing green, my little boy brought up the subject of the traveller and her sad, wet-eyed children.

I knew the woman, not personally, but recognised her from her kin, who usually winter-camped in bowed tents near Lochgilphead. Sometimes they favoured Double Dykes. This was a large boggy field on the outskirts of Perth, and now, thanks to the efforts of hardy travelling folks, it had been turned into a properly-run caravan site.

'Well, my lad,' I said, sitting him on my knee and squeezing him gently, 'that poor woman had no husband. Those bairns didn't have a daddy like you to bring in money for food.'

He asked where their dad was, but at six-years-old his young ears were not ready to hear that the man was burned to death in a warehouse fire in Glasgow. I simply said that he died of a bad illness.

I know telling lies is not a good parent thing, but Johnny was a sensitive child.

His little eyes widened, and I could see the brain cells painting a picture of kids without a dad. I went on, 'those tears were caused by their mother rubbing onions around their eyes to make them cry.' This seemed to horrify my child. He jumped off my knee, eyes wider than ever in disgust and wonderment. 'How could a mother do that?' he raised his voice. I looked into his little reddened face and calmed him down. 'Son', I assured him, 'no mother loves her children more than a travelling mother, but those kids had to beg, and that was her quick and authentic way of doing it. Long ago—well, if after the last war was long ago—that woman's menfolk would have owned tinkering tools to fix pitchforks and knives, pots and pans; in fact any kind of broken metal would have been sorted, and that would bring in money. She would have had a job if it were the olden days. They used to be called tinkers because of the noise their tools made as they carried them on horse bags or wee bogeys, and later, prams.'

He didn't understand much of what I told him, nor the word authentic, but he got enough of the explanation to learn that onions make you cry, and crying brings caring folks to part with a few coppers. 'If that mother had begged for money, folks would have looked the other way. The tears unwittingly made them give generously. Tears reach our souls. And I know that for every person who gave, she would have blessed them with a prayer to God.'

Silence followed, and both Dave and I could see our wee boy deep in thought. In time he went into the bathroom, and came out with tears flowing down his small face. 'What in heaven's name is wrong, laddie?' asked his concerned father, whilst I was busy feeding Barbara, our youngest, who was three at the time.

'Those wee tinker bairns without a daddy made onion tears. Well, I have cried some real ones for them.'

Johnnie was cradling in his hand a photograph of his dear departed Horace.

When our children grew older, I would often tell them stories of my own tinker childhood, and to this day they are proud that mother belongs to a cultural background rich in ballads, stories, and with a lifeline going back two thousand years.

Well, where will I start? Yes, let's go back to Crieff, just after Stephen, our second lad, was born. We were living in a rented flat, part of a large Georgian house. If you have refilled your cup, then let's walk back again, back down memory lane.

1

MAMMY, WHAT NICE PICTURES IN THIS CAR

Davie had a succession of jobs, but all paying next to nothing, and this meant very little money for anything other than the bare necessities. My in-laws, Margaret and Sandy, were super at keeping the kids in clothes, sometimes paying the odd bill when we struggled with other debts. Sandy worked at Naval Stores near Almondbank, three miles from Perth. In his spare time he excelled as a poulterer for John Lows, fishmonger in Crieff. Margaret had taken jobs cleaning hotels and offices. Davie had a younger brother, Alex, who was a wee brain-box. Much to his parents' delight, he was always studying, head down in books. Alistair had been their oldest son, but at twenty-one years old, while serving in Germany with Her Majesty's Royal Engineers, he was killed by an express train. Margaret never got over the loss of her boy, avoiding any conversation that might open her wounds. In her own way of dealing with his death, she kept quiet and to herself.

I sometimes wondered if I was good enough for her son, me being from travelling stock, but she made me welcome from the first moment we met, and we stayed friends until her death of cancer many years later.

Mammy and Daddy had uprooted themselves and headed for Macduff on the Moray coast. A picturesque house nestled at the top of the town became their home, and if memory serves me right the street they lived on was Patterson Street. Macduff is built on a steep hill, so the views of the ocean from that house were spectacular.

When we visited them for the first time I didn't want to go away, it was so fresh and beautiful. Even the sea-gulls had a kind of regal glide to their wings.

Dave and I bought a cheap scrap-heap of a car for the journey, a white Ford Popular it was, from a 'This is a bargain, honest, folks' mate. From Crieff to Macduff is 140 miles, and how we survived that trip was a miracle to say the least. Round about Perth it became apparent that the vehicle had a few more openings than just the doors and windows. Johnnie sat alone in the back, and kept telling us he could see brown and black ribbons, and what a bonny picture they made at his feet, also that he wasn't comfortable due to a lumpy bit on the seat. We ignored him, putting his remarks down to the vivid imaginings of a toddler. I sat in the front with Stephen on my knee. This was before seat-belts, and when I think on how danger-ous cars were back then, I'm certain a higher being was watching over us. Outside Perth, Davie heard a rattling sound and pulled over to investigate. It was then he discovered that Johnnie's ribbons were in fact the road beneath us. Our wee laddie had been staring down through a gaping hole in the car floor, which had given way not long into our journey. The rattling sound was another problem; the exhaust had decided to part company with us, causing the most horrendous roar all the way to Macduff. How the police didn't get wind of our travelling beats me. When we at last arrived at our destination, Daddy was horrified by the state of our transport, and flabbergasted the car had made it.

However we soon forgot about the car, because I was so happy being near my precious Mammy. After looking over her new home I thought, 'she'll be content here'.

This was the first time in thirty years that my parents had slept in a bed that didn't need folding up in the morning. Daddy felt un-comfortable at the change, and so spent most of his time scanning the horizon of the sea from a high wall circling the fine garden, like a mariner with a hand shading his eyes, rather than sitting inside at a nice warm fire. I must have got my travelling blood from him. Mammy, on the other hand, was in her element. She had her very own sink, oven, bath, washing line and much more. At long last she had arrived at her castle—a wee queen. She discovered, much to her delight, she had green fingers, and grew herbs, flowers and shrubs. She baked cakes. Boiled up, not just berries for jam, but countless pans of other culinary delights to store in large jars, which she delicately labelled and stored in the larder.

Meantime my younger sisters, Renie and Babs, took on jobs living as any normal lassies would do, and never mentioned their rich cultural background as travellers.

Daddy still had his health, and his spray-painting equipment that he used for contract work. He started up a small business, earning enough to live a comfortable existence. He furnished the house with all that was needed, and soon settled into the friendly neighbourhood. However, when asked if he was now a 'scaldy', he would reply, 'Nae way am I a hoose-dweller. I'll aye keep yin eye on the road, another yin on the sky.' What that meant was that if the mood and the weather suited him, he would go.

By then I couldn't have seen Mammy going with him, though. She loved her bus-travelling days, no doubting that, but now, older and stiffer, she'd settled for her cosy wee hoose. Anyway, she'd seen enough of Scotia's bit fields and wood-ends in her lifetime. There wasn't a B-road she didn't know, nor a landowner she cared to know; a lifetime as a gan-aboot for my dear Ma was well and truly over.

The only worry she had was that Daddy's habit of leaving doors open at night stayed with him. When a boy, because of claustrophobia, he'd throw open the tent flaps at night, and according to Granny Riley they'd all be near frozen stiff. Even the bus door would get drawn back; frost-covered eyebrows he'd wake up with many a winter morning. So once more, even although he'd found a spacious bedroom to sleep in, the daft gowk insisted on leaving the house door ajar. Nothing scunnered Mammy more than thinking a wee mouse was inside her larder, scoffing all those cheeses and cakes she stored so meticulously. Many a time she scolded him, 'Charlie, man, I'll feed the mice-droppings tae ye if I find them at the fit o' ma press. Honest tae God, I'll pit them in yer stew and tatties.'

He in turn would say, 'I dinna want that bloody door locked if a fire breaks oot.'

'Away an' no be so silly', she reminded him nightly. 'The fire's cinders and ash. Anyway, the safety screen is on.'

We couldn't drive home after that first visit because Davie was pulled up by the Banff police on account of our noisy exhaustless car. Banff is only a mile from Macduff, separated by a grand bridge.

There's a story from those parts about a certain fiddler I'll share with you soon, but not until I've told you about our car. Driving along the road, Davie noticed he was being followed by a police car. The officer who pulled him over had a wee look under the vehicle, and when he stood up said to Davie, 'Div ye ken there's a burst spring in that car, loon? It's a' down on the one side.'

My poor husband, who had not long had his driving license but acted like he knew all about motors, said, 'Och no, officer, there's nothing wrong with it, it's only a wee-er spring than on the ither side.'

The policeman took off his helmet, knelt down and said, 'Listen tae me noo, loon, an' no be makin a fule o' me. I ken enough aboot motors to tell when one has a burst spring. Now follow us and we'll gie this heap a guid going over.'

Well, to cut a long anxious story short for Davie, they told him to come back after two, and they'd have it inspected properly. Imagine his horror when he found his white Popular Ford sat at the rear of the yard, with a sticker on it saying 'non-roadworthy'. The lumpy bit that had made our wee Johnnie so uncomfortable was in fact the broken spring, held in place only by the metal frame of the back seat.

A visit to a scrappy left us with three pounds and car-less. Once again we were reliant on some kind soul to take us home. This time my Uncle Joe offered to take us, and boy, were we grateful.

2

A LOOSE MOOSE

Now, the mention of Mammy going on about mice made this memory come vividly back. I can't remember telling you about the time when we lived in the Bedford bus and my older sister Shirley, seething with thoughts of revenge, brought back a pet from the tattie-field.

This is how it went:

We had settled up for the winter in Tomaknock outside Crieff. It was tattie-lifting time and all hands were to the fields. All except Mammy, that is, because she had enough to do with Babsy, her youngest and not yet school age, and Janey who was working as a shop assistant in Scrimgeours (Crieff's high class department store). Renie and Mary were at school, but I was a fine tattie-lifting age of nine. I had an exemption certificate signifying that I was fit for hard work. Well, it didn't really mean that, but Daddy always made me feel a big lassie when he said it did.

In the fifties, traveller children were allowed to attend harvests as long as they attended school when they were finished. However, just in case some lazy travellers ignored the harvest time and kept their kids off school without working on the tatties, inspectors would randomly visit campsites and tattie fields checking for shirkers. I might add that their search was nearly always fruitless, because travellers knew just how much of a difference tattie money made to a cold winter existence. If my memory serves me right, these inspectors were known as the Spewers—this meant when folks saw them coming, it made certain bodies sick.

Shirley and Chrissie had been arguing all that morning, something to do with a Teddy-boy apprentice named Bobby. This said lad, with a headful of thick, sticky Brylcreemed hair, hadn't decided which of my sisters he wanted. Sixteen-years-old Shirley had already made up his mind for him, and didn't like the fact Chrissie, then nineteen, was homing in on her beau—so she threw a bowl of porridge over her.

Mammy slapped the both of them and refused to pack sandwiches, saying, 'Bloody stupid buggers, it'll serve ye baith right for filling yer heads with men when there's a ton o' tatties needin' lifted. Now, if you want food then walk back here, an' I'll have soup ready for dinnertime.'

'Mammy, for the love o' Jesus,' exclaimed Shirley, 'the farmer's fields are three miles from here.'

'Don't blaspheme! There's no so much as a nugget o' shame in ye.' Mammy hated to hear the Lord's name uttered in vain and warned Shirley to mind her tongue.

'What do you expect from a dung-face like her?' laughed Chrissie.

It was all my poor mother could do to stop them from cat-fighting, so rolling up a wet dish-cloth she gave them a nippit wallop into the back of their legs. It worked, as each of them ran off to await the early morning transport laid on by the farmer to collect his workers.

Chrissie heard the tractor and bogey coming, grabbed a welly under each arm, and called out to Mammy that she'd get a certain tractor lad to drive her home at dinnertime, but that Shirley would have to walk. Mammy gave me and oldest sister Mona sandwiches for the day, knowing the farm wife would supply milk, and ignored her haughty pair of daughters who were staring daggers at each other. Once on the bogey we all found a space to sit between thirty or more Crieffites, while the driver made his way to where the tattie field lay ready to be churned by mechanical diggers and flattened by a hundred pairs of eager feet.

The farmer guided us to our set 'bit' for the day, while we scooped up enough tatty skulls (potato-lifting baskets) scattered around from the previous day's work. I called out hellos to a family of Burkes (distant relatives to my father), especially to Elly who was nine like me. She was great fun, and not afraid to play the silver birch game at break time. Growing next to the field, these slender, thin-barked trees were ideal to shin up. When you reached the top, there was sufficient pliability in the trunks to bend them down, and when they couldn't bend any further you just let go, landing like Tarzan on the next tree along. A whole wood could be covered this way. Anyone who touched the forest floor with their feet had to fall out. This was just one of many games we traveller bairns had devised to play with Mother Nature. No one ever broke a tree, or if they did then it was understood they carried too much weight and couldn't take part in the game.

We could do a fair share of showing off as well. Once, when I had been at the berries in Blairgowrie, I told a lot of scaldie bairns who were bothying at a nearby farm to lie still and no' frighten the row o' rabbits at the brow of a hill. Stupid gowks, did they not lie stiff for an hour, not moving or saying a word. If a shepherd hadn't appeared when he did, shouting to them to be off, they'd still be there. No, they weren't rabbits, it was a row of neeps (turnips)! Anyway, let's get back to the story of my sisters, feuding over a Teddy-boy.

Chrissie settled onto her spot at the far end of the drills, with Shirley downwind. Shirley swore if she so much as smelt her arch-enemy on that day, she'd throw worms at her.

The hard back-breaking day dragged on, with every person on that field praying that the earth would throw up a giant boulder with enough bulk to render the digger powerless. But with the digger not hitting a single stone and stopping to give us a wee respite, the work was relentless. Up and down, down and up, no sooner were the skulls filled and emptied when up came the digger again. At piece time, all that could be heard was the munching of sandwiches and slurping of tea. This was provided by traveller women, though first they always carried on working their husbands' patches along with their own while the man made a fire and boiled the kettle.

Shirley asked me for a piece of bread and of course I gave her some, even though I knew I'd not have enough to get me through the day. But she and I were close, and what sister could eat while the other had nothing? Elly's mother Jean-Ann gave us soup, which helped. However Chrissie wasn't so fortunate. She'd found no generosity coming from the folks at the end drills, in fact these craturs refused to share a conversation with her, and I wouldn't blame them. She had a face like fizz, and a brow furrowed like the same drills she was lifting tatties from. But things were to change, when a very handsome tractor driver appeared to whisk her off for dinner. He offered to take Shirley back home too, but Chrissie warned him not to, or else. As I watched my older sisters, one on the back of a tractor, chest out and chin upwards in defiance, the other squeezing dozens of fleshy worms in her fists, I thought only one thought: the bus was going to be the scene of a war of the Amazons!

At long last the day came to a finish, and I can tell you there is no better sight for a tattie-lifter than a digger man turning his vehicle homewards.

We clambered onto the bogey, every bent-backit one of us, from teeny wee weans to decrepit auld bodies, praying the tractor driver would do his best to avoid the dozens of waterlogged pot-holes in the long farm-track road. He didn't though, the blasted sadist! Middle-aged women, not afraid to speak their minds, screamed the air blue, but from the safety of his tractor seat he grinned as we rolled and joggled from side to side.

At long last we jumped off the bogey at the bottom of Tomaknock Brae. Shirley pulled on my arm for me to look at something concealed within her trouser pocket. Gingerly I peered in, and near on died when I found a totty snout-faced wee mouse staring up at me.

'What in blue blazes are you going to do with that? Let it go! It's cruel to keep a helpless thing.'

'Shut up, I'm only going to put it into Chrissie's bed for a night. In the morning I'll set it free. That'll sort her to eye her own men and leave mine alone.'

'I thought you were going to pack worms into her pyjamas?'

'Well I was, but when the digger threw this wee lad into my skull I thought it would have a better effect. Dae ye mind when one ran intae her knickers while she wis peein under the railway arch at Ballinluig? God, did she no half shoot up ontae the track. If Daddy hadn't been there, a goods train heading tae Pilochry would have flattened her—no way would she have won the "Miss Logerait" beauty contest if it had. Mind you, if I wisna in bed at the time with a broken shin, it would have been a forgone conclusion who the winner would have been.'

Before I could say a word on that matter, a certain painter and decorator's apprentice with a stiffened head of jet-black hair came walking towards us. It was Bobby.

'Hello, darling, are we goan' dancin' the night?'

Shirley blushed, not at his request but at her grubby tattie clothes. Still, clothes don't maketh the man—or, in Shirley's case, the woman. Anyone who ever met my sister will tell you her beauty was awesome. Flawless complexion, hour-glass figure, shiny black hair, perfect height and sea-green eyes. Oh, indeed a beauty. And boy, did she flaunt it.

'How could I be such a twit to imagine he'd look sidey ways at weasel-face Chrissie, there's no comparison,' she reminded me, then called to him, 'I'll see you at seven,'—totally forgetting that helpless cratur which shivered in her pocket, unaware of its fate.

Chrissie was busy chatting with her tractor man and making her own plans for the evening. Mona too had a fancy-man, but with her flair for finding rich guys she kept him a secret. Mind you, I noticed the farmer's son spent more time giving her denim buttocks the eye than those of any other female tattie-lifter.

The three of them dashed into the bus to see what Mammy had cooked for supper, before the battle of soap and towels took place.

Mammy was in a great mood, because a nice lady had presented her with a massive box of the finest bed-linen. This person was in the throes of emigrating, and wondered if Mammy wanted her bedclothes. What kind of a question was that for a mother with eight lassies?

Chrissie and Shirley, who had by now settled their differences with a silent truce, lifted the great big box of bed-linen and sat it to the back of the bus, where Mammy would later put it under her and Daddy's bed, in a large storage box used for storing all the family's blankets and sheets. Daddy never let on, but we think he got it from an undertaker—still, it did the job.

Supper was mouth-watering, stovies and onions with stewed rhubarb and custard to follow. Mary and I did the dishes, while the she-devils made themselves into Marilyn Monroes and Gina Lollobrigidas. I loved watching them. Silk stockings would have been a bonus, but no one could afford them, so my sisters, being the Picassos that they were, improvised by very carefully drawing charcoal lines up the back of their legs. They looked just like stocking seams. Except for Mona, may I add. She had the real Mackay. She would save every penny until she had enough to buy them. When she dressed, it was an art form like no other. For a start, she never pulled on stockings without having cotton gloves on to avoid snags. Her shoulders were covered by a towel when she powdered her face. It would have been terrible if one particle of powder should come to rest on those fine silk blouses she often wore.

Now, I know you're having a hard time imagining that all this went on in a single-decker bus, but believe me it did. Not only that, but Daddy listened to his wireless through all the high-pitched chatter and Mammy told stories to her wee ones.

Now let's get back to another wee one—a certain mouse, to be exact. 'Where did Shirley put it?' I thought, as I watched my older sister saunter off arm-in-arm with Bobby, the Brylcreem king.

I quickly checked Chrissie's bedclothes, but they were neatly folded where she'd left them that morning. I didn't say anything to Mammy or anyone else; not wanting my sister to get a row and knowing that she would when Mammy found out. After a fruitless search, I gave up, thinking she'd disposed of the wee timorous beastie into a field of cropped corn next to our winter stopping-ground, and I forgot the matter.

Next day the lassies were all chatted-out by the lads and tired after their gyrating on the dance floor. The day went on at its usual pace, a replica of the previous one, until while shinning birchies I tore a great lump of material out of my trousers, and was presented with another pair by the farmer's wife. She had no females in her household, only young ploughmen—what a sight I was in my nicky tams!

Within three weeks, Mammy began complaining about a scratching noise beneath the bus somewhere. This was not unusual, so Daddy set some traps. The noise continued each night, driving my poor mother batty. Eventually, unable to stand the constant scratching, she sat bolt upright in her bed and screamed into the pitch dark night that we must all rise 'oot o' our pits and search for the moose!'

Damp matches were thrown all over the bus as Daddy tried to light some candles, tutting and moaning about broken sleep.

Suddenly I froze, and the same thought must have been flooding Shirley's mind, because she gave me a nudge. What if her wee mouse was hiding in the bus?

'What happened tae the moose?' I whispered.

She whispered back in my ear, 'I don't know. All I remember was taking off my trousers and laying them on that box of linen.' Her face drained of colour. 'Oh, oh, bucket o' shit, are you thinking what I'm thinking?' she said, tightly squeezing my arm.

'I hope for your sake those fine Irish linen sheets are intact,' I told her, unfolding her fingers from my pinched flesh.

Mammy threw up the mattress and opened her blanket box. 'Hold that candle down there,' she ordered Daddy. I swear, on my Granny's low grave, I have never seen such a sight; no wonder Mammy shrieked louder than the Banshee. Piled high inside the box were mounds and mounds of shredded sheets, blankets and eiderdowns, and curled in a corner was a terrified wee mouse with a dozen and more tiny weans, all squeaking and squirming.

Mammy never knew it was Shirley who caused that catastrophe by introducing a pregnant mouse to our home, but I knew, and boy, did I put the tighteners on her when I wanted something!

3

ON THE ROAD AGAIN

Now, back to the pokey flat in Crieff where Dave and I were living. The postman made me cringe each time he pushed mail through the letter-box—with me feeling trapped behind four concrete walls and a heavy oak door, it seemed to me that he was a prison warder having a peek.

Davie was born and reared in a house, how could he possibly understand my anguish? The poor man had enough to do keeping down a job without having to take my constant nagging about how unhappy I was in that house. 'Listen pet,' he assured me at nights when I tossed and turned in bed, 'you have more to think about nowadays than yourself.' He'd point across at our sleeping infants, and I knew what he meant.

In all honesty, though, as days turned into weeks, I began to hate my basic but comfortable home, and could hardly wait for morning, when my little boys were rushed into their clothes and popped into the pram. Like a miniature gypsy wagon, that pram was crammed with enough food and drink to last all day, as I got as far away from the four walls and into the fields and woodland surrounding Crieff. Stephen's baby milk was wrapped in tin-foil and nappies to keep it warm. When we stopped, out would come blankets for the kids to lie on. Then my shoes would be discarded, as Mother Earth and my feet joined again. It was as if I was retracing my steps to old tinker ground.

Listening to the different birds singing to each other, it seemed as if they were including me and my wee lads. I'd sing a lullaby to my tiny infant, then when he was asleep I'd teach Johnnie how to tell the difference between trees and bushes. Tell him tales of the Tree people who lived under bark, and Giant Mactavish who spent all his two hundred years living in the forest fighting off the Smelly Sock frogs. (When I recall how his big hazel green eyes lit up at those stories it makes a dull day disappear.)

Rain or shine, it made no difference, just so long as me and my little half-breeds could escape to the open spaces. When the sunshine of summer shone in cloudless skies, going back to the house was more than I could bear. Selfishly, I'd leave my wristwatch at home, and one day, when we eventually arrived back, it was a very angry, hungry husband who confronted me.

'Jess, I can hardly work for worrying about you.'

'Why?'

'Trekking lonely byways with my wee sons, that's why.'

'They're fine; do you think I'd put my boys in danger?'

'If you'd come down out of your silly cloud for one minute and listen to me. What if one of them got sick or something?'

'Davie, travelling people live like that, we cope with everything, even sickness.'

My stubbornness hit a raw nerve, he thumped the kitchen table so hard all four legs bounced off the floor. Cups wobbled in their saucers as sugar scattered between them.

'I am not a traveller, though, and these are my sons! And by God, I don't want them dragged around the countryside because their stupid mother won't let go of a dead lifestyle. Now stop it and get a grip.'

That night I wrote the longest letter of my life to Mammy.

Davie and I were like strangers after that night, with an iron atmosphere between us. Sandy brought a garden swing for Johnnie and Margaret gave me a Bero home-baking recipe book. Strange to imagine me being a good baker, but with my wandering curtailed I had to do something. Davie saw I was trying to adapt into scaldy life, and in time our marriage did strengthen again.

Then came the letter from Mammy.

Round the corner from her house was a wee low-roofed cottage,

Daddy knew the old man who lived there. He, getting too elderly, had decided to move over to Aberdeen with his niece. The rent would be affordable. 'Did we want to come up to Macduff?'

I was like a bairn on a Christmas morning. 'Oh Davie, please say we can go.' The thought of living in a new place beside my parents was drawing pictures of wonderful excitement.

I had deep pangs pounding in my breast. Would Davie, who was a Crieff man through and through, say no... or maybe yes. I watched his face, then he said, 'I'm away out to think this over.'

Hours passed, and there was still no sign. It made me think my long-suffering husband was not ready to up sticks and go far north; fifty miles north of Aberdeen, to be precise. However, just after midnight I heard his key in the door. If extra persuasion was needed I'd baked a thick chocolate cake.

'Well, lad?' I asked, pushing near half the cake under his nose, and waited on his answer.

'Yip!'

I could hardly contain my excitement, because when Davie said 'yip', it came without conditions. We were leaving Crieff and this nightmare prison of a house.

That night we cuddled and laughed with excitement at our forthcoming new ground.

'My birth sign is "Pisces", the two fishes. Macduff is a fishing port. All the signs are there—we will be happy.' I was heart-sure. Davie joked, reminding me his sign was Cancer. 'Plenty of them crawling among seaweed on the shores of the Moray Firth,' he said, and tickled me, pretending to be a crab.

We were both only twenty-one, a lifetime spread out before us. Macduff, I was certain, would be just the first place of many more.

Sandy and Margaret were heart-sorry to say goodbye, especially as we were taking their only grandchildren from them, but offers to visit would soon find them not far behind us.

4

THE BIG HUNTER WITH HIS POACHER COAT ON

I have a wee tale to share with you before we all take ourselves up north. John Macalister, a half cousin of mine who had promised to flit us in his wee van, was helping with our packing one night when he brought in a large rabbit some mate of his had trapped. I told him to take it away, because I'd no stomach for skinning or gutting. Anyway, all my cutlery and cooking utensils were packed in boxes. Over a bottle of beer, he and Davie got talking about poaching and trapping and so on. When John left, Davie said. 'I think I'll go out for a wee turn at the poaching.'

'What?' I asked.

'Catch myself a goose.'

'Davie, did you not hear me tell John all my utensils are in boxes?'

'Dad would pluck and skin it, if I caught one, and Mother would cook it. We could call it our going-away feast from Crieff.'

This was my husband's one and only attempt at goose-stalking.

Old Tam, a neighbour, had given Davie a long, heavy wool coat some time ago.

'A richt poacher's yin,' Tam joked, showing Davie all the concealed buttons and hidden pockets. Davie thanked his neighbour, but as he never considered wearing anything other than trendy Beatle jackets, he put it away, not intending to be seen in it. So imagine my surprise when he unearthed this sinister-looking garment to go goose-stalking.

All that day, fog and damp air covered the countryside. Geese and ducks could be heard flying above the blanket cover of mist. 'Surely I'll get myself one, there's hundreds up there,' he said, pointing upwards, the poacher's coat hanging loosely over his frame.

Before I could close my half-opened mouth he was gone, swallowed up by the mist that swirled round his ankles, billowing up into that coat. All he left behind was the eerie noise of his footsteps on the pavement outside our soon-to-be-vacated house. I imagined him rounding a corner in the street. 'My God,' I thought, 'he'll frighten folks to death. He looks like Jack the Ripper.' One glance at the mist, tinged orange by the street lights, and the door was slammed shut, and my kettle boiled for a nice warm cup of tea.

For a moment I peered through a slit in the kitchen curtains, convinced he was joking and that I would soon hear his knocking on the door, but no sound came and I began to worry. Feeling a wee bit uneasy about the thick, ghostly mist outside, I closed the window I'd left ajar, and then ran through the house, drawing the curtains. Johnnie pushed his tiny arm into mine and asked for a biscuit. I gave him several, along with a box of Lego. Then, when Stephen filled his nappy, thankfully concerns about Davie diminished while I busied myself with the bairns. The hours passed slowly, and my boys were long bedded and asleep when those familiar footsteps brought my man home. 'Is that you, Davie?' I asked, before opening the door.

'Woman of the house, open the door and let your hunter in,' he joked.

'Have you caught a goose, then?'

'Have I indeed. Feast you eyes on this big juicy fella.' Davie threw open his poacher's coat and rammed both hands eagerly inside the hidden pockets. From one he took out his father's priest (salmon thumper), and from the other a big, brightly-coloured, plastic, DECOY DUCK!

The sight in front of me I can only describe as unbelievable!

The fog had turned to rain and soaked him to the marrow. Exhausted, but still smiling, he made me promise hand on heart not to tell a living soul what had happened—that he had seen the duck sitting in a field and lay on his belly for ages stalking it. When he decided that it must be an injured bird, he jumped up and charged. Not until its head went one way, and body the other, did it dawn on him what it was he'd been stalking in thick mist as he crouched for hours on the freezing ground.

The poacher's coat was handed in to big Wull Swift, a real life rabbit man. He, standing well over six feet, would be better suited to its size.

I never was one for breaking promises, so only after getting my red-faced husband's permission have I ventured to reveal to you the tale of 'The Big Hunter, with His Poacher Coat On.'

5

THE REAL LOCH NESS MONSTER

Stories of hunting, shooting and fishing were common among travellers while I was a bairn. Depending on how they were told, certain tales stayed vividly cemented in my head. This tale I wish to share with you now is about the most feared hunter in the whole world, and for two reasons it has never left me. One is the legend that is intertwined with it, and the second is its theme of greed. Greed is a monumental sin, but one that can grant you the gift of immortality if the old Devil likes you for it.

Are you one of those who believes in the Loch Ness Monster? If you are, great! If not, then perhaps after this story you'll be of a different mind. I leave it entirely up to you, my dear friend. Sit down, and I hope you are near a pond or some other stretch of water, though it would be far better if you were sitting on the shoreline of Loch Ness. Never mind where you are, just let me paint the scene.

Around three centuries ago, Peggy Moore, a heaving giant of a woman, lived in a tent on the side of Loch Ness with her husband and son.

Quiet folks living over in Drumnadrochit kept well away from Mistress Moore's abode. Not because her family were tinkers, but simply because folks were terrified of her brute strength. For around the expanse of the loch it was well known that she was as uncouth and unkind a woman as ever breathed good air. Her long-suffering husband and son were kept back-weary working to feed and clothe that awful brute of a woman. She was not born with her huge bulk—oh no, it was sheer unadulterated greediness alone that was responsible. Folks said, as they were wont to do in wild and isolated places of Scotland, that she was the offspring of a witch's womb. They further said her husband had been put under a spell and enslaved to do her bidding. And adding to this household, the result of a single passionate night when the hypnotised husband was robbed of his reason, came the son.

When rising in the morning Peggy ate her way through pound upon pound of thick milky porridge and loaves of crusty bread. Mid-morning, she'd thump the bare earth outside her canvas home screaming for more food, and this, sad to say, was provided by her deathly-pale and emaciated kin.

'Get me meat, ye useless objects,' she'd howl at them, 'work and work until I have my fill.'

And this the sad pair did. Cutting trees and selling firewood from early morn until sundown, they chopped and sawed until exhaustion took over. Then, before falling onto their small, narrow, straw-filled mattresses, they handed over every penny they had earned.

This Mistress Moore was not just a greedy bisom—oh no, she also had cunning in her bones, so she did. Because some of the hard-earned money went into a purse she hid under a horse-hair bed, to be saved for the beef market. And on the day our tale unfolds, farmers were congregating over by Castle Urquhart to sell the best cuts of prime meat.

With a thump and a kick she sent her menfolk off earlier than usual that morning, followed by a sharp warning not to come home until the stars were sparkling in the sky above.

Keeking from her tent door, she watched until the men were gone into the forest before counting her money. 'Oh man, ye look fair braw, ma bonny bawbees, I'll git maself a rare bag o' the best juicy meat today, oh a grand day, tis this.'

No sooner had she lifted her massive frame—which, it may be said, weighed half a ton—onto two swollen feet, and pushed open her tent door, when two shepherds came coyly by.

'Hello tae ye, Mistress Moore,' they said, pulling cloth toories from their heads and making sure there was enough space between them and her tent. It was usual for the said woman to throw a punch and ask questions later. Not this day, however. Hardly glancing in their direction, she covered her shoulders with a shawl of grey wool, bigger than any normal family blanket, and began to waddle off down the road.

'Mistress, we have been having terrible times wi' a giant cat-like creature,' one said, still clutching his headgear and keeping a safe distance behind. The other made up to her and tried to get her attention by overtaking. Not one bit did she tolerate such intrusion, and lashed out at the poor fellow with an elbow to his chest. Several feet in the air went the poor man, landing hard on the rough shale shore.

The other shepherd stopped to assist his friend, shouting after Peggy Moore, 'it can rip a calf from its mother and crunch through a sheep's skull with one close of its jaw. We canna find it, so you had better mind yer back, tinker woman.'

The earth stopped shuddering as she halted her footsteps. Only her head did she turn to dart evil glances at the men, who stood there with plaidies covering their shoulders and cromachs to hand. One look in her direction, and the three accompanying sheepdogs curled around their masters' feet like earthworms.

'I hiv nae fear o' ony livin' creature.' She lifted a fist into the air.

'But Mistress Moore, this is a demon cat wi' the power of a lion, the jaw o' a tiger and the stealth o' a panther. Tak' care an' keep a fire burning in the darkest pairt o' the nicht.'

'Let it dae its worst. If it has the courage tae come within a hundred feet o' me, then little does it ken Peggy Moore.' With those words ringing over the still waters of Loch Ness, she rounded shoulders, laughed loudly like a witch cackling through the flames of a burning cauldron fire, and was gone, clutching her bulging purse.

At Castle Urquhart, heavy oak tables were covered by blood-dripping cuts of finest beef, lying in mouth-watering heaps.

'Oh, ma wee beauties,' she said, stroking at the sinews running through the pounds of flesh.

Bluebottles circled over the meat, but fell dead at one swat from her massive forearm. 'Deevils o' disease, dinna so much as glance at ma beef,' she whispered to several advancing flies, which took one look at her slit eyes and buzzed away. Beneath the tables a dog growled at a hissing cat over one scrap of meat that had fallen on the ground. Peggy stood hard on the cat's tail before sending it into oblivion with a kick.

'What can I get you this fine day, Mistress Moore? Maybe a handful o' this for stewing?' The blood-splattered butcher, with his cleaver clutched tightly just in case she fancied throwing a wallop at him, thought she'd be looking for stew beef, but this wasn't to her satisfaction, not that day. She'd enough money to afford the finest rump.

She half-smiled, not taking her greedy eyes off the ruby red flesh, and said, 'give me this lot'.

'I'll charge ye dear, for that's ma finest rump, is that.'

'Are ye saying ah canna pey fer ma grub?' her eyes narrowed and a growl came from deep within, as she produced the purse thick with money in her clenched hand.

'No way would I bring your guid self down, Peggy, my fine big lass. Yer money is as guid as ony others',' he said greedily, catching sight of how much the purse held.

Instantly the meat was rolled up and pushed inside her deerskin bag, and she hurried away home to cook and gorge before those weary men came back.

It was quite a distance from the Castle marketplace to her tent. Since she was so heavy, getting home usually took longer for her than for a body of normal frame. Several times she stopped to lean against a tree and get her breath before moving on.

Now, let us for a moment sneak back to the tent. Quiet it was, with nobody around. Silent enough to attract a certain accursed cat which was searching for cover to hide out until dark. All territory was forbidden to him, yet here seemed a place of sanctuary from those death-minded shepherds, in here there was peace. Night would bring him out, refreshed and ready for another kill, but in here he'd rest. Eyes darting in every direction the beast crept up to the tent. Inside it was near pitch-dark, perfect. One last sniff of the air to check that no human was on his tail, and in he went, until his body rubbed up against the natural covering of deer skin and bracken at the furthermost end of the tent where Peggy Moore would eventually lay down her body to sleep.

At long last Peggy stood panting outside her abode. Her weight, added to the bulk of raw meat with her, was all she could cope with, but the burden was forgotten when inside. She thrust her eager hand into a wooden box and retrieved a large iron pot. Quickly firing up the smouldering embers and adding more sticks to her fire, she soon had a pot ready for the contents of her skin bag. Sparks hissed and spat as the cold meat met the hot pan. Peggy could hardly contain her desire for food as the aroma curled up her nostrils, sending taste buds into spasms of ecstasy that only a greed-driven gourie (woman) could experience.

'Lovely, mmmm, my, what a feast I'll have.' She squirmed her gigantic wobbling buttocks from side to side, and like an eager kitten toying with a bird she poked a skewer into the frying flesh. The cooking meat sent smells of delight into every corner of the tent— aye, and the cat smelt it too. Awakened now, he'd been watching as she wobbled, muttering all the while. He half-closed his yellow eyes and opened keen nostrils. While she licked the meat juices from her fingers, he licked his lips. The meat was cooked and the feast began! She tore off strips with her bare hands, and no sooner had one slid down her gulping thrapple when another and another followed. She gorged like a demon possessed, running her tongue up and down her forearm and licking the juice that escaped. Gristle and bone were also crunched and gulped, until nothing, not even a saucer of gravy, remained that might feed her hungry menfolk when night would bring them home starving. But another creature was beginning to feel hunger pangs. It watched as Peggy shoved the meat down that gargling throat, and to his empty stomach that great bulk of a neck looked quite delectable. Her day had reached its fulfilment and now she was exhausted. After her trip to the market, cooking and eating, she just had to rest, so down onto the mattress went that massive frame with a great thud.

From the shadows of her tent a face, grinning with menace, watched her in deathly silence. Cats are not known as impulsive eaters, unlike dogs and certain humans; they have patience, and can wait to savour their moment. Yet how could he, this demonic creature of the shadows, stay patient when such a prize lay sprawled before him? Lifting his slender body with stealthy movements he crouched above the half-sleeping woman. For a little while he scanned the meat-stained face. Then very slowly he positioned one leg over her shoulders until he stood directly straddling her head.

Aware not all was right, she opened her eyes and stared into those yellow orbs! This was his time, when his prey froze in terror. He waited on the smell of fear. But it did not come from Peggy Moore!

'If ye think tae sink yer green and yella teeth intae ma neck, pussy, then think again!'

Suddenly the cat creature realised, as she picked him up and threw him the length of the tent, he'd met his match. This prey wouldn't go as easy to his stomach as the market meat went to hers. He stood rigid, stretched his spine, unsheathed sharp claws and pounced. Claws and teeth tore a lump from Peggy Moore's neck. Blood, hot and steaming, poured freely from the gaping wound. This should have shocked her to death. But instead of being sent into the throes of terror, the big woman rose onto splayed feet, sucked her head into her shoulders and screamed, 'give me all you've got, cat!'

From then on it was life or death for them both, as fist met claw and kick met paw. Scratching and ripping, punching and gouging, they rolled and wrestled, neither giving in. Peggy was torn and tattered, while the cat limped and bled. For a minute, when it seemed as if all strength was gone, they rallied and tore into each other again. They rolled out of the tent, among the shale, over boulders, tripping over dried tree roots at the loch's edge, then, in one last desperate grapple they met and rolled over, and were both swallowed by the deep waters of Loch Ness.

Down they gurgled, clinging to each other, neither giving in until their lungs filled to the top and death claimed them both. Only a tiny trail of air bubbles popped and evaporated into nothing as the monsters breathed their last: she a mistake of Nature, he a ferocious hunter who had met his match when he had taken on Mistress Moore.

Now, as it happens, never before had anyone seen such a spectacular contest. No human had witnessed the pair, but a water kelpie, that supernatural creature of myth and legend, had seen it all from the other side of the black water. Without a moment lost, he swam down into the fathomless depths. Down and down he sank, entering a world where nightmares and ghoulish creatures live.

'Your Majesty,' he shouted, awakening the horny Devil from a grand slumber, 'did ye no see Peggy Moore and the wild cat fechting?'

'Na,' answered the Hairy Man, angry at the intrusion. 'Now, water horse, it had better be good, this tale ye're about tae tell me, for I've a splinter in atween yin o' ma cloven hooves, and the black mood's on me.'

'You turn back yer clock, sir, an' then tell me if ah've wasted yer time.'

Auld Nick cleaned a fish bone out of his jaggy teeth with the point of his forked tail, sat down and pointed a finger upwards. Suddenly Peggy Moore and the cat appeared—scratching, rolling, screaming, and neither giving way for a moment.

The Devil laughed and slapped his goat-like thigh. 'Ye're richt enough Kelpie, yon's too guid a wrestling tae let finish, I'll gi'e the twa o' them immortality.'

So there you have it, folks. I bet there's many a time you've been sauntering about the shore of Loch Ness when the gloaming has come down. I can hear you say to whoever is in your company, 'Did ye see the shape o' thon thing in the water?' And in turn your friend will say, 'No, I didn't, what was it?' You'll scan the water and swear blind something moved along, a great bulk of a thing. But the water calms, and if there was a creature, then it's gone. You, being certain there was something, hope that somebody else saw it.

Next day as you open your morning newspaper there's a story catches your eye which reads: 'Last night two American tourists saw the "Loch Ness Monster". There were several humps in the water [Peggy's four bellies]. It had a thick neck and small head [her forearm thrusting upwards and fist thumping into the back of her opponent]. As quickly as it appeared, it was gone.' It was just her and her pussy cat fighting their way from the bottom to the top of the loch and down again—readers, that's all it was.

'But,' I hear you say, 'what of her kin, that poor sad pair who worked day and night. What was their explanation for Peggy's disappearance?'

Some said that when they saw the trail of blood going from tent to loch, they could only assume she'd been eaten by the wild cat. But with her demise they made a smaller tent, ate more food and did less work. And became a happy, contented pair, no doubt.

6

MACDUFF

Time to leave Crieff now and head to Macduff, courtesy of my half-cousin John and his wee Morris van. When I think back on how we all got inside that tiny vehicle I burst into a sweat.

Mammy had earlier promised she'd pick up cheap bits of furnishings to make the fisherman's low-roofed cottage habitable for us. That was just as well, because at that stage all our worldly goods consisted of two bonny bairns, some kitchen utensils, one pair of green cotton bed-sheets, towels, four woollen blankets, a duvet and our clothes. Mine were of no use on account of my extra weight. I'd put on two extra stone since taking possession of that blasted Be-Ro book. Still, nothing could spoil that day. I remember so well how I felt as we drove off, with Crieff getting smaller by the mile.

The boys and I had to make do in the back of the wee van, getting as comfortable as we could. Davie sat in the only seat next to John. Stephen was rolled inside some bath towels that Margaret had sent down the previous night. Johnnie, full of energy, bounced over everything, excited to be in a Morris van—to him it was a toy to be played with.

Earlier, an hour before we left, while giving a final dusting to our Crieff house, I said to Davie who was feeding Stephen his bottle, that I was concerned our bairn might not settle on the journey. I didn't think to ask Davie what he meant by, 'Och, this wee fella will sleep all the way there.' Because that he did!

When we arrived at Macduff, Mammy was there to greet us with lots of tattie soup, tea and scones. It was after we ate I asked Davie how he had been so sure about Stephen's long slumber. 'Oh, I slipped a teaspoon o' whiskey intae his bottle.' Now let me say right here and now, if I'd so much as had a whiff of the stuff on my baby's lips I'd have swung for his father. But, and this isn't any excuse, not a difference did it appear to make to our wee bouncing laddie, as he smiled broadly at everybody who tickled his chubby chin. Mind you, when I think on the swaying he did in his pram, I'm certain my eight-months-old was drunk.

Macduff was filled with a fresh sea breeze that blew gently through my new home to greet us each morning. Johnnie played safely at the front door, where the traffic was almost non-existent. Baby Stephen soon threw away his bottle, refusing to suck on it any more and craving solids instead. At nine months he was eating the same as us, scrambled eggs and milky tatties being his favourite.

Life began to settle into a regular pattern, one that suited me fine. Mammy and I would take the boys on a daily walk across the bridge to Banff for messages, although fresh fish and vegetables were delivered to our door by friendly Macduff van men.

Davie helped Daddy at the painting and was well paid. We managed to afford a three-piece-suite and new kitchen table and chairs. Davie put his skills as a joiner to good use by building a fitted kitchen, with permission of the house owner, of course.

Neighbours were friendly, not at all the gossiping or in your house kind, just there if you needed them. One old dear was Sarah. Let me tell you about her.

'Hello fine quine, fit like?' This was the Macduff way of saying, 'how are you this fine day?' I turned around to see a very old lady smiling at me as I washed my small windows. We chatted on the pavement, before the want o' a cuppy had me invite her in. She politely refused this invitation, saying when we got to know each other better then she'd take up my offer. Next day, as Davie was waving goodbye, Sarah appeared minutes behind him. It was seven o'clock in the morning, a very busy time of day for a young mum, but when she smiled and held out a hot steaming loaf of crusty bread, how could I refuse. When inside she found the best seat and sat down. 'Ah'll play wi' the bairns, while ye mak a fresh pot o' tea, Jessie.'

When I brought the buttered bread and cups of tea in, she'd washed and dressed both my boys. Who, may I add, loved her to bits. On a daily basis she'd pop along from her house to mine, which was a mere hundred yards away, never empty-handed. If it wasn't a pound of mince she had brought, then it was bread or cakes, and always sweeties. Thus began a wonderful friendship between an old woman of ninety-four-years old, and a young mum of twenty-one.

Davie and I seldom went out together, and this was sometimes noticed by Sarah who soon became a fixture in our busy house. In fact amongst our family noise she'd snooze happily. I got to the point many times of leaving her asleep and going off with the boys for a walk. One day she came in and said, 'There's a dance in Banffy this weekend—why don't you baith gang?' We told her my folks were away visiting family in Perthshire, and even though it would be nice to get out of the house for a time, there was nobody to baby-sit.

'Fit's wrang wi' me? I'll watch the bairnies.'

Sarah was a dear old soul, but there was no way she could cope with two bairns. After all, she'd never had any of her own, and at her age—oh no, we couldn't possibly burden her, the responsibilities were far too great for her to manage.

Sarah didn't see herself as old, and insisted, reminding us, as she constantly did, 'me and ma Wull, afore he deed, wid walk ten miles a day, an' he's only four year deed.' In other words this elderly lady was covering quite a distance at ninety!

So we gave way, and, on the night of the dance, as I put the finishing touches to my hair, Sarah's parting words were, 'dinna drink spirits, for the demons will fill yer heed.' Sarah hated alcohol, and would lecture us about how many a good man 'fell tae the demon o' the bottle'. I promised not to drink, but she'd wait on hell freezing over before Davie would make the same promise. A night out meant, to him, a guid dram.

The dance, which was run by the local fishermen, was great fun as I twirled and skirled the night away. We met lots of young couples who had kids of our age. As we walked home we left the bridge spanning the river Deveron, and with shoes in hand played upon a moonlit shore. Exhausted in a nice way, we slowly wandered home through the deserted streets of Macduff. All was silent at our wee house. There was never the need for locked doors then, so we very gently turned the handle and let ourselves in. I expected to see our old babysitter plopped on her favourite chair with the boys snoring from their bedroom, but boy oh boy, was I in for a shock! Johnnie was vrooming a toy lorry along the floor. Stephen was sound asleep in a basin, face covered with dried chocolate. And Sarah, the bold lass, sat on the floor with her back against a chair. Her legs were apart, and plonked between them was an empty bottle of Davie's OVD Rum, a present from his father to celebrate the New Year when it came. An old photograph of Wull lay inside Johnnie's toy lorry along with an empty glass, and the headscarf forever tied tightly under her chin was covering her face. She was totally unconscious, and no wonder, because the empty bottle had previously been full!

Davie put her into our bed and we made do with the settee. Stephen, who awoke screaming from his basin bed, probably with a stiff neck, curled up beside us. Next day, try as we might, there was no way we could raise her off that bed, so we left her there. She surfaced again only when it turned dark. Sarah never mentioned that night ever after; nor did she offer to baby-sit again.

The only 'blind blink' on our horizon was my weight gain. Within six months of moving to Macduff I'd piled it on. I was eight stone before the kids came, now I was fourteen and a half! What a fatty—and try as I might, not an ounce could I shift. This mystified me, because if anything I was exercising more and eating less. A visit to the doctor in Banff didn't help. He put it down to the extra pounds that pile on during pregnancy, and a slight imbalance in the body's make-up of cells etc. I must say, though, Doctor Mackenzie was a right braw lad. His mate was none other than Jimmy Mitchell, our Crieff doctor. They were both students at Aberdeen together and each hailed from the north. This medicine man from Banff will always stay dear in my heart, and this is the reason why.

Perhaps that cup of tea would come in handy now. If you are a parent, then you too may have had a similar experience to the one we're about to share.

It was around October's end, in fact Halloween time, when the usual thick sea haar turned everyone into blind folk. People called out to each other, groping along the street, searching for familiar voices. Davie and Daddy came home early, they couldn't do any painting because it was far too dangerous climbing ladders. Mammy brought me some milk and bread. I couldn't push a pram outside in case I knocked some elderly body over onto the road.

Stephen was sitting playing with a rubber toy when Johnnie began to complain of a stomach-ache. Nothing unusual in a toddler, but within four hours he was fevered and crying painfully. Mammy came round, saying he should be cooled. This I did, bathing him with tepid water, but one minute he shivered, next he was boiling to the touch. His eyes began to glaze over, and it soon became apparent our bairn was quite ill. Davie went over in Daddy's van to fetch Dr Mackenzie. Within half an hour he'd arrived home, doctor at his back. No sooner had he stepped inside, when Johnnie began vomiting brown and green slime. The poor wee mite also took diarrhoea, which was the same colour as his vomit. Dr Mackenzie examined him and said, 'this wee chap has gastro-enteritis, I'm sure of it.'

'What is that, Doctor? Can you give him something for the pain?'

'Firstly, it is when a stubborn bug finds its way into a bairn's digestive system, and it depends on the child's stamina how fast it gets out. Usually lots of fluids and tender care shifts it. As for pain, no, I can't give him anything. But now that's he's been sick he should pick up. I'll come back later on tonight to see how he is.'

I felt much better with my wee boy in his care, and after the door closed behind him, Johnnie said weakly, 'can I watch Thunderbirds?'

'Thank God,' I thought, 'that means he's feeling better.'

Davie switched on the black and white telly and sat Johnnie up against some cushions, but no sooner had he propped him up when our son began to vomit violently. Suddenly he stretched his spine, jerking his arms and legs. He was convulsing and I was shaking with fear.

'I'm away to fetch the Doctor.' Davie ran out the door and met the Doctor coming back. He'd not liked the look of Johnnie, and had gone back to his surgery to fetch his colleague for a second opinion.

All of a sudden my house was filled with ambulance men. Mammy, Daddy, Renie and Babsy all appeared. Wee Stephen, be-ing a baby, sat stunned by the commotion, and only when Mammy took him away did he cry for me.

Bairns guising the doors were singing and shouting, 'pennies for the guisers!' I distractedly apologised and told them to come back later.

'Johnnie is seriously ill,' Doctor Mackenzie whispered to me. 'I want him to go to Aberdeen Sick Children's Hospital. This will be a long night. Now you go with your wee lad in the ambulance. Keep talking to him.'

Daddy told Davie to follow in the van.

All the way there I clung to our child as he lay limp and pale in my arms.

The driver, aware of the poor visibility throughout the fifty-mile trip, put himself at terrible risk by speeding as best he could through that nightmarish sea haar. 'Slow down,' his mate whispered, hoping we wouldn't hear, as the ambulance screeched on bends. 'That wee laddie micht nae make it if ah dae,' was his answer. This made my fear all the more terrible.

Our arrival at the hospital saw a host of professionals tear into action, as our bairn became their property and not ours. Davie, following on our heels, was at my side in minutes. The waiting-room, with its yellow-painted walls, felt cold and uncaring. If it hadn't been for a certain nursing sister, I would have cried myself into a hysterical state. She came to tell us where Johnnie was and took us to him. What a fright we got, seeing him lie limp and thin with tubes coming out of his tiny wrists and ankles. 'Don't be alarmed by them,' she reassured us, 'that's food and water he's getting. Now come in here with me.'

We followed her into a warm room next to Johnnie's ward, and no sooner had we sat down when a young red-headed nurse brought us mugs of tea and plates of toast. 'If this isnae enough I'll dae ye twa eggs.' We had no stomach for food, but thanked her just the same.

Desperate in our ignorance, we pleaded with the sister to tell us about our son's state. 'I'll tell you truthfully, kids, that wee laddie will fight this night for his tiny life. It will be touch and go, but if by the morning he's still with us then he'll live to tell the tale.'

These days, if a health employee said that to worried parents, they'd be sued to the hilt. Her words entered my heart, and I had an overwhelming feeling that Mammy's Jesus had to be found. I closed my eyes and sat praying, sometimes inwardly, sometimes outwardly, but not once all through the longest night of my life did I cease. I must have repeated Jesus' name thousands of times.

'Come and see this,' said a voice. I opened my eyes: it was the friendly sister. We followed her, on legs stiff and aching, into the ward.

Sitting up, with arms outstretched towards us, was our beloved wee son, smiling. He'd made it! Whether it was Mammy's Saviour or a devoted caring staff who had helped him, I do not know, but our time with Johnnie had been extended. No questions needed answers, the only important thing was that the joy of life continued.

He would get home within two weeks, and by the end of this time he was a favourite patient with nurses and doctors alike.

7

THE CURSE OF A GOOD MAN

Winters along the Moray coast could be mighty cold, and the first one we endured there was no exception. Night entered when the afternoon had hardly had time to start. People disliked those long cold nights, especially fishermen's wives. Where Uncle Joe and his wife stayed by the shore, there also lived an old woman. Betty Lyall was her name, a woman who'd given to the sea two sons and a husband. Although her husband had come from the Moray coast she was a wife from the west, Kintyre to be precise. It was by chance, as I walked my two lads down by her door one day, she invited me in.

As we got chatting in her immaculate front room, it became apparent we shared the love of storytelling. This is a tale she told me from her home ground. Steeped in tradition, it held me spellbound. See what it does to you, reader.

Superstitious and fearful of strangers were the folk of the western Highlands, but not so the inhabitants of Morvane House, home of John McPherson and his family. He was not a big man in stature, but in heart and good nature there were few his equal. While he gave most of his time to rearing cattle, his wife opened their home to many a weary traveller passing by in need of a bed. No one was turned away. Over a wide area, folks knew if their journey was broken by wild weather then the light of Morvane would offer shelter, and no matter how poor the travellers were, they never failed to offer something in way of payment. A halfpenny, a penny, a spare pair of shoes, a plaid, hat, anything would do for payment, but not many left without handing over a morsel of sorts. If Mistress McPherson needed work undertaken then this too was offered in lieu of money.

McPherson, a busy man, spent long spells away at markets or doing deals connected with his cattle. Now, it was while he was away that his good wife allowed a certain stranger over her doorstep, and if he'd been there it's doubtful if he would have given night shelter to such a one. Exceptionally tall, head covered by a black hood attached to a long cloak, she stood in silence at the half-opened door of Morvane. 'What can I do for you this dreich nicht?' enquired Mistress McPherson.

No answer came from the mysterious stranger, so she began to close the door. Other visitors were complaining at the sharpness of the wind that found its way in to suck upon the burning sticks in the hearth, throwing spirals of smoke around the room. A long skeletal arm, thrust forth from underneath the cloak, stopped the door from closing. Mistress MacPherson looked at the woman, who stared back with a look that sent shivers running from her toe to her head. A white face without sign of life, and eyes cold as granite glared silently and sternly from beneath the hood. Shaking off the foreboding rising in her breast, the good wife further opened the door and offered hospitality.

'Come in, woman, for this night grows colder by the second. Now sit ye yonder by the kitchen door.'

Morvane was full that night, so the hostess could offer little in way of bed, but she brought the stranger some food and a blanket, and pointed out a place where she could find sleep upon a window bench. The eerie visitor refused food, but took the blanket and sat down on the bench seat, staring at each of the other guests who had fallen into an uneasy quiet. Before that knock on the door the house was full of laughter and good crack. One by one everybody made excuses and went to bed, not so much as looking sideways at the woman in her dark clothing.

When a seat by the fire emptied, she rose and warmed herself. Outside, rain lashed at the windows. Mistress McPherson wished her husband John was home, because she did not know what to do with this person who refused to utter a word. But tiredness was overtaking her, so she told the woman that if she wished more privacy then there was a small loft above the stables. The stranger nodded her head, took up the blankets, then turning slowly pointed at a box of candles. Mistress McPherson offered the box, and instead of one the dark-cloaked woman took seven; her hostess, wanting rid of her, said nothing.

By midnight, John, who'd decided to cut his business short, came trotting home. The hour was late, and, as was only to be expected, all of Morvane was in darkness. But there was a light coming from the little room above the stables. Why? Not wishing to waken his wife, John thought he'd find out whoever was in his stables using candles. It was stacked high with bundles of dry hay, and if a spark landed in the midst of it, the whole lot would burn. He called up the wooden ladder leading to the room, but no answer came. He climbed up and knocked upon the door, but it was not opened to him. Not to be beaten, he went outside and stood up in his horse's stirrups. As his eyes fell on the awful sight within, his heart almost stopped in his chest!

Stretched out on the floor lay the stranger, surrounded by seven lit candles, arranged like so—three on one side, three on the other, and one to her head. John McPherson was amazed, and for a moment spellbound. Then, without the woman touching them, three candles went out. Then two more, then another one. All were extinguished except for the one at the head. Then came the most terrifying minute of his life, as she rose up, turned towards him, and began to sway. In the little light that remained, he saw by her heinous appearance this was no mortal woman. To his utter horror, it was a creature he'd prayed never to see in his lifetime—it was the Banshee. Here at Morvane. This demon had come with a prediction from the dark country. As she moved from side to side, her long grey hair, thick and matted with swamp peat, also swayed to a hellish rhythm. She floated over towards him, smiled menacingly, and was gone as the final candle flickered out.

John had been brought up on tales of this apparition coming. Why did it appear? To herald doom, that's why. He trembled, thinking of his sons, all six of them.

Although shaken and terrified to the bone, McPherson wasn't one to show fear, especially before his dear wife. So without disturbing and alarming her, he slept downstairs at the fireside. Yet to say that he slept would be an exaggeration; he had more than enough to think about. Three of his sons were employed at the herring fishing. Because they had managed to buy a boat of their own, he was indeed a proud father. The eldest son, who'd recently married, named the boat after his young wife, Catherine.

Next morning he was troubled dearly, because the 'take of herring' season had begun. His fine sons knew that in Kilbrannan Sound there were silver darlings that would fill their boat to capacity.

John, at breakfast next morning, asked his wife who had lodged in the stable loft the previous night. Did she realise that by burning candles the stranger could have sent the whole place up in flames?

'Husband, I was feared by her appearance, but she refused to say who she was. We had a full house, so I let her stay in the loft.'

Not wishing to frighten his wife, John said nothing of what he'd witnessed. After lighting a fire and briefly chatting with two wanderers who'd stayed the night, he said to his wife: 'Bad weather comes, I feel it in my bones. Anyway, this is the time when it always blows the severest gusts, so I think I'll ride down to Campbeltown Loch to see if I can catch our lads in the fleet. If the weather gets any worse they'll do better not sailing till the sky shows clear.'

But what John was unaware of was his sons had set out a day early. They weren't near the port yet, and had little knowledge of the blackening sky heading toward the Kilbrannan Sound. John lost no time in galloping towards the shoreline. The raging water had many boats scurrying for safety. Some found the harbour, while others headed for the Saddel and Carradale. All of the boats had found safe havens—all, that is, except one. The McPherson boys had been far offshore when the huge black clouds released their fury. John from the back of his sweat-soaked steed saw them struggling alone in the raging sea.

Men and women, frightened at the boys' predicament, ran up and down, screaming for the lads to make inshore. But even if they'd been able to hear them it was useless, the sea was their mistress now, and she was screaming doom. Catherine stood among the crowd on the shore, calling from the depths of her heart, 'Duncan, ma man, beat ye the ocean and come hame tae me.'

John kept up his agonising vigil, galloping the length of Carradale's shore, calling all the time upon God who might just pity his beloved sons and render them safe. 'Oh mighty father in Heaven, if you need my sons, then take them now and do not prolong this agony further. Take them into your care and love them as I have done since their first breaths.'

He reached a point near Carradale where the ground allowed a wider view of the sea. Just at that moment his horse gave way beneath him, and at the same time the boat carrying his brave lads was swallowed by one enormous wave, never to surface again. John fell upon the wet earth, lifted his fist in a futile defiance of the elements, and cursed the demon Banshee with her mantle of despair.

Suddenly his heart grew cold with fear for the safety of his other children. Leaving his mount to the hungry sea birds he went down to the shore and took his daughter-in-law Catherine home. She would, if left to herself, have taken her own life, for so much had she and Duncan meant to each other.

After the period of mourning was over, John still hadn't told Mistress McPherson about the Banshee. Maybe, with the loss of the three boys, the curse would be ended. Perhaps his fears for his two sons, who were in the Americas with the 42nd regiment fighting the French, were unfounded.

But the doom-maker hadn't finished with the McPhersons. Rumours that many soldiers had been killed during recent battles circulated among the Highland folk. 'Rumours,' John told his worrying wife, 'just gossip gone mad.' Yet in his heart there began a terrible gnawing which would not go away.

Soon the word came—that dreaded news he prayed never to hear. A young man stood solemnly on the cold doorstep of Morvane, a letter sealed with black wax held tightly in his palm. Catherine carried it into the house. Mistress McPherson bit hard into her knuckles, asking a servant to go for the master.

John felt the icy fingers of death run up his spine as he broke the wax seal. Trembling, he slowly opened the letter. 'Sir, as Captain of the platoon in which your gallant sons, Hugh and Alister, served, it is my sad duty to inform you they have given their lives in the most heroic manner.'

The letter went on and on about the exemplary conduct of his sons in fighting for the 42nd, but it made no difference to him and his broken-hearted wife. Death had come once more. Where once six sons filled their happy home there remained but one, young Ian.

Circling his arms around his wife to comfort her, he said, 'My love, I have something to tell you. So awful is this I can scarce bring myself to speak. However in view of our loss I feel I should.' John held her close, and told of the vision he'd seen that night.

'You saw seven lights, my love—we have six sons. Oh please, do not tell me we are to lose wee Ian, and...'

'And me,' he whispered. 'Surely I am the seventh.'

This was far too much for a mother who had lost all but one of her children. She could and would not talk again on the matter. 'I will not believe,' she declared, 'that what has befallen us is any different than to any other parent who has lost loved ones to the sea and to war.'

Two months went by, and John refused to take young Ian anywhere near danger. The cattle might stampede him or he might fall overboard while fishing. Ladders were also forbidden. Like a hawk, John watched over his son, but another worry plagued him; who was the seventh? If his wife were to die, then how could he go on? Yet, unknown to him, she also felt the power of the dark supernatural curse, and feared dreadfully for him.

Time went on, and with it the diminishing fear of death. Spring brought a fragrance from pretty apple-blossom trees. Ian and John thought a gentle day's fishing at the small safe stream off the River Bran which ran by Morvane would produce nothing untoward. After a time John went into the house for some refreshment.

How Ian slipped and banged his head was a mystery. Yet there he was, face-down in the pool, bonny thick blonde hair floating like a lily.

'Oh God, how could you take them all, and it will be my love next. Is heaven so empty that you desire them all?'

No one heard John's agonising pleas, because as he made to pull his son from the water he too slipped and the seventh light went out.

Mistress McPherson and Catherine, from that day, as John would have wished, continued to offer shelter in the bosom of Morvane. It is doubtful though, if on a misty winter's night, they'd open the door to a tall, narrow-shouldered, hooded female!

8

IS THERE ANYBODY THERE?

Coming once more to our time in Macduff, I want to keep the subject of superstition alive if I may. This is a more modern tale, in fact it happened to Davie and me. Shivers run up and down my body as I recall this incident.

'Come down and have a go at the séance crack,' said Uncle Joe one morning. He was my father's youngest brother, and I thought the world of him, also of Doreen, his wife. They lived, as I said earlier, down on Low Shore. An old-style house it was, not the usual fishermen's cottage, more like a well-to-do body's place. They, like us, were renting, and when they first moved in it was dark and moody, but in no time they'd freshened the place up with their own special touch. Doreen loved flowers, they were everywhere. Joe loved music, which could be heard drifting from open windows and never-locked doors. The kettle was seldom off the boil for anybody happening by who was wanting of a cuppy.

If you have yours to hand, then let's go down to their place and touch the unknown. But before I go any further, I want to clarify something: what happened that night is in my opinion unexplainable. Perhaps those who were there were controlling the messages that came through unconsciously. But what if the messages came through by themselves?

These séance nights were becoming quite fashionable in and around the small coastal villages during the time we lived in Macduff. I thought it sounded like fun, something different. Davie and Uncle

Joe were out to take the mickey, but Doreen—well, she had taken a more serious look at the prospect of raising the dead. Youngest sister Babsy came along to make up numbers.

Sister Renie, who by now had a steady boyfriend, offered to baby-sit. Her gentle manner and quiet beauty had captivated a handsome young fisherman, and he was soon more than a visitor. He swept her into his own love net and she was caught, hook, line and sinker. They were later to marry and produce two lovely bairns, a boy and girl.

I remember setting foot in the big house that night. Darkness and a cold sea breeze had made Doreen close her curtains, giving the place a more enclosed feeling. Joe's record player had broken, it needed a needle, I think, but can't quite remember. Anyway, there was a deathly quietness. That could have been for two further reasons. Doreen had not long since had their first child, a bonny wee lassie who was sleeping soundly in a large Pedigree pram near the window; or perhaps she just wanted the proper atmosphere for our gathering!

On a large coffee table Doreen had arranged all the letters of the alphabet in a circle. Centred within the ring was a glass; not any special kind of glass, just a simple ordinary everyday one. She held out a notepad and pencil and said, 'who wants to write down the messages from the spirit?' I took the job, yet I don't know why.

Doreen instructed us to sit, this we did. Davie and Joe began laughing at how she was being so serious.

'I happen to think there are as many unexplained things on this earth as there are explained ones,' she said, raising her voice at their inability to control themselves.

Babsy agreed with her. Only sixteen was my wee sister, but sometimes she'd the mind of one far older.

Joe apologised to his wife, then said, 'Sorry pet, now who are you going to crack tae the night? Henry the 8th might have a tale tae tell, ask him why he had it in for women. Maybe the poor bugger wis a poof and didnae ken it.' I told him homosexuality was rampant in those days, but not among kings; Royals would get a bad name if it was broadcast that they didn't walk the straight line.

'Well, how about wee Harry Lauder tae give us a song?' My uncle was in fits laughing by now, and Doreen was not pleased. Even I began laughing at the antics of Uncle Joe. Once again she scolded him, 'Look, Joe, if you're not going to play the game, go and make a cup of tea.'

'OK, I'll stop. Now let's get started.' He promised to stop acting the clown. Davie didn't want to annoy Doreen, so if he'd a joke to tell, he sat on it.

So there we were, then, all sitting in a circle, me with pencil and paper at the ready, Doreen, Joe, Davie and Babsy all with their fingers on the top of the glass.

'Is there anybody there?' enquired Doreen, in quivering tones.

Joe bit down on his lip, trying hard to be serious, but at Doreen's second attempt in a more quivering voice than her first, he offered to make tea instead.

With him whistling about in the kitchen, we got down once more to reaching beyond the veil of life. Doreen took in a deep breath, as if willing a response from the glass, and said, louder this time, 'is there a spirit in this house?'

Suddenly, with all eyes on the glass, it moved very slowly. It seemed to be making up its mind whether or not to communicate with us, going from left to right, then stopping and moving again. Doreen opened her mouth to repeat her request, but before she'd half a word formed on her lips, the glass, in a most determined fashion, shot up to YES.

Doreen gave a wee squeal, so did Babsy, while Davie pulled away his finger as if it had been burned. Joe came dashing from the kitchen to see what the commotion was.

'Sit down, Joe, forget the tea,' whispered Doreen.

'Why, has King Henry decided tae crack?'

His wife peered inside the pram to check her sleeping infant and said, 'we've made contact. Our visitor has arrived.'

Her words sent shivers up my arms, and I could feel the hair rising on them. She told me to write everything down. Tightly I held the pencil, notepad unsteadily settled on my shaking knees.

'Who are you?' she asked the unseen being, which had turned us all into zombies with staring eyes and white faces. At first, no answer brought a little relief, colour returned to Babsy's face.

Then, slowly but methodically, the glass came to life. I wrote down each letter to form these sentences: *my name is Lyall this was my home I was a lawyer I do not want to be here why are you doing this?*

Joe's eyes widened with sheer excitement. 'What great fun. Ask the spirit questions, Doreen.'

'I can't do that Joe, I'll not mock the dead.'

'Oh, come on, what harm is there in asking it some questions? Will we win the football pools, ghosty? Or, let me think, how long is a piece o' thread?'

There was no movement from the glass. After all, we were exhausted and the baby was stirring. Doreen picked her up and went into the kitchen for the bottle feed.

For an hour we drank tea and chatted, then, when baby had fallen back to sleep, Doreen asked us if we wanted to have one more go, giving Joe the sternest look to tell him to behave.

'This is rubbish, Doreen,' he told her, 'it's all done by your own control of the glass.'

'Well, let's see if your finger will make a difference.' She bade him sit and take a place.

I felt unable to touch the thing and was happy to stick with my notepad.

'Are you willing to talk with us, Lyall?' was her next question into the void.

This time the glass shot violently towards the YES and back again to the centre. 'That was a bloody quick response, this bugger fair fancies a crack,' said Davie, who up to then had been fairly quiet. Doreen looked at each of us and said, 'who has a question for the spirit?'

Davie wondered if his dead brother was happy, and asked the spirit to speak with him. '*I am fine Mother isn't well keep an eye on her.*' I wrote without taking my eyes off the board.

Davie went pale and removed his finger. Babsy asked after someone, but I can't remember who. Doreen too asked to speak to some long-gone relative.

Then it was Joe's turn. Now, my uncle still wasn't convinced that we weren't subconsciously controlling the messages, and he asked to speak to a certain mass murderer he'd read about from the fifties. In fact he one of the last men to be hung in Scotland. This request had the glass stop dead and not move another inch. He asked twice, three times, yet no response came forth.

'There now, I told you it will only move when the answers are in your own heads. None of you know anything about that murderer, therefore it's unable to say anything, I knew it was all a bloody sham and you are all believing it.'

Thinking him right, we sat back, taking our fingers off the glass. What happened next would change forever my uncle's attitude towards such things as spirits. I still had my pencil and this is what the glass, without a finger touching it, spelt out—'*there is a baby in this room!*' The dead man whom Joe had asked to come had included, among his victims, little children!

That was the end of that kind of entertainment for me. From that moment on, the dead, as far as I was concerned, would stay just that.

9

CHAPBOOK TALES

The whole area along the coastline of the Highlands is steeped in superstition. When the rest of the country was embracing religion, it still adhered to old druid ways. Into this rich seam of dark history I want us to travel now.

'What's a chapbook, Jess?' I hear you ask, when you see the title of this chapter. Well, as far as clever folk have told me, it was the very first kind of book written for ordinary people. No words of great literature did it contain, just simple words with simple stories. A chapman would travel the land, selling his wee books to whoever could afford one. Centuries ago, gypsies were renowned for spreading news through ballads and poems, but so was the chapman.

I learned that this particular body whose story I am going to describe was also a gypsy wanderer. Travelling gypsies seldom drifted outside a certain area. I am part of the Perthshire travellers, who are known for a touch of blarney. Stewarts were mainly Highlanders. Young and Gordon were Borderers.

Not all travelling gypsies could read or write; truth is, they seldom did. Yet in every tribe one would aim to excel the others by teaching himself. Then, when stories were told, the writer would take down many a tale.

So here's a wee snippet of folklore from an old travelling gypsy's Highland chapbook. It's about a lass and a werewolf; the greatest shapeshifter of the supernatural world.

Many are the times I felt unable to go into the forest or play by a pond after hearing tales of the shapeshifters. Travelling bairns never failed to lie wakeful at night if it was thought a shapeshifter had prowled through their campsite. It was said that witches and war-locks seldom walked at night if the wolf howl was silent. Were-wolves were part and parcel of my parents' upbringing, long before Hollywood got wind of them. But I'm losing the thread. Let's go on with the tale.

Douglas loved Loarn greatly, yet how difficult it was for him, a mere woodcutter, to show her how much. Many times had he passed the big house where the master had her wearied by an enormous burden of work. One glance of affection in his direction was enough to cause her strict master to whip her hard. Only at night could she find time to slip away and meet him, yet night was also the time for the blessed relief of sleep, and her visits greatly diminished as she'd have to lie down upon her bed exhausted.

Douglas decided enough was enough, and that he would buy her from the evil man. He was met at the big house door by a manservant who ushered him in. When the master said that to buy her would take thirty pounds, poor love-torn Douglas knew it was impossible. Not in all his lifetime had he seen such an amount, nor was he ever likely to do so. As he walked away from the house, something floated from a high window. It was a small piece of paper, and on it were written the words, 'she of night will unleash our love.'

Obviously it was from his beloved, but why did she wish him to go where few would dare—into the deep forest to take counsel with *An Cheilach*, the Old Woman. Long had rumours followed one another of how she flitted over treetops straddling a broomstick, cackling at the moon. Her spells, when uttered, could herald death and worse. Yet if Loarn wished it, then he had no choice. That night, alone and a wee bit scared, Douglas crawled through brush-wood and briar, paddled moonlit streams, climbed hillock and glen, until beneath a canopy of forest trees he stood outside her dim-lit hovel. 'Can ye lower yer heed when enterin' ma hame, Dougie, ah've toads and bats, and een-gouged rats, hingin' drying by the door.'

'Mistress, ye have had word o' ma visit?'

'Aye, lad, I ken the thoughts in yer head afore ye have an inklin' yersel.'

'Loarn has sent me tae ye. Oor love will shrivel an' die if yon maister o' the Big Hoose is oucht tae dae wae it.'

The old biddy lifted her spirtle stick from a black stew in a cauldron from which nobody but Auld Nick from Hell would sup, and bade him sit. He obeyed and waited.

'Loarn, as ye ken, is a MacLennan. Dae ye ken whit that name means?' she said, adding a long worm to her pot.

'That I do, it means "son of the wolf."'

'Well, you're a clever yin, I'll gi'e ye that. Now listen tae me, Dougie, and listen well. Loarn is the daughter of John MacLennan, who was a "son o' the wolf". Her very name, Loarn, means wolf. There is more in a name than we ken, lad.' She stared upwards at flickers of moonlight coming through a crack in the roof, where spirals of unearthly smoke were allowed to escape. 'Time is slipping by. Now, I can see ye lo'e the lass, but how much? That will be the test.'

'Dinna doubt—ma heart will love nae other. If she escapes me, I'll gi'e up ma ain life.'

The old hag could see a determination in his face, etched there by his longing for Loarn. 'Come with me then, laddie, an' meet yer fate.'

Not understanding, he followed behind as she half-floated over the moss-carpeted floor of the dark forest, lit only by the spreading moonlight. An owl hooted eerily, then rose in slow motion to surprise, then rob some small unsuspecting creature of its last breath.

Douglas soon found himself in a clearing facing some form of den. Sticks and broken branches knitted together made a door. 'Go inside now, Dougie, and may the Earth serve you both well.' At those words she floated backwards, and was swallowed by shadows.

How long he waited for whatever was to come to him, he could not tell, yet all the while he felt eyes watching him, staring into his very soul. Then, from the den, he heard a low growl. His heart beat loudly like a drum, he wanted to run, to scream, to fight, but his body had frozen. It was like a dream. Just when he thought his heart would burst in his chest, a face loomed from the darkness. Eyes yellowy-red, fangs dripping, jaws open wide, it pounced and sank great teeth deep into the flesh of his neck. Then the wood was gone. He was fleeing into some long black passage, pursued by hundreds of howling wolves. He ran and ran until a mountain stood before him; he leapt upon a pinnacle of rock and began to fight the wolves—one by one they fell as he ripped their bodies in shreds. As the last one lay broken and bleeding, he stretched his head towards the clouds that skipped past the full moon and screamed. Mountain and earth shook. Then a smell entered his nostrils, one that called to him to follow and seek out. With speed never before afforded him, he leapt through the forest until he stood outside the big house. With the same haste he bounded up the stone steps, kicked open the front door and leapt the stairs to a small room. With brute force he pushed the door, which fell from its hinges to the floor. Loarn was waiting. Together, side by side, they left the big house and disappeared into the cover of trees.

Next day the master was unable to speak, let alone eat a morsel of breakfast. Later, when more composed, he asked if any of the servants had seen what he had seen, running over the gardens in the moonlight?

When asked what that was, he answered with eyes terrified and staring: 'Why, the wolves of course. Did naebody see them, the big black brute and the slender white yin?'

The seal too was known to shape-shift, under cover of dream-time, to become, once again, a human. In North Uist were found the origins of the seal folk. It is believed that the name MacCodrum means 'the son of the seal'. The song 'Mhairi Dhu' is the seal song. Mhairi was betrothed to Donal the boatman, but one night on the eve of her wedding she set off in a dream state and met a seal man. He transformed her into a seal, so that every night she would shape-shift into one. From this union, folks say, were descended the MacCodrums of North Uist, who were brown-haired, brown-skinned, had curiously-set ears and round, bullet-shaped heads. This is in contrast to most folk of that place, who have more of a Scandinavian appearance, with blonde hair and blue eyes. As I say, this is only a snippet from a chapbook, and I cannot confirm what are the real facts.

Hares too were shape-shifters. Once upon a time Donald, who had more than one run-in with a nasty old hag of a neighbour, was cutting peat when a monster hare ran past him, pursued by two hounds. Donald lifted his spade and brought it down so hard upon the beast that he split it in two. What a fright he got when the animal turned into none other than the old woman who lived nearby. When he got home, imagine his horror when his wife met him with the news that the old woman had been killed by a kick from a sheltie. He didn't tell his wife what he had seen on the bog—it was, in fact, the old woman's soul being chased by the Hounds of Hell.

Cats haven't escaped a reputation for shape-shifting either.

There are better-known stories of shape-shifting like 'Beauty and the Beast', and tales of water kelpies. Even Shakespeare told tales about such mythological beings. There's no end of stories about them—of goats, peacocks and rats which transformed themselves. It was said that the old witch who turned herself into a rat was recognised by the lack of a tail. This is interesting, because folk tradition says that for every limb in the human body there is one to correspond in the rat except for its tail. So a tailless rat would clearly be a witch.

My favourite shape-shifter is a drunken man on a Saturday night. It always amazes me, the difference in him from earlier, when sober and sensible, to his downright mental state with the alcohol in him.

We will no doubt wander back again through the pages of my chapbook, but meanwhile let's see what is happening on the home front.

10

FATTY

Davie and Daddy found the painting-jobs drying up—in both senses of the word—so what did my water-hating husband do? He took a job on a fishing-boat, and boy, did he learn the hard way that it's not an easy life on the choppy sea.

He looked terrified out of his skin standing on board that first day. We had walked the few hundred yards with him from our house to the harbour. Johnnie said, 'Daddy has a green face, Mummy.' And that he did, as the waves almost swallowed his vessel. My poor man, what he did to put food on the table. The boat was a trawler, with a crew of grand lads, especially the cook, who had his own ideas of the best way of filling my man's belly, and just as odd a way of causing him to empty it over the side of the boat.

Yet not being there out on the briny I have only what Davie told me to go by. In his words, 'it was a hard life, catching wee fish, big fish, and giants o' fish'. So let's leave him to the ocean for a while, and I'll tell you how that blasted weight problem of mine left me with more than a fleeting resemblance to the biggest fish Davie was netting on his trawler. I will take you on some of Davie's trips as a fisherman later on, but firstly we'll go through the tale of a fatty.

The Macduff folk were right proud of their swimming pool, Tarlair, a mile from town and lying on the brink of the ocean. Everybody from nine months to ninety swam in this man-made dam. The only problem was when the tide came in—there sometimes came with it an odd fish or jellyfish, you know the kind of thing. Not many big ones got in, because local lads were employed to clean the pool regularly. 'Nothing gets past us,' I once heard a guy say, and he wasn't kidding. Parents would sit about sunning themselves; picnics were enjoyed as the wee ones ran in and out of the sea-green water. My boys loved it, and so did I.

However there was a difficulty, not a big one, but a difficulty nevertheless: where would I purchase a swimming costume to accommodate my massive frame, all fourteen-and-a-half stone of it?

You might ask how I knew I weighed this amount? Well, one morning as the boats were unloading, I went down to the harbour for some free fish. It was usual for the man weighing in the catches to give a freebie to whoever was there. 'You're an awfy breadth for sic a wee quine,' the weighman said looking me up and down. To be honest, I'd never given my weight-gain that much thought, because my man said he loved me no matter how fat I got. He'd laugh and add—'more of you to cuddle.' So imagine my horror when the weighman told me I was too heavy for his scales. Of course he was kidding, but when I stood on them the needle did a jig.

'Fit are ye scoffing tae mak a bonny quine like yersel sae swelt?'

'Pavement, swallow me up,' was all I could think as I walked away. Suddenly I thought all eyes were on me, what a shaming it was. I turned and pushed my children back home, feeling every cursed pound of unwanted flesh.

'Get some exercise done, lassie.' This was Mammy's remedy for fatties.

Yet I seemed to walk miles every day, and although we'd a telly it only got switched on for Johnnie's programmes. But how could I bear to stay this weight? From that moment I decided I would lose the unnecessary flab.

'I saw some swimming costumes, Jess, there's a sale of them in the Co-op,' said my wee sister Babsy. 'All sizes, even ones to fit you.'

How awful she sounded, but she was only trying to help, I knew that. So I bought a Speedo, a nice black number. 'It slims one, they say,' said the assistant—who was three times fatter than me, cheeky imp.

Well, summer was upon us, and off I went with my laddies to Tarlair, Johnnie toddling by my side, Stephen in his pram which was loaded with goodies to eat, buckets and spades and swimming gear. Just in case I got stuck undressing, my Speedo was on under my clothes. Mammy came along too. Everybody from Macduff was of the same mind, and the place was heaving. 'God,' I thought, 'of all days to introduce my body-filled Speedo to the Moray coast, I have picked the worst.'

For ages I watched Johnnie paddling and splashing, running over to Mammy and me for a digestive biscuit, only to drop it into the water and cry for another one. Since his close escape with illness I would have given him the world, and he knew it, the fly wee devil. So after handing him a few digestives I gingerly stepped out from under a rainbow-coloured beach towel (another Co-op bargain), and while Mammy sat doing a word puzzle next to sleeping Stephen, I slid under the water at the deepest end.

It had been a long time since I swam, and in no time I was in my element. I always was a good swimmer, and could keep up with many a powerful travelling laddie with frog arms and lizard legs. Ever since my uncle threw me in one year at the Lunan burn pool at Gothans outside Blairgowrie, I have had the water powers of a mermaid.

At first I swam like a butterfly down the length of the pool, until a baldy man with the body hair of an ape began doing dives under me, emerging to smile into my face. 'What a show-off,' I remember thinking. Suddenly after his umpteenth dive, it dawned on me that this twit of a water zebra was having a good look at my bulk. And everybody knows we look twice as big under water as above it. That old cliché, 'if you can't beat 'em, join 'em' came to mind, so I too took to diving and soon felt a lot more comfortable. The hairy one, obviously exhausted, left the deep end to me and one old woman. She also got out of the pool and my happiness returned when it was apparent I was the only one left in. Not so at the shallow end, it was filled with squealing weans. As I threw everything into my swimming the crawl, diving, floating, backstroke and butterfly, I spoke to my bellies wobbling buoyantly under the fabric of the Speedo. 'I shall come up here everyday,' I told each pound, 'until every ounce is shed. Oh aye, you're for the chop, nothing surer.'

'One more length, then I'll call it a day,' I thought, swimming into shallower water. Suddenly the pitch of kids' noise grew louder and louder. I stopped swimming and stretched my head above water to see what alarmed the wee ones. My heart skipped a beat, thinking my lad was sick again, but when I saw Johnnie sitting beside Mammy my anxiety diminished. I took one more dive, then headed towards where my mother and kids were. Even under the water the screams were deafening. As I emerged onto the grassy bank, a pool attendant approached me. 'Thank God,' he said, 'the weans thought you were a basking shark. I'd get rid o' that black costume and wear a coloured yin, quiney!'

Well, definitely slimming was the order of the day after that awful experience. But a wee word of warning: if you too are feeling the effects of being overweight, then seek professional help. I didn't, and here's what happened.

Round the corner from where we lived was a chemist's shop. It had just received a batch of so-called slimming biscuits. These tasty treats had just entered the world of dieting. Women were scoffing them like hot cakes, they were flying off the shelves. A friendly assistant said that, if I wished, she'd sell me at a big discount a box of the biscuits which had come in wrongly coded. I bought the whole lot, and if memory serves me right it contained four months' supply. One biscuit instead of a meal, and the weight problem would disappear. Within six months I would see quite a visible difference. Aye, right!

What did greedy me do? Well, these tasty treats went down no bother with a cup of tea. Then, after a plate of my favourite stew and tatties, I enjoyed one as a pudding. Also, I'd better confess to you about something else. There was a chippy down a flight of stone stairs at the rear of our house, and if one bought anything after ten o' clock at night they got it half price. You must know by now I'm not one to snub a bargain, and my favourite was a 'polony supper'. Yes, I know, I know.

Another stone later, I was so depressed I could hardly put a foot over the door. My wee boys also were suffering, not getting the fresh air growing children need. Davie still never complained, not even when he came home one day after three weeks at sea and I threw myself into his open arms. The result was, he spent four days in bed with a strained back and sported a thick lip after coming in contact with my podgy nose. Ochone, ochone, what a mess I was in; totally out of control.

As I rolled from my bed one morning, I suddenly had a clear idea what to do. A visit and a chat with nice Doctor Mackenzie was what I needed. If anybody could help, it was him. Blood tests were taken, my weight properly monitored, and he prescribed for me a diet that would guide me back from the abyss. Did it heck! Along with watery chicken soup and butterless toast, I was still downing the slimming treats and going out to get late night polony suppers. I was a lost cause, with a mouth sucking in every morsel.

My young sisters gave me makeovers and hair-dos, but nothing could disguise the four chins all fighting for space somewhere in the region where I knew there was a neck. The only way to find my waistline was by running a finger inside my knickers and feeling for the elastic. Those were a laugh, those knickers. Mammy bought me some—yes, from the Co-op again; they were designed for elderly ladies who had 'difficulties'. I don't know what kind of problems these were meant to be, but if the Boy Scout movement had needed extra tents, then a visit to the Co-op for these knickers would have met their needs. Constant headaches were also plaguing me.

I went back to the doctor for the blood results. 'What are you eating?' he asked, with friendly concern.

'Along with your food stuff I've been eating biscuits, slimming ones.'

He was horrified on discovering the amount of them I was eating, and told me not to take any more.

'They are full of caffeine, Jessie, that would explain the headaches. Don't eat anything after six in the evening and forget the chippy suppers. I saw you one night popping out of the chippy with a great bundle under your arm, but you must stop them!'

I blushed red with guilt, knowing that Doctor Mackenzie had seen me sneaking about with yesterday's newspaper disguising comfort food.

I did lose weight but not in the way I'd planned.

It began with a headache, then a fever, then a horrendous bout of Asian flu. Up and down the country folks were dropping like flies. It was a merciless epidemic, and death followed like a flooded burn in its wake. Seven days I lay in bed, unable to keep a morsel of food down. Nightmares of drowning in giant middens of polony suppers provided hallucinations galore. Doctor Mackenzie and his team worked round the clock. The poor creatures were exhausted, working flat out tending flu-ridden Macduff, Banff and all the wee coastal villages scattered along the Moray coast. The local newspaper

One of the many rich traditions of travellers and gypsies—the coronation of the Gypsy King, Charles Faa Blythe, down in Yetholm in the Borders. (*Bob Dawson*)

A typical camp of Highland travellers. This one is at Pitlochry. (*Bob Dawson*)

The travellers earned a living by working at the traditional country trades. This is Isabella Macdonald, tinsmith, in 1889.

Every year these nineteenth-century travellers would head for Blairgowrie and the berry-picking, just as my family did.
(*Maurice Fleming*)

Strathdon tinkers getting the donkey ready for the day's journey.
(*Bob Dawson*)

Camps could be high up in the hills, like this one…
(*Bob Dawson*)

Jinklers' Cave, Wick

…or in even more unusual places, like this one in a cave in Wick!
Cave-dwelling gypsies are mentioned in the chapter 'The Curse
of the Mercat Cross'.
(*Bob Dawson*)

made depressing reading; it was terrible to see how many entries there were in the death columns.

I had youth on my side, however, and was soon back on my feet. It was a delight to see how much fat had turned to sweat and drenched itself into my bedclothes, I was two stones lighter, and liked what looked back at me from the mirror. So when I was fully recovered, I started on the odd day omitting breakfast. Lunch would be ignored and then teatime. I drank loads of water and felt great. I spent hours walking and exercising, and in time my weight on the freebie weighman's scales had registered the precious figure of ten stone. No more auld wives' breeks for me. My bum was sliding into silkies from then on.

When we skip through our twenties, we humans seem to have a 'nothing can hurt us' attitude. It is like we're superhuman. But some discover to their cost this isn't the case. 'Why am I so tired these days, Mammy?' I asked her one morning, with baggy eyes and sore bones. I'd a pile of washing to do, sweeping and washing of the floor (I had no hoover then). I usually took no time doing it, yet lately I could hardly wash a dish.

'I blame the slimming,' she scolded me. My food press, when she examined it, had only the bare necessities to feed the boys. When Davie was due home from the sea I'd get enough food for him. But now I'd just won a serious battle with food, and I loathed it! Never would I go down that nightmare route again. I could hardly look sideways at chips, those horrible things that piled fat onto my now eight-stone figure. Time for another visit to Doctor. More blood tests and questions. 'Are you sticking to that diet sheet I gave you, Jessie? You can eat more vegetables and fruit, it won't put weight on.'

'You can take a running jump,' I told him from my mind, adding to myself as I smiled and left his surgery, 'I'm beautiful now, and no way will I let so much as a loose hair live on my body.'

Within three days he came by to visit, saying he was in the area and so to save me a trip he'd brought the results of those blood tests over. 'Do you know what a normal blood count is, lass?' he asked, refusing to leave until I'd put a hot cup of tea in his hand.

'No, doctor.'

'It is twelve. Do you know what yours is? Well, it's six! You, my dear lass, are running on a half-empty tank of energy. Healthy blood cells are not being fed.'

'Big lumps of fat are not getting to crawl onto my body, doctor and I don't care a jot for blood-cell counts or anything else. You try being so fat the sheets on the bed suffocate you, try it, see how happy you are.'

'I won't let you kill yourself, lassie, and that's from a father whose kids love and depend on their mother. You're eight stone just now, but within three months you'll be seven. Let's see how cold those bed sheets will feel next to bone! And what about other children? Do you think your womb will carry a healthy bairn? No chance, you'll not have any nourishment to carry a baby nine months. You'll abort!'

I watched from the door as Doctor Mackenzie went into his car and drove away. I had visions in my head of a giant nurse with bulging biceps, sitting on my body and force-feeding me. That night Mammy came round and gave me a right talking to. Changing the subject eventually, she said that Chrissie and her family were moving up to Macduff; Uncle Joe had got them a house beside their family.

I had learned a lesson and been drawn back from the brink in the nick of time. Many young women are not so fortunate. From then on my weight stabilised. If I went over I cut back, and if I went under I ate more, but never again did I enjoy the taste of a dripping-thick battered polony supper.

Sadly, Doctor Mackenzie was right about aborting. Three months after his visit I miscarried.

11

POT HARRY

With Chrissie and her lot now living in Macduff, it felt more like a Riley clan gathering. Smashing ceilidhs were held in our parents' house, with singing, music and dancing. Neighbours were always welcome, and filled the house to bursting. Mammy and Daddy only drank a dram at New Year, so it was always soft drinks, and the best kind of entertainment comes this way.

Remember how in *Jessie's Journey* I shared my childhood days with you, travelling the shoreline in our old blue Bedford bus, and how my obsession with beachcombing had me with head hung, searching every inch of the beach for scrap metal washed up by the tide? Let me tell you of a man who shared this pastime with me. Pot Harry was his nickname and I think it was because of his trade—he was a real tinker.

In his day there wasn't a mile of Argyllshire he hadn't tramped. He knew every inch of coastline and everyone who lived on it. He was the last of his line. His father passed both his skills and tools on to Harry, little knowing that modern materials would replace tin and render his skill obsolete. 'Folks fair looked tae me coming before they bought aluminium things. With the old knives, forks, gairden tools, plenty o' need for Harry—but no noo, they didnae need me noo.' Those words I heard him mutter to himself one day as I played along a stretch of coast. I was seven years old, and remember like yesterday the colour of his old face and the sparkle in his blue eye. Bonnet tilted to the side of his head, he sat looking out to the ocean.

'What are you muttering, auld yin? Is the want on you?'

My honest childlike question was simple enough to understand. All I needed was as simple an answer. 'Ye wee imp, if ma leg wisnae broke, I'd skin ye fur that lip. There's nothing' wrong with my head. Now be away and leave me by myself.'

I could see my mother waving from the bus, which had been settled in a safe spot above the incoming tide. I ran back to the bus and my mother's stern instructions: 'You stop talking to strangers. Who is he, any road?'

'He's a live tinker, Mammy, mends pots like the auld folks done.'

This raised a curiosity in her, so taking my hand she walked to where he sat on a rock seat.

As we reached him recognition spread over Mammy's face. 'Hello, Pot Harry,' she said, greeting him with a hug, 'what are you daeing in these parts? Last time we met, you said the tinker days were over.'

However before an answer come forth, the old man let out a groan, touching his plastered leg. 'Wit have ye done tae yer leg?' my mother said, sitting beside Harry with a look of genuine concern on her face.

'Och Jeannie, ye'd never credit it, but all that ah did wis jump oot o' the road o' a train. I wis searching for auld tin cans for ma soldering over by Hoolit's Bend, when it jist came oot o' naewhere, bloody train wis on me before I heard it coming.'

'My God man, are ye deaf? A corpse in its coffin would hear yon rattling, puffing monster.' My mother laughed, shaking her head, saying the luck was on him for sure, then she asked where his camp was. He said it was into the wood, no more than a hundred yards from our bus. Then he began moaning once more. She thought maybe this old fellow was in need of some, as they say today, TLC.

Obviously he'd been hospitalised, hence the heavy stookied leg, but by the way he was going on you'd have thought he'd had to put the plaster on by himself.

'I think what you need, Harry my lad, is tae come back with us. I'll get Charlie to fetch yer bivvy and pitch it next tae the bus. What did the doctor say about the leg?'

'He telt me no tae dae any moving, in case ah did mair damage. But what bothers me, Jeannie...' his face turned quite serious: he was concerned about something and Mammy's second sight told her exactly what. 'You're worried the country hantel canny get their knives sharpened and pots soldered, aye, lad.'

'Ah'm nae sae bothered aboot the sharpening, they ken whaur ah am, they'll find me, nae doubting that. But ah've no a drop solder left tae sort the pots. Bloody stupid bugger that I am, for no rolling doon the bank away frae thon train. Trust me tae loup in the air and break the bloody leg.'

My mother shook her head and said, 'if a woman stood up and had her baby instead o' lying flat, then there's no many o' us would be going about.' Harry nodded, but I wondered what in the name o' Rabbie Burns did she mean? As we helped hoppy Harry back to our fire, I had to ask her. Both of them said in unison, 'all the bairns would chap their brains and heeds wid yet be empty!' None the wiser, I put it down to adult talk, and as every seven-year-old knows, adults are mad!

When Daddy came back from the moling he liked the idea of another male around to be able to talk man to man with, and soon we had Harry's wee tent plus his tinker tools nearby.

We later discovered travelling folks had taken him to hospital, and then when he had come out, left him where he wanted to be, back on the shore beside his tent. They weren't abandoning him, as you might think, reader. Travelling folks were always in and around that area, and those who had come to his rescue knew he'd be helped by them. Everybody knew the tinker would be thereabouts, and as well as his own kind, others needing his services would most certainly seek him out.

We liked Pot Harry, and next day after the breakfast dishes were washed, my family busied themselves in making him comfortable. One of my older sisters found a discarded armchair lying in the bushes. Daddy re-strapped it with slats of wood. After it had been cleaned up Mammy covered it with an old blanket, and with my three-legged stool for the elevation of his leg, Harry couldn't have been more comfortable. He was especially relieved by the knowledge that Daddy had promised to take him back to have his plaster removed in a fortnight, but still he was anxious, because his handicap prevented him from going out to search for solder.

Poor soul, this insurmountable problem weighed heavy on him. We told stories to entertain him, and sister Shirley formed from some tree branches a pair of crutches so that he could make his visits to wee behind trees, but I leave that picture to your imagination. Still, try as we might to help, our patient's worries grew deeper. Only one incident changed his mood for the better, when Mammy found a bag of minced beef he had long forgotten among his belongings. 'How long have ye had this, man?' she asked, holding it at arm's length. 'It's humming tae the high heavens.'

For the first time since we had set eyes on Harry, he opened his mouth and laughed from his belly. 'Ye ken this, Jeannie, that mince was rotten when I got it. I manged [asked] it frae a butcher, it's for my fishing, ye ragie mort ye!' (Cant for 'you silly woman you'.)

'Well, I'll put it down here beside this stone, and oor Jessie will rake out a can to keep them in.'

I was curious to see what contents the bag held—yuk, big yellow maggots, that's what!

'Go find a rusty can to keep them in, Jessie, and then me and you can go to the water's edge and fish.'

'You can pit them on the hooks, because I'll no hurt anything,' I told him defiantly.

In no time the battered can I'd found along the beach was crammed with yellow crawlies awaiting a watery death. Poor wee things, what harm did a maggot ever cause us?

Here's a riddle for you:

> *A wee, wee thing made o' leather*
> *Running up and down the heather,*
> *Through a rock, through a reel,*
> *Through my Grannie's spinning wheel,*
> *Through a miller's happer,*
> *Through a bag o' paper,*
> *Through sheepshank marrowbone.*
> *What is it?*

A wee maggot, of course.

Anyway, the sea kept her bounty of fish away from the hooked maggots that morning, and as the tide receded, back came Pot Harry's black mood. As young as I was, I could still feel his sadness, so asked if there might be something I could do to help.

'You're a great bairn, Jessie, but I need solder, and my leg hinders the finding of it. Now help me back intae that braw chair, ma leg's nipping right sore.'

'Great' I don't think I was, but I certainly was persistent. 'Tell me where tae get this solder, and I'll fetch some for you.' I told him I'd go everywhere except Hoolit's Bend.

He stared at the stones around his good foot. I'd given him brain food, he was thinking hard. He then bent over and gathered some of the stones. With a powerful throw, he made each one skim the water. It was like all his problems went skiff, skiffing with those stones. Somehow it seemed to me I'd either offered a helping hand or given him a difficulty. So, giving the dirty plaster on his leg a stroke, I told him of the time when, after sitting one day during a film matinee, I thought I could fly, like the screen hero, Batman. 'Broke ma leg intae bits, Harry. What a pain, and boy did it nip. Oh aye, thon's a horrible pain.'

When I'd finished, his smile returned and with it his spine straightened. 'That's an awfy stupid thing tae dae. God gave wings tae birds and no you or thon actor gadgie, Batman. I've seen him in heaps o' films, and he's as stiff as the plaster on ma leg. Now, kin ye rake the beach and ditches fer syrup and treacle tins?'

'Nae bother, Harry, I'm champion at raking. I'll even midden-rake, tae.'

'Oh lassie, that's music tae ma ears. Half a mile along the auld road is a braw midden. I never fail tae find dozens o' tins there. Better ask Mammy's permission afore ye go, though.'

I made off breathless with a big jute sack in my hand. Only a 'cheerio' did Mammy get, as my mission to find the precious solder galvanised my young legs!

It took me only ten minutes or so to come across a braw heaped midden which lay behind an unlocked metal gate. Before me and my bag could scour its contents, I waited as the 'churl, churl' growl of an old Brownie tractor-engine drifted off down the road leading away from the rubbish tip. The Brownie had just deposited a bogey full of rubbish. 'Great,' I smiled, in my element at being the first to get stuck into this new mountain of trash. I knew that nearby travelling bairns would not be long in joining me, so without inspecting the tins closely, I shovelled what I could into the jute sack. By the number of treacle and syrup cans I found, it was obvious the village folk in those parts had a liking for scones and sweeties. To make carrying simpler, I flattened them with a heavy stone. Soon, with a full bag, I made homewards to see Pot Harry. I can still to this day picture that wonderful smile spreading across his grey face when I appeared, filthy and bedraggled, dragging a jute sack full of rattling, clanking, solder-pocked cans.

Daddy set up a brazier made from an oil-drum cut in half and filled with coals, and set it by Harry. It was as if the broken leg had been forgotten as he carefully melted the solder, and saved it like gold into a metal cup, to be used to fix handles back onto pots and pans, mend pitchforks etc. While I had been collecting from the midden, Mammy had taken herself off round farms and houses, telling folks that Harry was able to do his work, hence the pile of jobs awaiting his expert attention. Pot Harry—a real 'trade tinkler'.

12

LIFE ON THE OCEAN WAVE

I promised to take you on board with my Davie during his brief career upon the wild ocean as one of that hardy breed who put their lives on the line, the Scottish fishermen.

I've a tail-wagging yellow Labrador by the name of Brigadoon, and a twelve-year-old Heinz variety with foul breath that both desperately need walking. So while Brig, auld Jake and I saunter off, I'll leave you in the expert hands of my man.

'She pestered me to death, did Jess, to take up my trade, but to be honest there were already plenty well-established joiners and carpenters around Banff and Macduff.

After Charlie and I finished painting, I did the odd homer with my tools, but everywhere a body goes in these parts the sea is never far away. Lads I'd met while having a pint kept me informed as to which boats were in need of deck-hands. There weren't many, sad to say, and if one did come up there was a long list of lads ready to set sail. I didnae fancy being thrown about on the ocean's swell, but the money sounded good. However taking to a life at sea had to be a serious business, not something you go in for lightly. So a visit to the Broo Office was first step. "Try it first," was the advice given, so I did. At twenty-two years old and eager to learn, I accepted a trial run on a sturdy seine netter. After it was over and the guts somersaulted a dozen times, I decided yes, it might be the very life for me. So off to Aberdeen to be schooled in the ways of fishing, staying at the Fisherman's Mission. First boat I was on, the *Ardenlea*, was a big trawler, with a great bunch of lads who made me welcome. I'll tell you about the cook who never (and this amazed me) entered a boat sober. When I saw him sway and bounce around the deck I thought, "what the hell am I daeing here?"

Yet as the boat set towards the wide ocean, he immediately sobered up. Captain, mate and crew batted not an eyelid as the man who would be sustaining us throughout our trip began the day as pie-eyed as a one-legged hen. "Why?" I hear you ask. Well, the reason was that this lad was as gourmet a ship's cook as you could find, a brilliant chef of very high standards. The only time we ate fish was on our final journey home. The rest of the time it was steak, beef, chicken and so on. But sad to say, my trial trip on *Ardenlea* soon came to an end.

While at the mission I met Danny, and what a lad he was. "Davie, boy," he asked minutes after being introduced, "will you do me a big favour?"

I always feel uncomfortable when strangers ask favours, but before I could answer him he continued, "if I give you half of my money, will you look after it until tomorrow?" Too young and too naive for my own good, I said yes. Then, on second thoughts, I wondered why he should part with a sum of money, big or small, to a stranger for safe-keeping.

"If I take all my money intae a pub, I'll come out fu' wi' empty pockets. If I take half of it, I'll still be rocking drunk. It's best to be sensible and leave enough for another time."

"This guy," I thought, "is mental!" However, I agreed, but only if another chap witnessed the transaction. So me and this witness, we waited outside the Fisherman's Mission for well over an hour past the agreed time, but no sign of Danny did we see. Next morning after breakfast, I wandered out to stretch my legs, and there, draped around a lamp-post singing to an empty bottle of rum, was the bold lad with not a penny to his name. Two wee black-clad nuns sped past, crossing themselves at the sight of the half naked torso. He was totally oblivious to the world and its wean.

When we later became better acquainted, he told me tales of his sea-faring days. Sine-die is the worse label that can ever be hung around a seaman's neck. It means he has been judged to be a degenerate and has forfeited the right to sail from the harbour where the sine-die is given to him. Danny, while working out of Grimsby, had been allowed little or no time off. His feet ached for a time on dry land, while his belly yearned for rum. In protest, he climbed a ship's mast, refusing to sail unless he was allowed time off. This act ended in his being sine-died out of Grimsby. Not long after that he came to Aberdeen, hence our meeting. He had a terrific sense of humour and never failed to make me laugh. Here is one of those times. We were together on my second boat, *Cedarlea*. This state-of-the-art vessel was fitted with all mod cons apart from the cook. He was as stern-faced a bloke as ever sailed the sea. Unlike my trial boat where our cook was of the finest, this teetotallar was as useless as they come. The food was bland and tasteless. Fish was served daily.

On the last day of our trip, and sick to death with watery soup and rubbish grub, someone insulted the cook by calling him a c—. "Who called the cook a c—?" demanded the Mate.

Danny stood up and replied, "who called the c— a cook!"

Well, folks, I can hear "she who must be obeyed" coming home with the jugals (her traveller word for dogs), so I'll say thanks for allowing me to share my time at sea with you.'

13

MY POETS

Before we go back to Macduff, I want to tell you a wee bitty about the poets who have freely contributed to my trilogy. Perhaps you may have wondered about them. Take my sister Charlotte, for instance, better known through these pages as Shirley, my honest as the day is long, 'I'll take on a giant if he annoys me' sister. Born on a freezing January afternoon in a small hut huddled between trees at the Bobbin Mill, she came into the world with (according to my mother's endearment) 'one eye open.' A tiny baby, who came into a war-torn world of uncertainty and misfortune. It was 1940, and Daddy was away some place in Europe, when Mammy, with three-year-old Chrissie on one side and four-year-old Mona on the other, gave birth to Shirley. When we chat about the Bobbin Mill, she laughs and wonders what other person can claim that on her first nights in the world, rats had to be swept out from beneath the bed before she was laid down. I sometimes think that maybe her honesty and forthright approach at calling a spade a spade might have led her to be isolated. Never one to tolerate fools gladly, she was left many times friendless and alone. Yet, if she lacked the art of tact, she excelled in having a natural beauty not many could match. Boys sometimes thought her aloof, and females looked on her as one so lovely she'd lure their men away from them.

At the young age of nineteen she met a handsome six-footer from Kirkcaldy. Within a few months they wed. Two children followed, first a girl, then a boy.

Everything in my dear sister's life seemed to be rosy, until deep in her throat a nasty growth began to flourish. Her thyroid was diseased. One illness followed closely behind another. Days spent in bed, soaking sheets in sweat, left her drained. Her moods swung from gentle to violent. Almost overnight that armour of strength she wore peeled away, leaving a weak and out-of-control young mother. This illness, undetected, crawled freely through her body for years. Only after a terrible pregnancy, ending with the tragic loss of a still-born son, did doctors discover what was slowly destroying my sister. The course of treatment was harsh and as violent as her mood swings. Her husband, a petted son of an over-protective mother, gave her no help and soon found another woman.

Left alone, the mountain seemed unclimbable, the road never-ending. Her only saving grace was her inner desire to become a song-writer, a verser, a poet. All the pain, the anxiety, the self-sacrifice, went into verse. Long nights she spent head down, scribbling feelings of love, hate and lost desires onto whatever piece of paper came to hand. This brought her back from the brink. Anger, hurt, heartache, the joys of watching her child's academic progress went into verse. If the words sang to her, she wrote the emotion; a haunting melody smoothed the feelings. Joy bounced over the page with loud operatic tones. Yet no one listened, nobody cared. The children grew and left home; this too she turned into songs with beautiful silent music; played them in her mixed-up head with a full orchestra.

She reminded me of a bluebell flourishing yearly in a field of nettles; one solitary flower wishing to be part of the bluebell wood. But no matter how she wanted to be like everyone else, it was never to be, because just as the bulb from which the bluebell lives withers and dies, it only emerges in spring once again to a solitary existence among those stinging nettles.

Then Dave Munro, ex-soldier, man about the house, came along, and they hit it off. Not only did he see the budding petals of her gift, he encouraged every minute of her life. Never far from her side, in fact close at hand when sleep-terrors filled her with nightmares, his strength guarded her vulnerability. Most of all, though, Dave encouraged her gift; installing a PC, recording equipment of every kind, books etc. Now, at long last, she is what she always thought it was her reason to be on the earth—a songwriter and poet. To date she has seventeen published works, is featured in Tim Neat's book as one of the 'voices of the Bards', and is working on her master-piece, *Kingdom of Marigolds.*

Here's a song she wrote for Dave who is her 'bees knees.'

BEES KNEES

You do not have the sight
To follow stars into the heavens.
You do not have the hearing
That can tell when mountains sway.
You do not have the reach
To touch the birds as they are leaving,
But to me
You are the bee's knees anyway.

You do not seek a quest
To pull the sword from out of that stone.
You do not have a plan
To save the day.
You do not have the means
To tackle poverty alone,
But to me
You are the bee's knees anyway.

You cannot solve the secrets
Beneath the desert sands.
You cannot sail the seven seas
By two o'clock on Sunday.
You can't control the high winds,
Or the waves that wash the beaches,
But to me
You are the bee's knees anyway.

You can become a legend,
Especially in my time.
You will release the magic
That I hope for when I pray.
You must be sure you love me,
Just as much as I love you,
For to me
You are the bee's knees anyway.

More of Shirley later, for now we'll talk about a real legend in his time—my friend Mamie's dad, Keith McPherson. He owned and ran a garage at the far end of Comrie in Perthshire. He's no longer with us, having passed away in 1973, yet the poems he left will remain. As long as his poems are enjoyed and respected, then how can oor lad be forgot?

Mamie trained as a nurse in the Western Infirmary in Glasgow, doing her training in the Royal Maternity, better known as Rotten Row. German POWs imprisoned at nearby Cultiebraggan Camp (those who posed no danger) would find a benevolence, seldom seen in one so young, from fourteen-years-old Mamie. When they visited Keith's garage she would give sweeties to the youngest and cigarettes to the older prisoners. In a recent television programme, Mamie met some of those POWs who came back to Comrie to say thanks for the kindness which helped them through a terrible time in history.

There were plenty of lads who, all the worse for a heavy night's drinking, found themselves sat in Crieff cottage hospital dreading a lecture from a local doctor. Worse still was the prospect of getting home to the wife, sporting another stitched head-wound and taking a tongue-lashing. It was Mamie they wanted to see, because never a lecture or a dressing-down or any other kind of warning about the evil drink did she administer. She would simply ask, while cleaning and bandaging, 'How is them weans o' yours, lad? Are you still working with so and so?' Gentle words from a dear lady, who knew her patient was punishing himself inwardly. Little did she realise it was her good nature that made him feel shame and remorse.

I have known Mamie for over thirty years, and to this day I've never heard her speak down to a living soul. Her couthy ways were inherited from Keith, and not only did he love his neighbours, but he made sure all the bairns living around Glenartney got to school on time. He owned and maintained the school taxi. His poem about this 'school taxi' speaks for itself.

THE AULD SCHULE CAR
(Sing it to the tune of 'Where the praties grow')

There's folk who like to travel,
And some foreign lands tae see,

Like sunny Spain or Italy,
Or even gay Capri.
But me I like the hameland,
So I dinna travel far,
I go driving up Glenartney,
Wi' ma auld schule car.

I have a wheen o' laddies,
Who are starting on life's road.
Wi' singin and wi' laughter,
Man, they mak a cheery load.
I join them in the chorus,
For I'm just as young they are,
When I'm drivin up Glenartney
Wi' ma auld schule car.

There's Billy an there's Bertie,
And Sandy one and two,
Wi' Stewart an wi' Jackie,
They complete the merry crew.
They sing a cornkister
Just as well as any star,
When we're driving up Glenartney
In the auld schule car.

I've got another laddie,
But like me he's left the schule,
We've made him leading tenor
Just tae earn his milk and meal.
He leads us in the singing,
And he keeps us up tae par,
When we're driving up Glenartney,
In the auld schule car.

The cuckoo in the season
Gi'es a call as we pass by,
The old cock grouse, he lifts his head,
An' winks a beady eye.
An' whispers tae his sittin' hen,

'Jist bide ye whaur ye are,
For ye ken its jist McPherson
Wi' his auld schule car.'

We dinna hae the golden sands,
Nor yet the sunny days,
But bonnie is the heather
Growing round Dalclathic Braes.
We see the winter shadows
On the snowclad Uam Var,
When we're driving up Glenartney
In the auld schule car.

We see the bonnie rowan trees,
Their flowers the summer's pride,
And then the scarlet berries come,
And deck the countryside.
Ye get a great contentment,
And a pleasure nane can mar,
When we're driving up Glenartney
In the auld schule car.

I've seen the glen in a' its moods,
In sunshine and in snow.
I've seen it at its brightest
When the autumn colours glow.
I turn quite sentimental,
Till a pothole gi'es a jar,
Then I ken I'm in Glenartney
Wi' ma auld schule car.

There's time when death's dark shadow
Haunts that lonely, lovely glen,
An' Grewer whispers tae his wife,
'We've lost anither hen.
It wisnae Fisher Ferguson,
Nor Pate frae Tighnablair,
It maun hae been McPherson
Wi' his auld schule car.'

So if you're bowed wi' trouble,
An' your sky seems dull an' grey,
If you think that fickle fortune's
Turned her head the other way,
Should you want to lose your sorrows
(An' be sure there's thousands waur),
Just come driving up Glenartney
In ma auld schule car.

My laddies a' hae left me,
Father Time has passed along,
I hope they face life's battles
Wi' the same auld cheery song,
As echoed round the hill tops
'Stron-e-moul tae Uam Var,'
When we sang gaun up Glenartney
In the auld schule car.

If you have read *Jessie's Journey*, my first book, you will recall John Gilbert, that fine gent who gave me permission to use his grandfather's moving poem 'The Tinker's Grave'. I knew little about him at that time. I simply read the verses, researched who it was that penned them, and discovered I had to ask permission from his grandson.

The poet lived in Perthshire, ran a fruit and veg. shop in Comrie, and was gifted, as we all now know, with the art of beautiful verse. Since *Jessie's Journey*, his grandson has very kindly given me the following information about the poem:

'One evening towards the end of the Napoleonic Wars, a young man, Peter MacEwan by name, was watching for smugglers in the woods of Strath Bran. He saw no smugglers; instead he saw a strange sight, the burial of an old tinker. When Peter MacEwan was an old man he described the scene to my grandfather when he was a young boy.

Each autumn a group of tinkers were in the habit of camping near my Grandfather's home. On one occasion he noticed that one of their numbers was missing and naturally asked where he was. "We left him sleeping 'tween the licht and the dark," was the mysterious reply.

That incident in Strath Bran and that reply inspired my Grandfather to write the poem.'

Travelling tinkers didn't always bury their dead without marking the spot. Up until the reign of Henry VIII they were renowned for their elaborate way of sending loved ones into heaven with precious belongings and lots more. Stones were erected over them and it was apparent what lay beneath the earth. Well, the king became obsessed with gypsies, whom he believed were carriers of the plague. It was for this reason he decreed that burials of these 'verminous creatures' be halted, and the remains duly dug up and burned. Certain undesirables looked upon this duty as a trade, because when remains were brought to court a small payment was paid to the grave-robber. From then on, English gypsies burned their deceased and all they owned.

Like wildfire the king's ruling spread to Scotland, and soon burials were carried out under a cloak of secrecy and darkness. No sign was left to signify that a dear one lay sleeping beneath the soil. The only witnesses were kin, and no stranger was allowed anywhere near.

Being from travelling folk, this was a story repeated many times to me as a bairn. If you don't mind I'd love to repeat John Gilbert's beautiful poem for you, just in case it has passed you by.

THE TINKER'S GRAVE

In the drowsie sound o' a murmurin burn
Far ben in the hert o' a boskie glen,
There they left the tinker sleepin,
But whaur? There's nane but the tinkers ken.

Was it close tae the silvery stream o' the Earn
Or set by the Ruchill's rockie bed?
The fairies that dance on the Leadnaig's banks,
Do they lull his sleep wi' their airy tread?

His bed was lined wi' the saft green mosses,
His shroud was the tent he had sleepit in.
His dirge was the tune o' that wimplin burnie
Played on the sough o' the saft west wind.

Owre him they made the tinker ritual,
They merched roond the grave an they keepit time,

Chatterin aye wi' a mystic mutter
Some cryptic words in a queer auld rhyme.

The lovelorn merl there in the lerac,
Singin his mate tae sleep fur the nicht,
Soondit the last post owre the tinker,
Full and clear in the fadin licht.

Never a mound did they raise abune him,
Nor chiseled a stane fer his grave tae mark
That unkent spot in the phantom country,
That lies merched in twixt the licht an the dark.

There in the land o' mellowin gloamin
Whaur the evenin shadows begin tae fa',
Whaur the nicht comes quietly creepin forrit,
An the day goes gently wastin awa.

In the drowsie soond o' that murmurin burnie,
Far ben in the hert' that bowskie glen,
There they left the tinker sleepin—
Whaur? There's nane but the tinkers ken.

That beautiful picture in verse, written in the old Perthshire tongue, never fails to bring a tear to my eye. However moving it is, my favourite poem of all that has been written is 'The Last o' the Tinklers' by Violet Jacob. Honest, I challenge the sturdiest heart among you to read it and not to feel a tiny tear welling at the corner of your eye.

THE LAST O' THE TINKLERS

Lay me in yon place, lad,
The gloamin's thick wi' nicht;
Ah canna see yer face, lad
Fer ma een's no richt.
But its ower late fur leein,
Fer ah ken fine ah'm deein,
Like an auld craw fleein,
Tae the last o' the light.

The kye gan tae the byre, lad,
The sheep tae the fauld,
Ye'll mak a spunk o' fire, lad,
Fer ma hert's growin cauld;
And whaur the trees are meetin,
There's a sound like waters beatin,
An the birds seem near tae greetin
That was aye singin bauld.

There's just the tent tae leave, lad,
Ah've gaithered little gear,
There's just yersel' tae grieve, lad,
An the auld dug lyin here;
But when the morn comes creepin
And the waukin birds are cheepin,
Ye'll find me lyin sleepin,
As I've slept saxty year.

Ye'll rise tae meet the sun, lad,
An baith be trevellin west,
But me that's auld an done, lad,
Ah'll bide an' take ma rest;
For the grey heed is bendin
And this auld shoe needs mendin,
But the trevellin's near its endin
An' the endin's aye the best.

Is that not the saddest poem? It is in my world. Say it aloud to
anyone who might listen, it sounds as bonny as it reads.

14

ENEMY AT THE DOOR

Talking about worlds, this tale we're about to share deals with a certain group of travellers living in their own world—Glen Lyon. We'll drift on down there now. It's 1944 and Daisy is beside herself with worry.

'Donald, ma man, where dae ye think yon Germans are the day?'

Donald grasped the neck of the struggling cock pheasant between the two middle fingers of his right hand and pulled, threw the jerking bird at her feet. He said, 'Daisy, I'll tell ye till I'm sick o' telling ye; the Germans dinna come this far south.'

'Better no leave ma washing hingin ower the dyke just in case, though.' Pushing her bouncing breasts up with clasped hands she went on, much to the annoyance of a long-suffering husband, 'Minnie Robertson said she'd heard—and by god, thon woman is as honest as the lang day—that a troop o' the buggers were seen in aboot Kingussie. Donald, my heart is feart, 'cause you ken that's no far awa frae us here in Glen Lyon.'

Poor Donald, ever since a lone tramp had brought news that Britain was at war with Germany, his wife hadn't given a minute's piece to his wind-battered ears. He put some more sticks onto the low burning fire, lifted a big black kettle and wandered off to fill it at a fast-flowing burn near their camp site. Her shrill tones pierced through his head. 'Aye, dinna answer me—go on, walk away, an' thon buggers nae mair than six miles frae my tent door.'

Wearily he turned and said, 'Kingussie is mair than six mile away lassie, I'd say nearer sixty.'

Truth be told, neither of them had the foggiest idea where anywhere was outside Perthshire.

'You're a good man, Donald, I ken you're telling me that to keep me frae worrying.' Once more she shoved her large breasts under her chin, folding arms beneath her cleavage to stop them going the way of all gravity-controlled flesh. He gazed at her and thought, 'my goodness, whit German wi' two good eyes would come near ma Daisy? She's long past her best, and one scud frae her power-loaded fist could split an oak log. He'd need tae get a pot shot aff afore she kent it.'

Yet, in spite of her failings, she was a good-hearted woman who'd never failed to brose and bannock a cold winter night; her cuddles fair warmed his bones when a long day helping out a glen shepherd had frozen him near solid.

He slowly walked back and hung his kettle on a metal hook suspended over the flames from a tripod of iron. As he dropped some twigs into the container, 'to better flavour the tea', Daisy spurted off again. 'I don't care whit ye say, there's nae way I'm hingin oot ma washed knickers over the dyke this night, or any other, until I've heard yon Germans have followed the craws.'

Donald was too tired, and frankly too bored with all this anxious talk. He'd a good cosh under his bed, and a couple of hardwood spears topped with sharpened ewe horns. If the Germans did come into Glen Lyon, then he'd not go without a fight. That night, as his wife fidgeted and rolled from side to side on a coarse hay-filled mattress under the shelter of their canvas home, he decided a long walk into the Lawers mountains would be just the rest he needed from Daisy's tongue. Especially since, from the highest viewpoint in all Perthshire, he'd soon spot the enemy. Earlier than a red kite he was trekking away into thick Scots mist before his wife had stirred on her bed, and by midday was standing upon the summit of Ben Lawer itself. As far as the eye could see, all that lay below him belonged to the red deer and white balls of sheep dotting the green slopes. The blue heaven above was the domain of ravens, crows and the mighty eagle.

'I kent it,' he said to himself, scanning the horizon, 'not a German in sight.'

Far down below, dots of homes with thin spirals of smoke re-minded him that Daisy would have a pot of kale boiling around some ribs of ham. The thought made his mouth water. 'Best get awa hame, jist in case yon Germans are dab hands at the camouflage cerry on.'

How many times he marvelled at a scene of nature's disguising, like the antics of a green frog upon a patch of sphagnum moss; it simply could not be detected, yet he knew it was there. The old adder could disguise itself into looking like a bent root of heather. The more this thought pestered him, the faster he strode along the sheep track homewards. So hard was he going that he almost knocked over a tramp coming the opposite way. 'Man, ah didnae see ye,' said Donald, apologising, 'can I help with yer load?'

The elderly gent had a heavy box upon his back, cross-tied with a thick rope.

'Would you help me with this thing, I have been carrying it for almost a week.'

Donald carefully untied the box and sat it gently on the path. He wondered what it was.

'This, dear fellow,' said his new acquaintance, 'is a wireless.'

Not wanting to seem stupid, he being a tinker and all that, Donald pretended he'd seen something similar, somewhere. Imagine his terror when the old man turned a knob at the front of the box, and voices came forth. Donald lost the power in his legs and fell back into the heather. 'Who the bloody hell have ye got prisoner inside the box? Wid thon be a wee Irish leprechaun?'

The old man, being a toff who'd fallen on hard times, said, 'my dear friend, this wireless is a voice-box for the whole world. Listen.' He turned the knob round until more voices poured forth. Some were women, others well-spoke gents, like his mate here, some made crackling sounds, making Donald think a Banshee lived inside the magic box along with many more strange creatures.

'Well, well, wonders will never cease,' said Donald, 'and all I dae is turn this knob and the world speaks tae me?'

'Yes, my friend, that is all that is needed. Now I was thinking, I haven't got an ounce of energy left, would you have enough money on your person to purchase my wonderful contraption?'

'No, no, I've plenty to do with my lowy. Any road, a thing like that would frighten ma Daisy tae death, her being aye looking oot fer Germans.'

The old man seemed stunned by this answer, and asked why the Germans, who were so far removed from Perthshire, should worry his wife who was snuggled safely in Glen Lyon.

'Dae you know where they are, sir?' asked Donald, glad that at long last someone might have the knowledge to relieve the glen tinkers of their fear.

'Well, according to the voice of the BBC world broadcaster, they are on the retreat somewhere in Europe.'

Donald's eyes grew wide with excitement, as he rammed both fists deep inside his pockets. 'Here's all the lowy I have tae ma name.' It was hardly anything, maybe in total thirty bob, but it was enough to relieve the wireless owner of his cumbersome load, and to see the sheer joy on the tinker's face was well worth it.

Farewells were made, and soon Donald was at home and delighting Daisy with a voice-box capable of informing them where exactly German snipers might be hiding.

She birled and danced, swinging arms and legs in every direction. The silly woman forgot in her excitement how large were those bosoms, and one jump too far resulted in them connecting under her chin with as powerful an uppercut as any champion boxer. When she asked Donald where Europe was, he said, 'Up by the Minch, some place near Sutherland.' These were places he'd heard other travellers mention, yet had no idea where they were. It was enough to satisfy his wife, who soon spent more time in front of the talking box than she did plucking fowl.

Weeks passed, with Daisy twirling the knobs on her box, neglecting all her duties as a good tinker woman. Poor Donald, as hard as he tried, she was not for moving. Every step of the war she followed through the magic wireless, never missing a battle report. Yet for all the place-names reported, not once did she realise that a channel of water was splitting Europe from Britain. To her it was all one big place, with the enemy being forced back from every town in Perthshire.

Once a year her two brothers, Dougal and Thomas, came by to visit. Like their sister and her man, they too had no idea where the Germans were. Daisy sat lording it at her tent mouth, with the crackling patter of the World Service booming out through the glen, feeling like a queen among the heather. Her brothers never stayed more than a week, because a great deal of alcohol consumption would eventually result in fisticuffs between the foursome. But with a war on, and the BBC giving a remarkable day-by-day account, they stayed on to be entertained.

It was the morning of 8th May 1945. Donald rose first and lit a fire, Thomas and Dougal filled the kettle and made a pot of porridge. Suddenly, like a female mallard being gang-banged by fifty sex-starved drays, Daisy emerged from the tent mouth screaming and dancing with whoops and yells. 'They are leaving, man, oh man, the bloody Germans are finished! Donald, Dougal, Thomas, doon tae the burn and wash yourselves. Hurry noo, we're going tae Killin for a wild party.'

Stunned into zombies with gaping holes for mouths, the three men could hardly manage a blink between them, and each thought she'd gone mad. All the worry and obsession about enemies stealing her bloomers off the dyke had turned her head and left her pure moich.

Donald put the last stick on his fire, stood up and said, 'Daisy, as big as you are, I'll put you over my lap and skelp some sense intae ye. An' another thing, if ye dinna want that wireless sat in flames on ma fire, calm doon.'

'Listen tae me, the three o' ye, the Germans are leaving Killin, I heard it wi' me ain ears as clear as day! The bool-moothed woman said "THE GERMANS ARE LEAVING KILLIN"!'

That was enough for the boys, who were desperately in need of a celebration drink. However, when they at last arrived in Killin, smelling of braxy water and carbolic soap, it was apparent from the usual sober mood of its inhabitants that they'd already celebrated in their own quiet way.

No, of course buxom Daisy hadn't heard in the broadcast that the Germans were leaving Killin. But what she had heard sparked a worldwide celebration—'The German forces were leaving Berlin.'

I love tales like that, and believe me there were plenty, but we'll sneak back later and peek again at tinkers huddled in lonely glens. Meanwhile, let's go back to Macduff.

15

THE MORNING VISITOR

Johnnie heard the knocking on our door one morning while I had my new-fangled washing machine churning away. It was state of the art, my wee white washer, because it came complete with wringer attachment. I honestly don't care what any woman thinks, those first washers did a far cleaner job of clothes than the computerised wallies of the present day. I loved my washing smelling fresh, with not a stain anywhere. I felt much more in tune with being a house-wife. I took pride in those duties frowned upon by many modern day quines. On second thoughts, maybe my upbringing had a lot to do with my attitude.

Anyway, as I said, wee Johnnie pulled on my skirt to tell of someone at the door. Along with the chuggie-chump-churnie of my washer, Connie Francis was in full voice singing 'Carolina Moon' on the radio. No wonder I failed to hear a visitor. It was a strange time to hawk, but standing on my doorstep, that very busy Monday morning, was a real life gypsy. Grey-black hair, pleated and piled upon her head, ear-lobes stretched by solid gold loops, hands heavy with the weight of rings adorning each finger, she was about seventy years old.

Drying my hands on my apron, I waited on the spiel: 'I brings the luck to you, don't turn me away, you've a lucky face, but ups and downs of life tell me something waits around the corner...' etc., but I was wrong. 'Perhaps there's a different approach,' I thought, waiting on her to speak. I searched her face; it had a tired look, pained even.

For a moment she stared, said nothing, obviously her technique. I spoke first. 'I'm awfy busy trying to get a big washing on the line before rain comes.' Stupid me, there wasn't so much as a puff of cloud. It was the bluest sky I'd seen for a long time. I continued, 'are you English? It's just that you're a right bonny dark colour and all the gold. Dae ye ken Maggie Ellen Young?' (She was the only real gypsy who lived in Scotland that I was aware of.) 'She's a fortune-teller, by God a good yin tae. Put a spell on an angry farmer's prize-winning bull, and it dropped doon dead!'

The woman wasn't impressed by my tale, she'd heard it all before, no doubt; nor did she answer my questioning. She seemed preoccupied.

'Can I come in? My heel is painful, look.' She eased a shoe off with one hand, steadying herself against my harled, white-washed wall. A great blister bubbled at her heel. I asked if she wanted me to burst it. 'I'll clean it and put some powder on to dry it up for you.'

'No thank you, girlie, but if you have a kettle boiling, tea would be a blessing.'

Never in my life did I see Mammy turn a gypsy from her door, and I wasn't about to change our welcome no matter how busy or Connie Francis-obsessed I was. 'Come in.' I held her arm as she hopped into my low-roofed cottage, gently lowering her body onto my settee. I made some space for her among kiddie toys and cloths. 'I'll get some tea now, but I've no biscuits or cakes, sorry.'

My visitor stretched her neck and laid her head to rest on a cushion. 'Tea will be blessed,' she said in a low whisper. Those gold-clad hands could hardly hold the full mug of tea, so she asked for a saucer. It made me smile watching her delicately pour some tea into the saucer and sip it like a cat. When sufficiently refreshed she told me who she was.

'I'm a Penfold from Kent country. I never come up these parts, but recently I lost me mother. She never said where it was she'd been born until her final days, when she told me it was a town in these parts. Her own mother died giving birth to her, leaving me grandfather unable to look after her and big brother Barley. Travellers took them in, adopted them, brings them up as their own. They were known as Riley, but I don't know a single thing about them. Me mother married me father, Leonard Penfold, and lived south of the border ever since.

'My folks are Riley,' I told her eagerly, 'well, Daddy's people, he lives just round the corner. Keep your eye on my boys, I'll go fetch him in a minute. What have you been doing here? I ask because we don't see much of the old ways in these parts. These are all fisherfolks, very holy, don't hold to fortune-telling.'

'I've been walking all over these parts doing the dukkering [fortune-telling] and hawking with a tushni of lace. Me old fella is dead this past seven years. Young Barley, me son, is in the town over the bridge, I forgot its name.'

'Banff,' I interrupted.

'Yes Banif, he's fixing on the lorry engine, it's a 'mergency. We have parked our wagon, well, caravan, on a beach; lovely it is, but my God if it's not a cold spot. Praise to God we don't have to puv the gries [field the horses] in these parts. Me husband's people still grie-draw wagons, and if their gries [horses] depended on hay in these wind-blown flat-lands, they'd all be gotten stiff.'

I laughed and thought on the many times I'd pushed our wee chaps in the open pram, noses blood-red, and frozen drips of snotters stuck hard onto their wee faces. 'Aye, wife, the wind blows for championship in these parts, right enough.' Johnnie, bless his heart, had brought a stool and lifted my guest's sore foot onto it. She sighed in relief and gave him a lucky charm from her basket. Stephen had teething trouble, so she gave him a plastic ring which went straight into his mouth. I rushed round to fetch Daddy, but he'd left early for a trip to Aberdeen, and Mammy had gone with him. Somehow, with him being a Riley, this pair may have known snippets of history I didn't, and could have shared them.

'What's yer first name?' I asked her. Penfold was a lovely old gypsy name, but I wondered if her forename was Scottish.

'Morag.'

Aye, it was a right bonny Highland handle, no doubt.

Well, this visitor of half-Scots, half-English blood soon relaxed to the point when I wondered if she had intentions of leaving. She hung out my washing while I swept floors and made beds, and by now we all needed lunch. She'd discarded her hard shoes, adopting my baffies, shuffling from area to area of the cottage. That was a strange thing to do, because everybody knew that travelling gypsies do not nose into people's houses. They usually sit still and move only on invitation.

Afternoon arrived, and already my friend was intending on a wee siesta. Nowhere in my mind was there any hint she should go, yet I felt maybe being hospitable wasn't such a good thing, was I stuck with her? I popped out for baby milk, taking my boys with me, leaving Morag sleeping peacefully on the settee.

Arriving home, I saw a red lorry with flashy painted doors at the far end of Patterson Street. 'It can only be her son, Barley,' I thought.

'Hello,' I called out, 'are you looking for Morag?'

A young man of maybe twenty or so came towards me. 'Yes, is she with you?'

'Aye, I've left her asleep. Follow me, I live in this wee house here.'

'In this house?' he asked strangely, as if some memory hung around the place.

'Aye, come on in.' I opened the door, calling out to Morag that I'd found Barley. My boys were making a racket as we entered the house, and it seemed unusual that she failed to hear them. Barley was a right impatient lad, pushing by me, almost forcing entry.

'Oh Mother, Mother,' he cried.

'What's wrong with you, she's fine!' I shouted, picking up Stephen, who stopped crying at my touch. Morag, however, wasn't just sleeping as I thought. Barley was cradling her in his arms, sobbing deeply. She hung loosely in his grip. It was the most horrible shock to discover my visitor had died. She was stone dead!

'I'll fetch Doctor MacKenzie,' I called out, wishing that my parents were home, even one of them. Chrissie also was away that day: I was alone with strangers, one dead. Davie was at sea and I was left feeling totally vulnerable. 'Look,' I said again, 'if you put her in my bed I'll fetch the Doctor.' Johnnie, at my sternest request, went outside to play. Stephen fell asleep.

Barley smiled and laid her gently down. 'No need for a doctor, or minister, or anyone. She's done what she meant to do. Now, if you could hold back the door, we'll be gone.'

'What was it she meant to do?' I turned his head to face mine.

He wiped a hand across his tear-stained face. 'Her mother was born in this house a long time ago. This is where she wanted to die.'

'Then that's why she came here—this wee house of ours she looked upon as a resting place?'

'Yes, we would have stayed in this area for as long as it took, but

86

she knew the heart was pegging and there wasn't much time. Her grandmother went into labour while hawking Macduff. Just as she limped along this way all those years ago, the woman of this house took her in, helped with the birth. My mother recently discovered she'd not long to live and had me take her up here to die. Now, please don't tell a doctor, 'cause stardy [police] would hinder things, questions and all that stuff.'

I assured him. 'I'm a traveller and know enough about death ways; police won't hear from me. Will it be a long time before you reach home?'

'I have her coffin in the back of the lorry. When I get back, the funeral pyre will take place. Thank you for all you've done.'

'I haven't done anything, Barley.'

'Oh, you've done a lot more than you know, giving her the time of day. Not many folks would do that, but I see now the traveller in you, I feel some things are meant. For her last hours spent a while in the place where her mother began, thank you.'

Whatever had taken place in my home that day seemed outwith my control, I felt that others were planning a stranger's life and death. I watched in total silence as he carried his mother, Morag, my morning visitor, away. I wanted to call out she'd a really bad blister on her heel, but somehow the words didn't come. I saw him open a door at the rear of his lorry, pull an oblong box from the back, and lay her gently in. I watched him reverse, and then he was gone. I never heard or saw so much as a raindrop of them from that day to this.

Brief encounters, like falling dandelion seeds, have neither rhyme nor reason to them, yet I felt that for a whole lifetime a gypsy woman had planned her end, and whoever happened to be living in her mother's birth-home at her destined time would have been involved in that finale. It just happened to be me.

My washing dried soft and crisp and Stephen's tooth broke through that night.

The sight of death has never bothered me. I take heed of wisdom words spoken many times by auld yins at funerals—'just another turn intae a lang road.'

16

EWE MOTHER

Now I think I'll tell you a story of another Morag—a shepherd's wife who lived inland from here. Hughie was her man's name, and around by Turriff they lived, oh maybe a hundred years past. Get the kettle on again and listen to the tale of the Ewe Mother.

Tied to a strong bough of an old warped oak hung a rope swing, weakened and battered by many winters past. It grew, that tree, at the bottom of a garden—well, not so much a flowery garden, more a small field circling a but-and-ben, home to Hughie and Morag. Sitting on that swing, trailing her feet over the worn earth, sat Morag, reminiscing. She remembered the day Hughie strung it up for the big family they'd so eagerly planned and awaited, but which had never come. So long ago now, yet clear as a crystal stream in her memory, were the wonderful summer days when love was all their joy. Just sixteen she was when Hughie plonked himself down onto one knee and asked, no, begged her to marry him. Right in among the sheep. She knew long before then what her answer would be, but her youthful mischief teased and played with his emotions.

'Hughie, I think my fancy would be better applied to a man with more status than yourself. Surely, if you love me this much, then you'd not wish a shepherd life on me.' Before he could say a word she continued, 'my delicate hands are more suited to lifting wine glasses and giving written orders to servants in a big house. Don't you want me to be a fine gentleman's wife, Hughie

Macintosh?' Laughing loudly, she pushed poor big clumsy Hughie backwards and ran off.

'But if you can catch me, then I'll marry you,' she called out, scattering sheep in different directions while running for the heather track.

Those sweet words fell around him like clover heads bouncing in the air from the cut of a sharp scythe. In seconds they were joined together with kisses and cuddles, a day never forgotten.

They wed with promises and oaths of devotion, and within months settled easily together. He'd chosen well, because even at such a delicate age she immersed herself in the hard life as if born to it. The sheep became as important to her as they were to him. Winter found them both trekking cold desolate regions, shepherding through snow, wild weather, short days and long nights tending to lost sheep. They had a small herd of cows, and from them her country knowledge of milking filled a fine larder. Cheeses and butter, expertly churned, were in abundance. Bread too, yeasted and baked to perfection. Sometimes Hughie wondered if an angel had fallen from heaven and married him, his cup ran over.

Yet, as years passed, there was a lack spreading like doom in the small cosy house, so deep it cut into them both. So awful it was that her young face did not smile any more, and her days dragged by. In five years her womb had rejected three babies. She never reached beyond seven months in her pregnancy, with a pained premature labour. Oh, those terrible endless nights when her fruit trees produced no yield, and they were followed by months of sorrow. The country people, their neighbours, felt nothing but sadness for the pair. They'd see them herding the sheep off the hills, she blooming with motherhood, a bowed belly, his big, strong arms supporting her precious frame; then that sad sight of her at his side, both carrying cromacks, collies circling around, each alone in their painful thoughts.

It was after losing the fourth baby that Morag began to fear the bad time—the shedding. This was the only time when her heart broke, not for herself, but for the ewe mothers being forced from their lambs. September nights were filled with the bleating and crying of those mothers, aching for the lambs they'd never see again. It was then Hughie's bed emptied as Morag slept with the ewes. She tried to comfort them by singing lullabies, stroking their woollen coats, desperately bonding through her own pain with the loss of their infants. Her babies were gone to a cold earth, theirs to a butcher's slab.

Although his wife's behaviour was uncanny, unnatural, her husband had no heart to stop it. During shedding he'd enter the field in the early morning to find her snuggling between ewe mothers. The strange thing was, the nights quietened when she joined those grieving animals. It seemed her presence did help them. Then, after eager tups were fielded with the ewes, beginning the whole process over again, Morag slept in her own bed, things returned to normality. The sheep, when pregnant, got down to facing another fierce winter; and yes, once more, Morag too was pregnant.

However, her joy, like before, was short-lived, and in its place came the fear of yet another dead baby. She begged Mother Nature to help her miscarry, her body shook with fear at feeling the icy cold fingers of Death creeping into her womb and stilling the heart of her baby. But her belly like before began to swell. Hughie made her promise not to come out with him, but to stay at home and rest whenever possible. 'Stay in bed all day if need be, but don't lose this baby.'

So, with the greatest care for the contents of her womb, she slowed to a gentle pace of life. Months passed, and as before, the first kick of the unborn had them both filled with joy at one minute, apprehension the next. She went for gentle walks among the ewe mothers, telling them about her own little lamb kicking inside. Seven months came round once more. Hughie was lambing in full swing and rushing into the house on the hour to check on Morag, but thanks be, her labour didn't start. By the end of the eighth month they began to think—is this it, will we see a child, healthy and strong? Nine months came, a full-term pregnancy; everything was ready.

That morning she went outside to wave at the ewe mothers, who for some strange reason had closed in around the house to graze. Little lambs bleated and frolicked in small rows, trying to mount the dry stane dyke at the bottom of the field, making her smile through a mixture of fear and joy at what was to come.

In the late afternoon, claws of sharp tight pain shot up her spine, down her back and gnawed at her swollen abdomen. She screamed to Hughie, who was chopping firewood. He dropped his axe and was by her side, apprehension mixed with hope. Such awful pains kept coming now, each one harder and seething worse than the last. Fast and furious, only minutes apart, they stole valuable breath from her body, leaving her lungs tight and sore. Hours passed with anchors of stone on them, sweat oozed from her in buckets. His arms were torn as she clung on, then when she thought her heart would burst she gave one last push: one final moment waiting on that first cry.

A small lifeless baby boy lay limp, not breathing. Morag bit into the pillow, screaming at cruel, cruel Mother Nature, wicked, evil, hateful nature, as Hughie carried yet another dead infant from her. Tears ran over his face, shoulders heaved with torturing heartache. Nothing but a spark from the dimmed fire could be heard all through the lonely glen. Death had once more visited; would he ever tire of this place?

Hughie wrapped the baby in a sheet; he would bury it down by the oak, but not tonight. Morag needed some comfort. Poor sad Morag, never to mother a child. As they lay in silence holding each other, a ewe mother began bleating outside; the noise made when her lamb had died. Hughie thought the worse of his sheep, at a time like this to lose a lamb. He waited until his exhausted wife fell asleep before investigating, and by then the animal was becoming quite stressed, constantly bleating. Putting on his heavy coat, for he had heard rain earlier, he stepped outside.

There, a sight never before seen, were thirty or so ewes all standing together as if waiting on news. One, however, wasn't standing, she was lying on his door step, obviously the bleater. It was dark, so to get a better look he opened his door. The elderly ewe sighed, gave a loud cough as sheep are prone to do and stretched her legs. Hughie opened the door further to reveal, lying there naked with tiny fists punching at the air, a newborn baby boy, snuggled into his foster mother's fleece for warmth.

The big shepherd instinctively looked upwards as he thanked whoever it was that had deemed his insignificant household worthy of a miracle! A gift had been presented to them that night. He rushed inside with his tiny baby, and looked at the shawl which supposedly held the dead baby wrapped inside, but the shawl was folded neatly over his wife's feet. There was no sign of the other child.

Morag was stirring as he kissed her cheek. She opened her tired eyes to see Hughie hold something out to her. 'A present for you, my love, from the ewe mothers.'

Morag stirred from her swing, one more glance at the ewes in the field and she pulled a woollen shawl over her shoulders and walked back to the house. Soon Hughie and their son Angus would be home, hungry and needing fed. All life in the glen was a joy.

While on the subject of mothers, I want to speak a wee bit about my own dear blessed soul.

Mammy was, as mothers go, a gem. She wasn't a strict mother, but we always knew when we'd overstepped the line. Punishment could range from a 'you wash the dishes, ma lass', to 'just you wait until I get my hands on you!' I never remember a time when punishment wasn't deserved.

Recently, while discussing a manuscript of mine with Carl MacDougall, a prominent Scottish writer, I was reminded by him that readers who had any knowledge of travellers knew it didn't make for an easy life. 'Jess, don't cover your pages with roses, because folks won't believe it.' But to me, life was a bed of roses; in fact it was simply marvellous. Being chauffeured around the country in a bus, playing on picturesque hill-tops one day, miles of yellow-sanded beaches the next. If Daddy took the mood, off we would go, without a single tie. School exemption certificates allowed us freedom to leave our learning books and fly away.

Mammy, therefore, had to have a similar attitude to her roots as he had. Not so much in the beginning when the bus life began—she preferred a house, one where her older daughters could stretch their legs and enjoy a form of privacy not afforded in the bus. I loved it, though, and never grew tired of it, as you'll have gathered from my previous books.

Being so close to my mother, I found it easy to study her ways. Sometimes she'd say things that had me in stitches laughing, for instance I remember once while we were hawking in Perth. It was to the monastery on the hill we climbed. She said 'if anybody will buy, then it's the monks, no matter what the weather, the nice men wi' cloaks will aye gi'e.' That day, as always, she was correct, because they bought lace, threads, buttons, in fact everything in her basket—the only thing they kindly declined was to have their fortunes told. As we walked away, she smiled and gave the man at the gate a wave. She turned to me, linked our arms and said, 'I feel awfy sorry for the braw lads, Jess.'

'Why, Mammy, there's nothing coming over them. They're living a life they chose.'

'Och aye, fine I ken, but it's still an awfy waste.'

'They have a warm bed, home-grown food, aye, an' by the colour o' yon wee fat yin's nose, a guid dram tae boot. God himself takes care o' them, Mammy, how should you feel sorry for them?'

'Well, imagine how Daddy would feel if he didnae get his cuddles. He'd be a grumpy auld bisom. Poor craturs spending all their days like that!'

'Like what Mammy?'

'*Halibut*, that's what! Could you see your father lasting without a cuddle?'

'No, Mammy,' I told her, 'just as much as thon "*monkfish*" could go without a smoke or a drink!'

And there was that time, while I was recuperating in Perth Royal Infirmary, that she sent me a get well card addressed to Mrs Smith RIP (Royal Infirmary Perth)!

When Daddy met her, it was love at first sight. Ah, nice, I hear you say, but wait until I tell you about his own mother's reaction. Well, it might come as a big surprise, but the class obsession of Britain is prevalent throughout travelling folk as well. During Granny Riley's time there were the high and mighty house-dwellers, who looked down noses at their kinsfolk for still living in tents. The middle-class travellers roamed in bonny caravans, and there were the lowest class of tinkers who lived near rubbish tips. Mammy's folks, according to Granny, were the 'midden rakers'.

'Charlie, you can do better for yourself than her kind.'

'No, mother, Jeannie and I were meant for each other, I love the lassie.'

And, of course, as history has witnessed, my parents stayed together until death. So my Granny, bless her, accepted Jeannie, but always kept her opinions to herself.

'Two groups of people who will never lie to you are teachers and churchmen,' she told us. 'Teachers tell you what is in books, and preachers about the good book.' Those words of old-fashioned wisdom were her teaching to her brood. Many times we'd sit huddled around her black, shiny range at 'Lettoch Beag', the Riley home on the hill outside Moulin, Pitlochry, listening to tales from the Bible.

'Always question what folks say to you, except if it be a teacher or preacher.'

Now imagine my surprise when one day at school we were taught Darwin's 'Theory of Evolution'. I could hardly contain myself. 'Granny must know this,' was all I could think of, 'she'll go pure horn moich when she hears what my teacher told us.'

So there I was, standing outside, not allowed in until she'd finished blackening her range. 'Granny, wait till you hear what I have to say, hurry up and let me in.'

At long last the door was opened to me, and with strict orders to walk on the newspaper spread over the linoleum, I stepped in. She sat me down with a big piece of raspberry jam. 'Well, bairn, who disnae ken a thing about patience, what is it?'

'You telt me that Adam and Eve are the mither and faither o' a' mankind, Granny, isn't that true?'

Furrows wrinkled her wee brow, eyes narrowed. 'Aye, and who has been filling yer heed wi' lies?'

'My teacher at the school, Granny, he said we're frae "apes". Every brother, mother, father, daughter and dog o' us comes from monkeys, what dae ye think o' that, Granny?'

I left my chair because although she was a wee cratur, there was still plenty power in the fist. Standing by a blue vase of flowers on the window ledge I waited.

For a while she said nothing, then, like a light bulb had lit up in her head, she smiled broadly and said, 'Oh aye, Jessie, I ken what that nice teacher was telling you—he was talking about your mother's folk!'

17

THE FOX, THE COW, THE DEAD MAN AND THE WEE
LADDIE IN THE BARREL

I want to take you back to my father's life now, which according to him was a hard one, walking behind the horse pulling the heavy cart, gutters and horse-dung caking onto his trousers with each cold step of the way.

As the song says:

> Come all you tramps and hawker lads,
> That gi'ed the way a blaw,
> That tramped the country round and round,
> Come listen one and a',
> An' I'll tell tae ye a roving tale o' sichts that I hae seen,
> Far up and to the snowy north and doon by Gretna Green.

My father wasn't a great one for storytelling, but when it came, boy was it big. One of my favourite tales of sights that he had seen is this one. It's as tall a tale as you're likely to hear, but I love it, and might I add that I've heard versions of it in Wales, London, Yorkshire, Norwich and on the banks of the Manchester Canal, all told by travellers.

'James, ma boy, do your old father a favour and exercise these ponies on the moor for me.'

'Aye, father, I'll steer them over the moor, let them loose to graze.'

'While you're wandering, son, fetch your dear old mother a trout for tea.'

The moor was a cantankerous place: one minute there would be a clear blue sky, next a fog thick enough to throw cover over a field of cows a few feet from you.

James was a good lad, but much to the annoyance of his mother, a lazy streak had come upon him. With this in mind, she called after him, 'don't dare forget to guddle the trout; there'll be no tea for any of us if you do.'

A gentle wave of the hand saw him reach the brow of the hill; then he and the dappled ponies were out of sight. On the expanse of heather intermingled with patches of green grass, he sent his ponies to graze at leisure. There wasn't a single human being for miles. He sent his jaw into a giant yawn. 'I'll lay down here for a few moments while they fill their bellies, plenty time to search for a burn. There's enough of the day left to guddle trout for tea.' Soon lazy James was fast asleep. The 'kweek, kweek' of a buzzard soaring brought his slumber to a halt. He sat up, and oh my, had the thickest fog not covered the moor. Whistling and calling should have brought the horses, but it didn't. Panic crept in. 'Surely they've not wandered off,' he thought. 'Father will tan my hide if I've lost his two newly-bought ponies that recently cost him an arm and a leg.' Thinking about limbs, his were shivering. This was a dreich cold fog, a right pea-souper.

Although it was still summer, he'd enough knowledge of the mist-shrouded moor to know if one got lost in it the situation could be hazardous and even fatal. 'I'll search for the animals later, first off, best find somewhere to get a bit warmth,' he said, rubbing his cold body. Fog over the moorland can be a devil, just what direction had he come and where was he going? On and on he stomped, until, praise be, he saw a light; far off at the top of a hill, a flickering salvation awaited him. His step quickened; getting nearer he could just make out the outline of a small cottage. At last he stood inspecting the door, then knocked wildly, hoping for a kind word and a wee bit shelter. He didn't have long to wait before a couthie-faced woman opened it. 'What can I do for you, son?' she asked.

'I need shelter until the fog lifts, can I stay here?'

For a moment she gave it some thought, then her face lit up. 'Of course you can, but only if you do me a favour.'

'Anything, wife, what is it?'

'My man needs looking after. Can you sit with him until I get back? My neighbour needs me, I'll only be gone a half hour at most.'

James smiled and stepped inside. 'Where's the man then?' he enquired, then thought to himself, 'strange request this—I canny see a soul.'

The only answer she gave was the door slamming shut behind her and the noise of her footsteps trailing off as she hurried away. The first thing he did was make for the glowing flames of a grand fire. Soup bubbling in a black pot brought a rumble to his belly, but what of the man? 'Hello,' he gingerly whispered, thinking that the husband might be sick in bed, 'where are you, sir?'

From a dark shadowy corner of the kitchen came a low growl of a male voice, 'I'm over here.'

James near fell flat on his face, for tip-toeing very cautiously across to where the sound came from, all he could see upon a pine table was a long oblong box, draped with a black cloth. 'What in hell's blazes is this, I'm still asleep on the moor, for surely I'm not alone wi' a corpse?' He peered inside, shaking like jelly. 'I'm James, and all's that I want is a heat at the fire. Now can you please show yourself, for the presence of a death-box brings a want on me to empty my bowels.'

'Dinna fret, laddie, I'm here in the box, but it's not what you think. You see, I'm not dead. An old gypsy woman gave me a po- tion to fake death, but my reasons are my business.'

Then, to put the lid on matters, the so-called corpse rose up and got down from the table.

James headed for the door, shouting at the dead-like stranger, 'to hell with fog, I'd rather take my chances than stay in here.'

'Look lad,' said the man, putting a hand on James's shaking shoul- ders. 'You away ben the room and have a sleep; take no notice of me, leave whenever the fog clears.'

Slipping into the wee bedroom, James quickly shut the door, leaning a chair against it for safety. Soon, lazy as ever, he was fast asleep, only to be abruptly wakened by an almighty crack from a shot-gun. Throwing back the chair he was soon standing in the kitchen. What a horrible thing had happened. Two people—the woman he recog- nised, but her companion a stranger—lay dead on the floor, and gaping holes in each of their chests. The husband, sitting up in the coffin, had forgotten about James. 'I hadn't reckoned on you seeing this, boy, but I've had suspicions that this man was having an affair with my wife. And I was right, because the pair o' them laughed at me dead in the box, but they're no laughing now, are they laddie? Oh no, this gun wiped the smiles off their faces for good.'

James edged his terrified body inch by inch towards the door, trying not to look at the pools of blood oozing from the dead bodies. His hand fumbled for the door handle.

'Where do you think you're sneaking off to? No doubt the nearest police station. Well, sorry son, but you're a witness, I can't let you go.'

'I'm a tinker, here today, gone tomorrow, what harm can I do you? Shoot everyone in the place if you like, it makes no odds to me. The polis give me nightmares, they're the last folk I'd be running tae.'

'Sorry son, but I can't take that chance.' He grabbed hold of James, wrapping a strong arm around his throat. A vase of flowers stood upon a barrel in the corner of the room. Smash went the vase; flowers scattered over the murdered couple. Suddenly, poor weak laddie that he was, he found himself being pushed down into the barrel. In terrifying seconds the murderer was hammering the barrel-lid tight shut with several big nails.

'Right, my boy, away you go.' Round and round, bumping and rolling from side to side, rapidly gathering speed as he plummeted downhill to God knows where, went James in his wooden-slatted coffin. On and on, thump, bang, faster and faster. He closed his eyes and waited on the crash that would surely see him dashed to smithereens on rocks somewhere below. However, and a million thanks to someone on high came from that desolate youngster, the barrel landed on soft ground. But wait on, it wasn't earth where he'd landed, it was water—he'd rolled out on a pond or something. He opened his eyes; much to his horror water was seeping through the staves of the barrel. Quickly he retrieved a small pen-knife from his pocket, and began chiselling a wee hole. From his peephole he could just make out a cow drinking at the grass edge. It was impossible to turn the barrel to the shore, so he set about scooping handfuls of water, pouring them out of the hole.

'Make the hole bigger and catch me a trout,' came a demand from the pond edge.

'Who's out there? Please help me. I'll guddle trout all day for you, but I'm drowning in here—hurry.'

'Look back through the hole.'

James frantically peered out, only to see an old red fox staring back at him. 'Am I going mad?' he asked himself. 'Two murdered folk and a corpse, now a blinking talking fox.'

'If you think on any longer, that water will be the end of you, now do you want out or not?'

'What stupid kind of a question is that? Wait and I'll have that fish.' James sliced bits of the barrel until he'd a hole wide enough to take his hand, then, with a turn of his body he flipped over the barrel, and in went a trout as he flipped it round again. Taking the head of the struggling fish, he pushed it through the hole. 'See, now will you save me, fox?'

In went the furry red streak, swimming up to the barrel, and before James could do a thing to stop him, the fox was heading back to the bank with the trout secured in his strong jaws.

'Fox, what kind of a double-cross is that?'

'Who in their right mind would trust a fox? Stupid, that's what you are, laddie. A great looking fish, I'll eat it later. Bye-bye, and thanks again.'

So there he was, stuck fast in a barrel rapidly taking in gallons of water; there seemed no escape. One last look from his peep-hole, and as the water filled his nostrils a last desperate thought—that cow! Was she still there? 'Hey cow, there's a bull looking for you.'

Abruptly the animal lifted her head, stomped the water and swatted her tail violently from side to side. No bull would get as much as a sniff of her out of season. Another swish-swat, and the tail went straight. James thrust his hand out of the hole and grabbed hold. Thinking a brute bull was about to violate her, the frightened cow went helter-skelter forward, barrel and its contents hanging on for grim death. Crash went the barrel as she lodged it between rocks, and out rolled the most grateful laddie that ever lived. He lay back and stared upwards at a clear blue sky—the fog was gone. Quickly he was on his feet now, and a sight to match any wonder was his father's ponies grazing happily on the brae-side. Soaked but happy, he made towards them, when he heard a sound coming from thick bracken. As quiet as a mouse he peered into an opening, and there, snoring snugly, was wily old Slee Tod Lowrie, the red fox. Now what do you think lay untouched at his side? A fine fresh trout, just big enough for his family's tea.

A short while later, as James walked over the brow of the hill, a spiral of reek wound its way from the camp-fire to meet him. He smiled broadly, holding the horses with one hand, and a juicy fish in the other. He gazed over the peaceful scene below and called out, 'get the pan on, Mammy, I've guddled'.

A tall tale that one, no doubt.

18

UNDER THE BLACK WATCH COAT

I'd like now to go back into our bus of many summers, and tell you a story of a tramp who just happened to be on any road or by-way as long as it wasn't ours. You see, Mammy had a thing about the flea-infested men of the road. Daddy was aware of this, and she'd warned him dozens of times—'don't dare offer them lifts. I have a hard enough time keeping my lassies' hair clean, without thon dirty buggers bringing their vermin in among my weans.'

Daddy, just out of pure devilment, on seeing one of Mammy's tramps at a bend in the road, would slow down until level with the scabby gent, and say through the bus window, 'are ye for a lift, man?'

I laugh now as I write this, seeing her anger-reddened face, crochet needle whirling like a piston ring as the man, poor innocent cratur, stepped into her domain, her palace.

'Sit doon right there on the step, an' don't you dare come intae my hame.'

He, being a gentleman fallen on hard times, would silently remove his cloth bunnet and sit on the floor next to Daddy's driving seat. These were Mammy's conditions—her home, her family, her responsibility. Not many tramps of the road would so much as open their mouths after hearing the orders being rapped at them; they were to be 'on the bus and off again'.

However, life has a twisting road, so it does, and after the episode I am about to describe, she not only opened her door to the tramp, but a grateful heart as well. I was eleven years old.

It was August, and we had a healthy berry-picking season behind us. 'Where to now then, girls, will we go west to Argyll, or for a change try rock pools at Dingwall?' Daddy's smiling face meant his pockets were full. 'We'll not starve this winter,' he said, as he patted his wallet, which was thick to bursting in a back-pocket of his corduroy trousers. With a high price for pure wool that year, he'd made a packet cleaning brock from fields. The hot summer sent sheep scraping themselves at every available fence-post, leaving in some cases whole discarded fleeces. June saw them lose coats to the shearing scissors but April and May were unusually hot, hence the long strips of wool everywhere. Mammy had jarred pounds of early raspberry jam, strawberry too. My older sisters headed off to spend time in other relatives' nests, leaving me and my three younger sisters to be spoiled rotten by our parents. Chrissie had married two years past, so she had her own wee corner of the world.

'Well, come on now, I canna wait a' day, east or west?'

Renie, Mary and Babsy, much to my disappointment, shouted, 'rock pools, Daddy'.

I stamped my foot down hard on the floor, a cup wobbled in its saucer and did a wee ring dance, and before I could bring my bottom lip to meet the top it crashed onto the floor. Smithereens it was. Mammy's face dropped at the sound of her favourite cup shattering.

'I wanted to go west, Jessie,' she cried, 'but now you, wi' yer tantrums, has went an' broke ma bonny wee cup, so we'll head east. Look what that temper of yours has done!'

Daddy half-smiled at me, then at the cup being brushed off the floor by Mammy, who was speaking to it as if the bloody thing was alive: 'ma braw wee chenie cup; who could mak ma tea taste like you did? Look at ye intae bits wi' that Argyllshire-loving wean.'

I sat well to the back of the bus on the journey, in a place not many like to be (you'd call it Coventry). Swallows and house martins, strengthening wee wings for their own journey come September, circled in every available blue space high above. As I always did when seeing them, I whispered a prayer to the angels that cared for birds to keep them safe, especially the late arrivals with their feathers still baby fluff.

We stopped overnight south of Inverness. You may recall the story I told you in *Jessie's Journey* about how Mammy feared being close to the killing moor of Culloden, and about Arras, my saviour with a flair for bagpipes. Well, not wanting to upset her, Daddy pulled onto a wood-end several miles or so before the moor. I resigned myself to the fact that Dingwall, with its cold water, would be our stopping place before heading back to Perthshire for the tattie-lifting.

Well, there we were camped up in the wooded place, and according to my Daddy he was born just down the road from there, ahent a dyke. He always gave the same answer when I asked him where he was born—'ahent a dyke, lassie, in a wee snow-covered canvas mansion. December it was, and by God did it no half start wi' a wild gale, and me taking ma first breath. Ma Father broke the icy water in the burn and dipped me intae it. He telt me, did my father, that I squealt sae hard a herd o' red deer ran back up the mountain.'

He wasn't lying about the icy water, because one day I asked Granny and she said, 'aye, I'll ne'er forget poor wee Charlie, he didnae half squeal when Granddad plonked his wee naked body, head first, intae the burn.'

I was horrified and said, 'what kind of a cruelty was that; his heart could have stopped wi' the shock!'

'Jessie,' she turned me around to face her, 'if he could take that, he could take anything life threw at him.'

There might be truth in that. What other man could stand eight pairs of wet knickers drying on a string suspended above his head, while doing his football coupons on a rainy Saturday afternoon?

Anyway, let's go back to our campsite. The fire was reeking away good style, kettle boiling on the hook hung from iron chitties. Daddy whistled in fine tune, while Mammy sang 'Busk, Busk, Bonnie Lassie' like an angel, at the top of her voice.

Sisters played nearby—and me? Well, I was still being ignored, so I thought I'd distance myself from the family, who were grating my nerves good-style.

I found a braw deep burn hurling with fish, so broke a thin branch from an ash and went home to unwind some strong thread from a pirn kept in Mammy's sowing box. As I rifled through it, I helped myself to a safety pin. Back at the stream, the uplifting of a few flat stones exposed some big worms, too big for my hook, so I put them back and raked for thinner ones. I unearthed two or three and plopped them into a wee flat fag tin I'd found in a midden heap.

But I have never had the nerve to stick a hook into an innocent worm, so they stayed in the tin while I made a fly from pieces of a crow-feather I'd found. Voices drifted from our bus over to the burnside where I sat fishing. I heard Daddy and Mammy with raised voices, unlike their earlier mood, which was a jolly one. Leaning my makeshift fishing rod against a tree, I went back to see why. 'Och, nae wonder,' I thought, seeing the tramp. 'Mammy did our hair the night before and isn't about to expose us to an army of nits.'

'Give the bloke a drink o' tea, Jeannie, for God sake, woman.'

Daddy took his life in his hands speaking to her in that tone. He knew she was a sweetie, but that it was us she was protecting—well, our cleanliness to be exact. Tramps didn't put her up nor down, if they would only pay a wee bit more attention to personal hygiene.

'You sit away from my weans,' she told the man, sternly pointing to a tree stump. Turning to Daddy, she said, handing him a mug of tea, 'here, you give him that, and he gets not a single bit of food.'

I couldn't understand why my gentle mother felt that way, because she'd give her last penny to whoever asked her. I know, though, it wasn't so much a personal thing. Keeping us free from nits meant that when school came around once more, we wouldn't have the fingers pointed or names called. If weans had nits, then to her they weren't clean enough.

So there he was, a small-made tramp of the road with not a tooth in his head, sitting on a tree-stump wearing a massive army coat. Daddy told him to take it off and be comfortable. He apologised for Mammy and sat by the old fellow blethering. Now, as you well know, I loved these colourful chappies, and just had to join in the blether. Mammy ignored the situation, getting on with peeling tatties for supper. The look she sank me spoke volumes, though, something like 'I'll be dipping you intae the burn the minute he's away!'

He didn't say much, this guy, he wasn't a storyteller, so my thoughts wandered back to my fishing rod. But when I got back to the burn, it had gone. I ran upstream a bit, and could just make it out bobbing in deep water. Being so young I shan't tell you what I was muttering to myself: suffice to say it wasn't the language of an eleven-year-old.

Aware of the fast-flowing current's strength, I lay flat on the bank and stretched. Too short was my reach, leaving only one option left, to wade in. Dangerous waters flowed swiftly around my legs as I sank into a nightmarish slurry of algae and mud. I was being dragged down, sucked by a whirlpool. My danger did not become apparent at first, because this was no big river, just a stream, deep in parts, shallow in others. However, one heavy shower of rain high upon the mountain can turn a quiet burn into a raging river, so it could well have been in spate. I thrust an arm forward, yet missing its target, a hanging branch of willow. I was losing my struggle and felt stupid.

'What will they say when I walk back like a drookit rat?' was all my mind could think, before panic gripped me. 'Perhaps I'll not walk anywhere again?' I felt fingers of long grasses wind around my legs and pull me further, deeper in. The burn began to take on the form of a monstrous ocean trying to gulp me down. 'Help me!' came those desperate screams that all near-drowning victims must utter, 'I'm trapped, Mammy, Daddy, help.'

Water cascaded into my open mouth, choking my futile calls, filling my lungs. Bubbles started popping in my head; it was then that the strangest thing happened, I began to feel warm and good. My struggling slowed down, then stopped, as those gentle, dancing, fingers of water formed into slender arms swaying in motion. I was aware of currents rushing violently above my head, yet not down here.

My body began to float back and forth in rhythm, while a beautiful girl with long dancing silver hair held out arms to embrace me. Who was she, this smiling mermaid with long flowing hair? Words came from her lips as she pointed downwards, but what was she saying and where was she pointing? She then began to fade into the reed grass, leaving me alone in the merciless depth.

It got very dark; my spine arched, forcing back my head, and I could feel my lungs bursting with water. Then a terrible pain tightened around my upper body and brought back my panic. I opened my mouth to scream, and then came the most terrifying sight—a beast grabbed me, pulling on my neck. I looked up: it had no teeth and was smiling with an evil grin, then total darkness engulfed me. I was running down a long black passage, when other hands began to pull at me. They rolled me over and over, until a great thumping noise bounded in my head. Lights of immense brightness burst into my eyeballs, and then a fountain of warm sticky fluid came pouring from my mouth. My eyes opened, to reveal the toothless demon standing over me. It was a small man wearing a torn semmit and long johns; water was pouring from the crotch.

I didn't recognise him minus his coat. My saviour, of all people, was the road tramp. He had jumped in to investigate the air bubbles coming from a patch of clear water in a thicket of reeds and saved my life. My family were running up and down the burn frantically searching for me, but it was his eagle eye that detected the near drowning wean, me! I later discovered that the toothless, grinning monster who felt my kicks while attempting to rescue me, a common occurrence when someone is drowning, was that poor tramp who my mother had detested—but never again.

That night a saint sat at our fire, one wearing a heavy wool coat, and it mattered not a jot to my mother that an army of Black Watch nits infested his collar, they were welcome too.

After my near-death experience our visit to the east side of Scotland's coastline was breathtakingly spectacular. But so was each breath I inhaled. Rock pools filled with green water as the North Sea brought back and forth her tides. I didn't swim once though; I was too afraid to allow water above my neckline.

Ah, but what made my days there so joyous? A coastline bursting with goodies, that's what. Two stappit-full jute sacks of scrap metal, paying four pound sterling, meant that I became rich. And the first thing I purchased? A beautiful china cup for Mammy's tea!

Seriously, what did the 'wench from the watery depth' say to me as I struggled to keep my last pocket of air in my lungs? I've asked dozens of people after telling them of my experience, and they all said the same thing—'if you knew, then you'd be dead'. It's the same as falling from a great height in a dream. You always waken before hitting the ground.

Not that long ago I put my experience to an expert, who informed me that it would have been the water reeds, which can grow to a great length, that I mistook for a wispy female. 'Yes, of course it was water reeds of great length, but what did they say—?'

So much mystery surrounds rivers in Scotland, and a Pitlochry man, a fine poet who goes by the name of Douglas Petrie, gave me his description of one such mysterious waterway in his series of river verses.

THE RIVER

Where do you come from?
Where do you go?
With your never-ending flow,
Down through valleys
And along the glens,
Your sparkling body twists and bends,
And as you pass along your way,
Every night and every day,
Sometimes rushing, sometimes slow,
But never saying where you go,
In your splendid pools so deep,
What are the secrets that you keep?
O lovely river, so serene,
Where are you going?
Where have you been?

A RIVER HOME

It's in the glen you sparkle, twist and run,
And really dazzle in the sun,
Here will always be your home,
And not the place you will roam.
In the glens you're clear and free,
Further on must troubles be,
But although you journey away each day,
I know it's here you wish to stay,
For in the glens your beauty's best,
Its here I know you love to rest.

MY DREAM HOME

Just an old wooden shack
By the side of a track,
With a stream running close at the rear,
Where my neighbours and friends are the deer.
In the little loch, not far away,
I can see trout rising in a gentle ribble today.

The view down the valley
And up the glen, it's heaven here at my but and ben.
With no daily junk mail or rubbish TV,
Only realities have I to see.
I know some ways of life I would miss,
I can gain far more,
Just need to go and look outside my front door.

Douglas and I met by chance recently while I was researching into my family's background whilst they lived in Pitlochry. A phone-call had come from Radio Scotland, the producer of 'The Robbie Shepherd Show', inviting me to take part in a set of summer programmes they were planning. Now, you know what a show-off I am, so I didn't have to be asked twice. 'Choose your favourite places and several pieces of music,' was the request. I chose Pitlochry. It was there in Walker's Field over the bridge that Daddy introduced me to my home of many summers, the old blue bus. Blairgowrie was my second choice—those wonderful days at the berries, my friends, laughter, singers, camp-fires. Choosing music was fun, because there were umpteen songs I loved. So before I met up with Robbie and Jennifer, his producer, I took a jaunt over to see if some of the old places were still there. It was sad to see many places no longer existed or were changed dramatically. All except Granny Power's wee green hut where she lived at the Bobbin Mill, under a canopy of bushes, but still withstanding the ravages of time.

It was hungry work trekking around, so I went into a nice riverside café and it was here I met Douglas. It turned out he remembered some of my family, in particular daddy's brothers, Wullie, Joe and Eddy. We had a brilliant chat, and as I was leaving he handed me a sheet of folded A4 paper. 'If you write any more o' thon stories o' yours, lassie,' he smiled broadly, 'find a wee space for these'.

I thanked him and said goodbye. When arriving home I examined the paper, and on it were scribbled the above verses. I hope one day, Douglas, you find that but-and-ben by the stream.

19

CURSE OF THE MERCAT CROSS

I'll take us back to Macduff now folks, and, sad to say, for the last time.

Davie wasn't born to the sea. This hadn't taken long to dawn on him—in fact, poor lad, he had been overburdened with his dislike of the ocean from the word go, but being a good provider he decided to plod on and say nothing. He came home one day, and sat for ages allowing the contours of an ancient torn armchair Sarah had given us to almost swallow him, before telling me he'd quit, finished.

'It takes a certain kind of man, Jess, to leave his family and walk into the bosom of an ocean. You can be floating on a carpet of peaceful water one minute, and sinking fingers into wood and metal the next as you hang on for grim death, while twenty-foot waves throw you in every direction. I've seen myself heaving a newly eaten meal over the side, as those born to the sea to be fishermen laughed and played cards. I'm first to admit, it's not for me. Give me a building site any day. Let's go back to Perthshire. What do you say?'

I couldn't say much, as my thoughts about leaving my parents and family left a cold unwelcome mind. I should have seen it coming, he'd been showing signs of unrest for several weeks, always seeming preoccupied, unhappy with things. I thought it was a sore back I'd caused him by an over-zealous attempt to prove my love. I'd not lost much weight at the time, and ran into his arms after a longer time than usual at sea. The poor lad went backwards like a ton of tatties, me on top of him. But it wasn't that. No, in hindsight I think he needed to be back on home soil.

Well, I won't lie, there were very noisy arguments as I dug in my heels, adamant we were staying put, and he'd have to find another job here in Aberdeenshire, while he was determined to go home. Mammy solved the problem by suggesting we go somewhere new, like Fife. Glenrothes, where Shirley lived, was doubling in size; there was lots of building work on offer, and whole families were flooding the area.

I softened, as did he, and with everything packed up we said our goodbyes to everyone and left our wee low-roofed rented cottage for good.

I loved Macduff for many reasons. And like many places in my life little pieces of me remained there; Sarah for one, and Doctor Mackenzie another. It was there our son nearly died, and a nearly-baby changed its mind about being a human and leaving my womb; it became just a few joined-up cells. Behind closed doors I brushed shoulders with the shadow world. A ruddy-faced harbour chappie told me I had a weight problem, cutting me off forever from polony suppers. Oh aye, Macduff (which incidentally was Daddy's pet name for Mammy) would not leave me, we were joined just like Banff and Macduff with its bridge spanning the River Deveron.

So before we head to Glenrothes to take up residence with Shirley, here's that story I promised you of a half-caste rogue, the fiddler McPherson.

Legend has it he was the illegitimate son of a Highland gentleman and a gypsy girl. It may have been because of his mother's background that men of substance shunned him. Not many looked on gypsies as anything other than human vermin. Unable to find acceptance in mainstream society, he turned to his mother's people. There he could be a proud man, and grow strong in their midst. Musicians abounded among the gypsies. He acquired a grand fiddle, and from his mother, a deep love and understanding of music. This should have been the reason for his name passing into history, had it not been for a gang of cattle-lifters operating in the shire of Moray in the late seventeenth century.

Whether they were guilty mattered not—they were gypsies. On 7 November 1700, McPherson, along with a cousin of the name of Gordon, and a weak-minded lad called Brown, were brought before the Sheriff of Banffshire to face numerous charges. 'You are hereby charged with being "Egyptian" rogues and vagabonds, of keeping the markets in their ordinary manner of thieving and purse-cutting, also being of masterful bangstrie [violence against a person or property] and oppression.'

The peculiar language spoken between the gypsies may well have helped seal their fate. It was mentioned, not in their favour, that their nights were spent in debauchery, dancing and singing.

Guilty verdicts were levelled at McPherson and Gordon. At the Market Cross in Banff, the next day, they kept their appointment with the hangman's rope. There is a well attested story that the Banff authorities, anticipating a royal pardon, hung them before the stated time of the execution. McPherson composed in his final hours his famous rant, the song which inspired Burns' 'Farewell, ye Dungeons Dark and Strong'.

That was the traditional story that has been handed down.

But this one we now share has only been told round campfires by folks who swear it is the truth. I heard it myself one misty gloaming filled with the onset of night.

Once there was a handsome young gentleman who noticed, while out riding one fine day along the Moray coast, a vision of loveliness that stopped him dead in his tracks. So beautiful was the dark-haired girl singing to the sea, that he felt compelled to dismount and watch her from behind a windswept tree. He sat down among dune grass, completely spellbound by her sultry beauty. She was a shy songstress, and sang so bonny until her eye caught sight of him watching and listening. She smiled across on seeing him, waved her slender arm, rose, then ran off, and before he regained composure had gone from his view. 'Where did she go?' he asked his bewildered steed, as if the horse would know.

Remounted, he galloped for miles along sand and rock, but she'd just disappeared, gone.

Night found him tossing restlessly in the feather-down bed he slept upon. 'Sleep will', he thought, 'be an impossibility if I do not find the dusky maiden'.

This fine young man, heir to the estate of his father the Honourable James McPherson, had fallen in love at first sight. Next day, abandoning his usual duties, he set off once more in the hope of catching a glimpse of the maiden. As luck would have it, she too was hoping to see him; and in the place where they'd first seen each other they met properly. 'I am James,' he held out a hand.

'And I am Mary-Ann Gordon,' she told him, lowering velvet black eyelashes over smouldering brown eyes.

Sadly though, his dreams of courting this fine young maid and one day introducing her into his circle of family and friends were soon dashed, when he discovered she was a member of the Cave Gypsies, those mysterious people associated with the lowest forms of existence. Certainly she was not the kind a gentleman of blue blood would be found near. Yet love is a taskmaster like no other, and soon they were meeting in secret with a fondness growing stronger by the minute.

One day he decided she would be his wife, and no matter what the response a decision was made to tell his parents. Oh my, the wailing and beating of breasts that morning. His father hit him hard across the face, while his mother begged that he forget the wench. There were others, far more suitable ladies, who'd give anything to be his bride. They pleaded that he give up the cave dweller. It was a problem the McPherson family had never encountered before. James senior met with an old friend, the Laird o' Grant, and asked what could be done.

'There's documents needing taken south to Edinburgh, send him there for a few months!'

So McPherson ordered his son to complete this task. He promised that when he came home, and if she was still on his mind, then he'd receive the blessing of his parents to court the gypsy girl.

Happier now, with a clearer view of his future, James met his love on the windswept beach and relayed the news. They parted with a long and loving embrace. 'I shall take ye tae be mine when I come home, Mary-Ann, will ye wait on me?'

'Aye, that I shall, my bonny laddie, but heed these words afore ye go. For three nights in a row, auld Michtie Jean has been wailing intae the night. She telt me she *saw my blood running frae the gallows o' the Merket Cross in Banff*. I havenae been able tae sleep fer worrying.'

'Nobody will herm ye, lassie, and I'll be back yince ma business is done. The Michtie wife is shrivelled wi' gossip, and you'd dae weel no tae pay heed tae her.'

She touched his lips, smiled, then with a nod of her head she disappeared along the cliff tops, wind blowing through her raven-black hair.

She could have told him her news, but thought better of it. If he came to her it had to be without compulsion; the baby shifting in her womb might have forced the young gentleman in him to do the proper thing. She didn't want that: she wanted his love for her, and not his heir.

Next day James set off for the capital, leaving her worried for his safety, while his family worried more about a bloodline staying intact.

When he was due back she had news: a son, a child from his loins. One who'd be brought up proud and strong? But weary is the heart that seeks and never finds, for poor young McPherson never saw his boy. He fell as the victim of a raging storm which caused his horse to stumble, sending his body over a deep ravine to be shattered far below on jagged rock.

Mary Ann was destitute, heartbroken. It was almost as if they were never meant to be together. But mother and child needed protection, and it was her people who rallied to her, giving support and security.

When word reached them that their son had fathered an only grandchild, the McPhersons tried to influence Mary-Ann into giving him to them. He would be brought up as a gentleman, even although his blood was half-caste.

'No,' she screamed at old McPherson and Grant when they approached her cave north of Cullen, 'I will feed and claithe my ain wean!'

Big burly men chased the pair away, and so it was that the young James McPherson was brought up by the Gypsies. His grandfather left the area after that. Some say he and his lady found shelter with a cousin in England.

A fine fiddle was a gift to the boy from his beloved mother for his seventh birthday and he took to it like a natural: its music flowed from his expert hand.

He grew strong in the midst of wild pastures, with a fine physique that caught many a lassie's twinkling eye. He'd be heard oft times under summer moonlit skies serenading a wench or two on his violin.

'Dark shadows hold evil eyes,' announced auld Michtie Jean one night as she brushed against him on a cliff top. 'Watch oot fer the black hert o' Grant,' was her parting warning. He laughed and paid no heed to the back-bent old hag, who spent more time whistling among the wind and rocks after dark than she did in womanly duties during daylight hours. Yet it would have been better had he heeded the old woman, because soon a braggart came among the quiet folk of the Moray country. And the one I speak of was related in some dubious way to Grant himself; he was Donald by name. I say dubious, because rumours followed him from the Border country, where he had dealings with cattle reivers. He had blamed them for stealing a neighbour's beasts, whereas the truth was that it was he who had paid the thieves to carry out the dirty deed. On being discovered, he fled with his daughter to live under the protection of his kinsman, Grant.

The story went on that Mirrell, his daughter, was fond of visiting houses of ill repute. One night, in one of these ale-houses, 'Maggie Mair's Well Hole', she heard McPherson buskering. He was playing a kilt-rousing reel, which had a full house of revellers clapping hands and stomping feet. When she saw him, something stirred in her breast, her heart filled with desire. 'Will you dance with me, handsome fiddler?' she asked, tucking a handkerchief between her sweat-soaked bosoms and running her hand across his thighs. Embarrassment forced him to push her hand away, while he still managed to hold his bow.

'Take me home, handsome fiddler,' she demanded, thinking a simple gypsy would rise to her command and do exactly as asked. But James was no ordinary beggar, and being his own man, politely refused. Used to getting her own way, she stamped her foot down and again ordered him to see her safely home!

Unnerved by her manner, he stopped playing his fiddle, draped a tweed plaid over his shoulders, and disappeared into the night. He'd little time for women who drank alongside men, half-clothed and loud-mouthed. On his way home, his cousin Gordon reminded him of who she was, adding, 'best not to annoy the Grants, they have power tae hang every gypsy in Scotland if they take it on themselves.'

James couldn't have cared less, his love was his music. What harm could come to a musician?

Well, as it happened Grant had taken a grudge against a family of gypsy basket-weavers who'd taken up residence on the outskirts of Banff. One market day he whipped a half-wit boy who was seen annoying his horse. A simple altercation between the boy's father and Grant began a simmering hatred that would drive him to rid the county of all gypsies. Mishaps of little or no criminal intent started to be used against them. If one lost something and didn't find it, then a gypsy had stolen it. If a cow took sick, or dog or goat, then a gypsy curse was to blame. Blue babies were the result of an 'evil eye'. On and on flew the accusations. To avoid harm, many gypsy families left the area rather than face the gallows.

Mary Ann Gordon decided she and her son should uproot and go inland, where the peat moors would offer more in the way of a safe haven.

'I'll play ma fiddle, mither, in the Buckie Inn afore we gang awa. I hear tell it's tae be full o' fisherfolk; yin o' them's gittin merried.'

Strange, but at that precise minute his mother heard auld Michtie Jean whistling in the wind; it made hair rise at the base of her skull. She pulled a shawl over her head and begged him not to go.

'For why, mither? I'll tak a few bawbees at a weddin'; surely ye ken hoo generous the fisherfolk are?'

'Forget these people, Jamie. The Laird o' Grant and his wicked friends are death-dealers. And there's stories that yon Mirrell would pay money tae see ye pert wi' yer breeth fer spurnin' her advances yon nicht in Maggie Mair's Well Hole.'

'Thon's a spoilt lass, gi'en far too much her ain way as a bairn. I have nae fear o' the likes o' her. Some pair cratur will tak her fer a wife, and may the devil be his uncle if he does.'

The sea splashing on seaweed-covered rocks, mingled with a far-off whistle of auld Michtie Jean, was all she heard as her Jamie set off to entertain the friendly fisherfolk.

Leopards don't change spots, and so it was with Donald Grant, who had slipped back into his clandestine ways of cattle-lifting. He employed several wild men who were always happy to do his bidding for a few pennies and a bellyful of drink. After all, what blame could be cast on them, when everybody knew it was gypsies who were the real culprits?

Now, as the devil would have it, on the night of that wedding a great many beasts had been spirited away from pastures green. 'The gypsies have stolen near on fifty cattle,' came the accusation from a young man running breathless into the crowd of good folk who were enjoying the festivities at the Buckie Inn.

All eyes turned to the fiddler. 'Is this your doing?' demanded Grant.

'I heard him telling his cousin Gordon he'd keep us all busy.' Merrill screamed, seeing her chance for revenge, adding, 'He's the leader, and I tell you it's his men out there stealing our guid beasts.' Merrill had her platform, inciting the crowd of wedding guests who were filled and fired by the whisky. 'Black-faced vagabonds, they would rather steal from decent honest folk than pay for a morsel of meat!'

James knew these people were not going to allow him to leave the inn, so he made no attempt to escape as eager men ran forward with ropes to tie him.

'I am innocent o' this crime, and all ye ken it. But God and a fair judge will set me free.'

Grant leaned forward and whispered to the heavily ensnared prisoner, 'You'll swing like a pendulum, McPherson, for I'll be your judge. You and that witch o' a mother will leave nae mark on the land o' Moray.'

Mary Ann begged Grant not to condemn her innocent son, but no amount of pleading would change his mind. 'Have ye ever heard o' a braggart that plays a fiddle like an angel?' she cried. 'Ye must ken his father and grandfather, Sire, there was nae bad in them neither. Please let him go away with me, I promise ye never a sound o' us will ye hear again.' But all the pleading in the world failed to move the stone that was Grant's heart: James McPherson had to die. This was a travesty of justice. Mary Ann knew that if she got word to the High Court, her son would be fairly treated. Her determination led her to pay a rider to take news of this unlawful case to the High Court in Aberdeen, and she prayed some form of justice might prevail.

On the sixth of November, the eve of the execution of James and his cousin Gordon, he asked for his fiddle. The wish of a condemned man was granted, and as the wild and desolate cliffs screamed with an early winter storm he wrote a final piece. His Rant was filled with hatred for all who would do him harm. His innocence and the injustice he suffered ran through his fingers into his bow to yield a masterpiece.

It was not known either by him or his mother that the High Sheriff of Aberdeen had taken an interest in the trial. He saw a miscarriage of justice and so sent a pardon. It should have arrived at noon, but during the night the town clock in Banff was put forward an hour. This was because news of the imminent pardon had been leaked to Grant, and he had the clock interfered with.

A crowd gathered on the ring of twelve. The hooded hangman waited, fingers running over the knotted rope. Mary Ann lay at her son's feet, sobbing, and Grant sneered from his official window overlooking the Mercat Cross.

'Give tae me yer fiddle, McPherson,' shouted a lone woman: it was Michtie Jean.

'I'd rather burst it ower ma knee as gi'e you, ye auld witch, ma precious fiddle.' As he brought it up and down heavily against his leg, the pull on the rope around his neck tightened; the fiddle splintered; a jagged piece tore into his thigh and blood oozed freely.

'McPherson blood shall spill upon the Merket Cross,' whispered the old hag into Mary Ann's ear, 'your son's blood!'

Gordon's body followed James's with an instant break upon his neck. No sooner had the noose squeezed away their last breath, when a shout rent the air. Hooves tore hard into the cobbled street, an exhausted horse snorted with hot sharp pants as its rider ran in haste, waving a paper above his head. 'Hold the execution, I have a pardon frae Eberdeen!' Too late: both men were at that moment being pronounced dead.

Grant never had much status from that day, and it is thought he spent many an hour looking over his shoulder. His sleepless nights sent him into a mad state and Merrill ended in a whorehouse.

The good people of Macduff were able to substantiate the falsification of the clock in neighbouring Banff, because the timepiece there kept the right time. According to my storyteller, relations between the two towns were strained from then on.

Aye, this was a great story: fact and fiction mingling together, one gently easing the other along. I was fourteen when I heard it told. There was a man in the campsite that night listening around our fire who told another version, but needless to say his was just as entertaining. Before we upped sticks and left there, I can honestly say I felt as close to Jamie McPherson as a long-devoted sister might.

20

BAGREL

It had been my pleasure, while growing up as one of Perthshire's agricultural travellers, to enjoy the rich vein of diversity among them that even as a youngster I was keenly aware of. To the outsider it was easy to imagine all of us were the same, but that was simply a myth. 'We're all Jock Thamson's bairns,' is a true saying, but who's to say Jock didn't put it around a bit?

Let me share some characters with you now, and a cup of tea might be a good idea at this point.

Now you've poured that tea or coffee, what better place to start than by the campfire, kettle boiling away. Auld Tam Troot had just brought home a great big bunch of kindling. Nancy, his spouse of forty years, was in the process of ladling his broth into a cracked bowl, when without warning a great muckle cow galloped right into their midst. We won't linger on the spot as soup, bowl, ladle and burning water went heavenward, then showered back down to cover auld Tam, Nancy and their visitor.

Lurid oaths rent the sky, and that's why we won't tarry there. Instead it's to a worried farmer trudging through fields of mushy gutters that we'll go.

'Last time I let yon ba' heid o' a man near ma coo. Every time she sees him, her backsprent rises intae the air, she shak's her bahookie an' awa she goes. Lord A'mighty, whit will ah dae without ma Sally? When I git ma hands on that wee bagrel, I'll squash him like a worm.'

The ba' heid he referred to was a tiny wee man, almost dwarf-like, who tramped the country. He wasn't a traveller, tinker, gypsy or vagrant, in fact nobody knew what group laid claim to him, because he couldn't speak—as dumb as a mountain bawd [hare] was the wee man.

In glen areas he might have been looked upon as a 'Broonie', that mystical wee creature who, for a scone and a drink of milk, would do jobs around farmyards that no other hands would do. For instance, cleaning the hen pen and spreading the chicken dung onto fields. This foul-smelling stuff made even stones grow, such was its richness of compost. He'd clean the sties of dirty 'roll-in-gutter' pigs until they were spotless. In fact he'd undertake any job unfit for human nostrils without a word; just a wee bite and drink and then he'd be gone. The difference between our little lad and the Broonie was that the latter was expected to turn anyone who saw him to stone. This superstition forced him to live in caves or under trees, creeping out only under a night sky.

Well, that very morning, while our wee bagrel was simply minding his own business, not bothering a soul, his appearance at her field entrance had obviously stirred Sally into a panic. Her one-cow stampede, however, didn't half make a mush of Tam and Nancy's tent—flattened to a pancake, it was.

Tam caught the tired cow and was tying her to a tree, when our little man came whistling up the road, totally unaware of the havoc in his wake.

Nancy, like everyone else who laid an eye upon him, smiled, but didn't leave her stare too long upon his face which, and God forgive me for saying this, was not very bonny! Well, for starters, he'd a wart on his chin like a river stone, and a huge hump on his back. His windswept black and grey hair, thick and wiry with white streaks, danced down around his waist. His eyeballs rolled in their sockets as if they had a life of their own. But the beauty of him was in his strength. Some say he could lift a raging bull with one kick. Maybe that's why very few approached the bagrel, who stood four feet tall on a Sunday.

When he saw the devastation and debris scattered throughout the usually tidy campsite, he lifted his shoulders, throwing his hands out and palms up, asking with his gesture, 'what happened here?'

Still not making full eye-contact, Nancy used her hands to imitate horns, and slapped her bum to indicate a large back end such as a cow might sport.

The wee man smiled, making his acknowledgement with a thumbs-up.

Auld Tam came back from securing the cow and said his hellos. 'Gi'e the bagrel a drink o' tea, Nancy,' he said.

His able spouse had already built the fire and refilled the kettle, which was just beginning to boil, as a very irate farmer rushed into their midst. On seeing the reason for the disappearance of his only cow he lifted his cromach to bring it down upon the bagrel's back. 'You bloody half a man, I'll tan ye for spurring ma coo, the devil's in ye!'

'No in ma company, fairmer,' hissed Tam, wrenching the stick from his hand.

'I own this land ye're campit on, Tam, an I swear if ye so much as lift a finger tae stop me whipping this curse frae a witch's womb, I'll mak sure ye niver set a fit here agin!'

Tam knew full well there wasn't a place for miles where he and Nancy could winter-settle, yet he was a godly man; and what kind of sleep would his conscience allow him, if he let a poor defenceless creature take a whipping for simply being ugly? And he had never believed stories of the wee man's brute strength; how could someone so small hurt anyone?

'Sorry, fairmer, about yon cow o' yours, but I canna stand back and see a six-fitter like yersel take a rochet temper oot on a wee bagrel.' He turned and threw the stick into a now blazing fire.

'Ye kin pack whit ye have and be off my land within the hour; an' thank that lump o' useless flesh fer yer ruin,' the farmer said, pointing at the dumb dwarf who seemed rigid with fear. Red-faced and spitting with temper, he turned about and was soon gone to console himself at the loss of Sally.

'Well, handy man you are, eh Tam? Now where dae we go with the first snows roaring down frae the north? You've left us hameless, and all because o' him.'

Tam shook his head at Nancy's lack of tact towards a helpless dwarf who never bothered a soul, and began gathering what little hadn't been crushed by the cow. Then something dawned on him: where was the wee lad? In all the commotion they had failed to see him slip away after the farmer left.

'Now look what's happened, the wee leprechaun has gone aff in the huff. I bet he'll pit a curse on us for you being sae hostile.'

'Don't talk rot. Anyway, he's no' a pokey man and I blame your Irish mother for teaching you rubbish like that.'

'Rubbish is it? What about you, feart tae look at the wee man in case ye turned tae stone.' As the pair argued back and forth among the ruins of their canvas home, they realised that something else had slipped their mind—the cow. Tam had forgotten to show the farmer she was safe.

'Go, take her back to the field. Then tell him what happened. He'll let us stay if he thinks you found the cow. Tell him you fought wi' the dwarf and saved it. Go on, Tam.'

Tam listened to his wife and thought long and hard. 'Aye, I'd best get up tae yon farm, cap in hand,' he said eventually. 'Yet what kind of rat would I be if I lied like that? No, I'll just say the cow ran through us. Mind you, if thon wee dwarf hadn't frightened her, then she wouldn't have bolted oor tent. Bloody wee pest, thon leprechaun, he disnae even deserve a drap tea. Pitting fear intae a puir chowing-cud cow. Ah think he might be in cahoots wi' a "Green Man." I've niver telt ye this, Nancy, but once ma mither saw one crawling along the grun, cracking tae an adder.'

Totally convinced now that the cause of their predicament lay at the small feet of a dumb dwarf, he led the cow into her field before walking gingerly to face the farmer. He must have seen him coming, because the door near-on lifted its hinges as he swung it open.

'I telt you tae get aff my land, Tam Troot, I wisnae joking. Noo, is it the back o' ma hand or will ye go quietly?'

'Calm doon noo, fairmer, ye ken how much ye mean tae me an Nancy. This morning, if yer prize cow hadnae taken flight at the sight o' yon horrible wee man, then life wid hae been a gey sight milder. He put the evil eye on me, ye ken, had it stiff intae ma heed.' (Tam's godly scruples had fallen by the wayside.) Tam had passed the point of no return; lies fell from his forked tongue and he continued unashamedly. 'Why dae ye think I had tae defend him frae yer guid self? I had nae choice. He warned me and Nancy we'd be turned tae cauld marble if we let you belt him. But it's alright now, man, because I battled hard wi' the devil and chased him aff. He had the power in him, ye ken, but me—well, I said tae myself, "yon fairmer's a good man, and this demon isnae getting tae steal his cow." Go see for yourself, she's safely in her field.'

'Safe, ye say, Tam? Ma Sally is alright?'

'Aye, man, and no' a scratch on her.'

Chest puffed like a champion cock, Tam led the farmer down the track to where he'd just left Sally. He could see Nancy coming to meet him, in the hope that things were now sorted. A cold wind blowing from the north, flaked with snow, made her cover her head with a grey shawl. They met together at the field gate, she, her husband and the farmer.

'I hope ye're telling me the truth, now, Tam, for I'll no' be pleased if she's a mark on her.'

By now the wind had dropped slightly. The snow thickened and fell around them as they stood unable to think, let alone speak about what stood before them. Sally had stopped chewing. And it wasn't for the lack of food, because plenty of the best hay lay scattered around her stone hooves; she would never eat another morsel of anything again, that solitary statue of grey granite.

Stunned into silence, they then turned slowly when they heard a noise behind them. The wee man was jigging in the air and laughing hysterically. Then with a puff of blue reek he turned his behind towards them, patted it and was gone, never to be seen again.

21

THE DAY OF THE HAIRY LIP

I thought I had turned into a monster once. It all happened one morning while we were camped on waste ground near Oban, which had, during the war, been a Royal Navy base. After the wooden buildings had been dismantled, grand concrete bases were left in place and many travellers found clean floors to use for their caravans and tents. I was thirteen years old, at that nightmare age when a tiny spot on the cheek looks like a volcano about to erupt.

September followed a beautiful summer with hardly a drop of rain. We had chocolate-coloured skin under sleeveless tops and shorts. I can to this very day feel the horror of that particular morning, the day my life changed for ever.

I had been fascinated by two large white swans which had taken up residence in a patch of dry seaweed down by the beach. We'd camped on no man's land for almost a month, and the swans had got used to me beachcombing by their nest. I felt sorry for them because, according to locals, the bonny pair of birds had failed to produce any offspring. I knew several travellers who never had bairns. They were always kindly treated by folks who felt sorry for their barren state.

Perhaps it was because they did not have cygnets to protect that those regal birds didn't attack as I rummaged around, searching for scrap metal for my jute sack. Well, that's where I'd planned to go after Mammy went hawking and we'd finished cleaning the bus. But, as Rabbie was wont to write, 'the best laid plans o' mice and men', etc—a plan is best discussed in hindsight.

I positioned my gilt-edged mirror on a wee chair to give everything above shoulder level its usual third degree. This braw-looking glass I'd recently found abandoned on a rubbish tip.

It suddenly dawned on me, as I brushed my hair, my mirror needed a good clean. I'd left it out from the day before, and the mist was still clinging to it along with two spiders' gossamer webs. It soon shone bright, illuminating my shiny black hair and two new plooks at each side of my nose. 'I wonder if I could squeeze them buggers away?' I thought, as every human does when confronted by such face hangers-on. But as I moved close up to the mirror it wasn't the red plooks that caught my eye: oh no, it was something so terrible I felt cold at the very sight. Yet how could it be? Surely this wasn't possible? I wiped a frantic hankie once more over the mirror, even used it on my eyes, yet still, there it was, no mistake—a thin line of hair had sprouted above my top lip. I WAS TURNING INTO A LADDIE!!

I ran behind the bus, tucked my chin onto shivering knees and covered the monstrosity with my forearm. What was going on? How long would it grow? Would I sprout that thing that I had mistaken for a slow-worm which grew below Cousin Joey's belly button? I'd have to wear trousers and keep my hands in pockets. Oh God, what terrible thing had I done to deserve this? My knuckles would also grow hair. How could I tell fortunes with digits like the Wolfman? Ochone, ochone, heel, weel, heel, weel.

I must have sat rocking back and forth like a dafty for hours, when Mammy called my name.

'I'm roond the back o' the bus, Mammy, an' I'll stay here if it's a'richt wi' you.'

Her head peered round at my secluded spot between two gorse bushes. She smiled, then when she saw my red eyes, said with concern, 'Baby lassie, what's the matter with ye, hen? I thought you were away combing the beach or cracking tae the Queen's swans.'

I had sat so long imagining such terrible changes from girl to boy that waves of emotion suddenly brought floods of tears. 'Mammy, look what's growing on my top lip.' I shoved out my face; she quickly examined it, laughed and said, 'That's your celtic beauty.'

Shock and horror! I thought at least she'd show some compassion, after all the only women who have hairy faces are sat in cages in the circus. Then I wondered if perhaps all Mammy's prayers in years gone by to give Daddy a son were now being answered. Mother Nature had decreed I was to be a laddie. Oh no!

'Jessie, there is nothing ugly about a thin layer of fluff. As I said, all celtic lassies have it, it attracts the men.'

'Poofs mair like!' I screamed, then remembered how hurtful that word could be to certain individuals born to their lot. Still, I wasn't about to start wearing greasy jeans and a cravat on Sundays. If Mammy hadn't taken hold of my arm, God alone knows where I'd have run to—joined the swans in their barren nest, no doubt. Come to think of it, maybe they too were poofs. I went with my mother into the bus, protesting, with one hand over my lip hiding the hairy curse. She sat me down and opened a small wooden box concealed under the 'courie doon' bed at the rear of the bus. In it were all her womanly things—powder, rouge, lipstick and 'lily of the valley' perfume (her favourite). A small bottle of twenty volumes peroxide came out, and was placed very carefully on the thick chopping board. She pushed her hand down further and took out a ribbed bottle marked 'dangerous substance'. I near fainted. Was she about to poison me, ashamed of her daughter's metamorphosis into a man?

I felt my body shake, but only momentarily, as she produced a small dish and poured a tablespoon of peroxide into it. 'Hold your nose, now, because this stuff is lethal.' She warned me also to cover my eyes. I covered them and with a dropper she plopped five drops into the dish. The fumes were awful, but not for long. 'Now,' she assured me, 'let's magic this away, although too be truthful I can hardly see it.' With cotton soaked in the solution she applied it to my skin. There was quite a degree of stinging, but hey, 'no pain no gain'. We waited until, according to my beautician of a mother, the treatment had taken effect. After ten minutes she held my face gently with one hand, with the other she wiped a cool damp cloth over my painless top lip, dried it, then said, 'let's go look in your mirror.'

I swear sweat was dripping freely down my back as each step took me nearer that mirror. What would I see? 'Now tell me, Jessie, where's the moustache?'

What magic—it had disappeared. Oh, the joy of seeing nothing there made heaven meet my earth. I smothered my mother in kisses, and hugged her to death, when suddenly she spied the spots at each side of my nose. 'Get that face washed properly, and don't let me catch you squeezing,' she skelped my backside. Then, with a wee wink of her bonny brown eye, she said, 'Now you have a hairy lip like your Mammy.'

'No, it's away, gone, look.'

'It's been bleached, Jessie, and in several months' time when it reappears, let me know and this time I'll show you how to mix the liquids yourself.'

I spent the day in a state of nerves at the knowledge that I'd a hairy lip, and like the invisible man who took off his bandages to be unseen, I'd have to concoct a vile-smelling poison to spread over my lip. 'God,' I thought recoiling in horror, 'I hope my body doesn't start sprouting any more hair!'

I know, I know, but those tattie shaws under my armpits were dealt with in another way.

Secrets of the female form—eh, girls? It might be the right time to add that, on inspection of my new mirror, my father informed me it was a magnifying one.

Now, I should leave this topic, but I have another surprise for you, folks. This new hair-removing mixture could, as I later discovered through experimentation, be put to other uses. Let me tell you how my mother's wrath was pushed beyond boiling point.

Still at Oban, and only days after my traumatic experience, I was at a loose end. My swans had taken flight to another place, probably further down the coastline. With no more tidal scrap to collect, I decided to find out if my bleach would make head-hair disappear. Not mine, dear me no—but I had innocent wee sisters who hadn't a clue about anything other than building sandcastles and greeting for sweeties.

Mammy and Daddy had gone hawking through neighbouring villages along the coastline, leaving me to watch over my blessed siblings with strict instructions not to get them dirty or allow them to play on the beach. Other travellers were there, who also kept their eye on parentless bairns. My older sisters weren't with us at the time, so I was the big, wise sister. Aye, right.

Mary really didn't need looking after, in fact I'd challenge any-body who knew her to so much as try to keep that wild lassie in one place. Mammy told her, though, to obey me or else she'd feel the back of the hand when she got home. But as I said, Mary was un-tamed, so as soon as the van drove off she was off herself.

'Don't get stuck on rocks,' I called out with my so grown-up voice, 'if ye dae, bide there until the tide goes out.' I knew if this happened Mammy would be home and fuming at her disobedience, and at me for not keeping the wee madam in check.

Renie was swingeing at not being allowed to go with her, and Babsy joined in for support. There had to be something I could do to amuse them.

'Can we play at cards?' asked Renie.

'Snap, or I won't play,' said Babsy, sniffing the air like a meercat.

Cards it was, but where did Mammy put them? I checked everywhere, and while I looked under her bed, my hand ran over the beauty box. Suddenly thoughts so spectacular popped into my head it was a mini-Blackpool Illuminations as lights switched on in my brain.

'Forget the cards, lassies, we'll play at hairdressers!' I looked at them for a reaction, but before they could guess my plan I'd put two seats side by side and said, 'please, madams, will you be seated.' Giggles followed as I draped a towel around their shoulders.

'Listen now ladies, I shall give you both a Marilyn Monroe fringe, but while I'm preparing the mixture, feel free to have a chat. Coffee?' I asked, pretending to pour into invisible cups.

'Yes, please,' they said in unison, adding, 'cream and sugar lumps.'

As they sat chatting and sipping non-existent coffee from invisible cups, I went outside to prepare that lethal mix of peroxide and ammonia. Standing with a spoon in one hand and bottle in the other, it dawned on me I'd forgotten how much was needed, so I stupidly poured the whole bottle of peroxide into a soup bowl, then tipped in enough ammonia to send a fizz of torment up my nose, which joined tears and snotters to escape and run down my cheeks. Daddy's toothbrush had fine strong bristles, so I used that to lavish my home-made bleach onto my victims' hair. They thought this playtime was fun as I applied more bleach. In fact I used the lot. You might think me a bit of a show-off, but when I swear on my Granny's grave that my siblings had turned from dark-haired weans into lightning-streaked freaks, you may believe me. What a state! I'd created two brides for Frankenstein. Mammy would kill me.

'Well, Jessie, can we look in the mirror?'

'Yikes! No, ye canny, I mean there's no mirror, it's broken.' Before I could prevent them, they'd run from the bus and looked at their new hairdos in the bus wing-mirrors. What a screaming and yelly-hooing. Off down the road they ran, to tell anybody who'd listen that I'd turned them into monsters. I ran after them, only to meet Mammy and Daddy driving up the track.

I'd no idea my mother could dislocate her jaw like that. What a monumental roar.

Two leatherings I got after my beautician escapade; one for creating yellow-haired greetin'-faced weans, and the other for my seal sister, who had to be rescued from rocks because I didn't keep her in about.

I was not into babysitting, me—hairdressing neither.

22

MY BROTHER'S SHARE

Robbie Shepherd called me a right romantic, and of course he was right. This next story I share with you about two brothers describes a common scenario, especially during the pre-war years.

Along with several cousins, Janet and Drummond shared a campsite with her mother and his brother Robin. Nothing much happened in the way of excitement, and life wandered on at a snail's pace, yet there was joy when baby Muriel was born, and again at the safe arrival of Drummond junior. These had been the highlights of life on the campsite in over three years. A large farm provided year-round work, so they gave up travelling round Aberdeenshire and hoped one day they'd be offered houses. Tents could be mighty cold in winter, and the farmer did have a row of dilapidated cottages in need of renovation. One day the old farmer, as a way of thanking them, told Drummond and Robin, along with the other workers, that if they repaired the houses he'd let them have them rent-free so long as they stayed under his employment. Although the work to be done was back-breaking, it had its rewards in the end. Roofs were re-thatched, loose windows puttied into oak frames, doors replaced and gardens dug over for planting. It meant that for the first time in two thousand years the tinkers would have a place to call home. The womenfolk weren't idle either. With bairns tied to their backs, they scrubbed the slabs of stone floors, brushed away cobwebs, and made curtains and carpets from rags of ribbons all sown together.

Robin was born with the skilled hands of a carpenter, so it fell to him to build beds, tables and chairs. He even threw together bunkers at the rear of each house for winter firewood. One by one the families helped each other move into their new homes, abandoning the old campsite to be taken over again by its long burned and flattened grass. Soon it was once more the home of the rabbit, fox and weasel.

Three years later the row of cottar houses was as a bonny a picture as one could wish to see: the whitewashed walls were covered with honeysuckle and ivy, paths leading to each unlocked door were lovingly paved with broken granite in mosaic patterns.

Much as we'd like to see this continue, with our small band of tinkers toddling happily on through life, one day two momentous changes took place—the outbreak of war and the demise of the old farmer.

The war came in like a lamb, but soon turned into the most ferocious of lions. Drummond had no doubt that his loyal duty lay in taking arms against the enemy. Robin also followed his brother to the enlistment office but an accident with a saw had deprived his right hand of two fingers, so he was turned down. Drummond consoled him by saying that the women needed a man, a strong one, to be their guardian. The other men were posted to different regiments. The care of everyone and all the farm work were now the responsibility of Robin and two old workers.

It was at this time, while spending many days with Janet, that he began to feel drawn to her. At first he believed it was a brotherly affection that he was feeling, and as the country was thrown into the midst of war and its uncertainty, people certainly did draw strength from friends and neighbours. She too took the comfort that he offered, and many a night the pair sat cracking about old relatives round the hearth of a small fire. Little Muriel began adding another person to her prayers, and each night before she went to bed she'd be heard saying 'God bless my Mammy, Daddy, wee Drummond and Daddy two,' meaning Uncle Robin.

He worked hard, did that lad. He was as tough as three ploughmen, and although the missing fingers might have hindered his aim with a rifle, it didn't stop him with a plough. Janet especially needed his company during the long nights when she and Drummond used to cuddle together in bed and fall asleep, embracing in true love. She so longed for her husband and tried hard not to rely on his brother, but one night while a blizzard raged outside, she welcomed

Robin in to share her bed. From then on they were as one. Yes, this robbed each of dignity, but who can afford that luxury during a war?

Only once did a letter arrive from Drummond. It gave Robin and Janet an insight into the horrors of battle, but not wishing to upset his family he finished with a cheerful, 'no need for snivelling, I'm eating like a horse.'

Then it happened—the letter from a weary War Office: Drummond was missing, presumed dead! Weeks of closed curtains and tea-sipping left Janet's exhausted mind in turmoil. Robin said he'd not let the wind blow on her or the weans, and that once her heart wore off its pain they'd marry. Her own frail old mother gave them her blessing, saying he'd make a good man for her. So one sunny day, three years later, Robin and Janet wed.

Another two years passed, with the arrival of a son to bless their union: then great public celebrations brought the final chapters of war to a close.

The farm work was undertaken without supervision; the jobs needed to be done and the tinkers did them. The late farmer had left instructions with his factor that wages were to continue to be paid to his tinkers as funds allowed. However he hadn't reckoned on his heir: a nephew with a heart coated in iron. He liked the look of the houses occupied by the tinkers, and wondered what they'd fetch if sold. The farm could make a good sale also, bringing him cash; he was a lover of money, obviously. So one day the bombshell came with a letter to each tenant saying it was time to move. Oh yes, they met him and protested all they could, but there wasn't a drop of his uncle's benevolence in the nephew, and with deep sadness the tinkers took once more to the tent and travelling the trails.

For a while small amounts of money were earned through rat-catching and rabbit-snaring, but it barely provided the necessities of existence for the sad, weary tinkers. Janet's mother died of influenza. One young mother died in childbirth, and soon the severe weather took its toll on Robin. His chest proved weak, and as each day passed he began a downward spiral of ill health. By 1948 he'd seen his last winter. Janet, now alone with four children, took to begging the streets of Aberdeen.

One day, after a long sore day's begging, she headed home—which was a wood-end on the outskirts of Dyce. Walking along the road, young Muriel thought she recognised a man passing on the other side. She ran after the bedraggled man with black beard. He shoo'ed her away, but there was a distinct familiarity in this tramp. She called a name; one she'd long spoken under her breath. The tramp froze, then turned. It was her father: none other than Drummond, presumed dead, who'd been captured and spent the rest of the war as a POW. He'd suffered shell shock, not regaining his memory for some time. When it had returned, he made a long journey to find his family.

'Blessings come in strange packaging,' was all Janet could think as she kissed her lost husband. Now, with him returned home, she could see a future for her children. There were no recriminations about her marriage to Robin, because Drummond's sentiments all his life were 'what's mine's my brother's, and what's my brother's is mine.'

When the above story was given to me, not much detail came from its narrator. However it wasn't my place to elaborate or re-touch it. I have told you the version I heard.

23

GLENROTHES

We emptied our wee low-roofed cottage house of its meagre amount of furniture, giving it to whoever wanted it. Then we piled into Daddy's van (a bit larger than John's) and set off to Glenrothes, to live with Shirley in her new house. It was to be a tight squeeze sharing with her, but as far as Davie was concerned it was a step nearer Crieff. Fife skirted Perthshire, and he'd not be happy until we were back in his beloved home town. However, this, may I say, was a pipe-dream carried around in my husband's head. As far as I was concerned, Crieff was in the past, and would firmly bide there! Yet if you've read my previous book, then you will know that, in the end, he won.

From Woodside, the ancient part of Glenrothes, sprang Scotland's second modern 'shopping centre' (Livingston, I'm informed, gave us the first). By shopping centre, I mean shops gathered together under one roof. The birth of 'you will spend your money here', and the death of family-run businesses began in these places. Years of shopping with the personal touch died beneath those Perspex roofs. The old shopkeepers were unable to compete with 'buy one, get one free' smiley faces behind miles of walled glass. Like zombies we give them hard-earned money for cheap, shabby goods, and turned our backs for ever on the 'this is quality' businesses that had been handed down from father to son, pushing them into little drawers of past times. Yes, new town shopping centres like those in Glenrothes and Livingston had us hook, line and pork-linkers.

Nowadays, like locusts, those centres have arrived in every town, ruling our credit and controlling spending on a gigantic scale. Gone forever is the personal touch, lost to banks and building societies who determine what, where and when we spend.

Personally I blame these centres for destroying the art of conversation. We tend to eye up a nearby stranger as a hovering hawk ready to pounce and steal our credit cards from tightly held purses. I used to enjoy shopping—now I spend more time trying to avoid eye-contact with security guards than wondering if the garment I just purchased could be dry-cleaned or machine-washed.

Talking about credit cards, here's a poem on the subject penned by Shirley:

THE PLASTIC PATCH

With symbolic layers of plastic,
We procure some flexible friends.
This warrants idle fancies,
Able choices in the end.

With the touching face of plastic,
We inhale the telephone.
The moving arrow travels on,
Words unspoken, minutes gone.

With fine moulded, mounted plastic,
We acquire Baird's progression—
Beware this T.V. madness,
It dictates without permission.

When steel encircles plastic,
Enter now the vehicle maze,
The happy wanderers' wanderlust
Enslaved to wheel and brace.

With the ultimate in plastic
We replace our tired hearts,
A hip, a leg, whatever next,
In this Hi-Tech paradise...

Shirley was working in a chicken and egg factory named Eastwoods. Her then husband had a good job managing a department within the local paper mill. My Davie got a job working on a building site (Glenrothes was rapidly expanding) and guess who held the fort. That's right, me. I made certain Christine and Hughie, Shirley's wee ones, got off to school on time, sandwiches were prepared for the workers to their satisfaction, the house cleaned (it was a big one) and dinner cooked for all eight of us. Could life get any better? Nope!

24

BELLS AND GHOSTLY CHAINS

So why don't we all take another trip down memory lane? To a time when Daddy was a laddie of fourteen years old.

Every year Daddy's family trekked over the old drove road leading to Ballater, to spend the winter working on a large estate. Their allotted campsite was behind a high dry-stane dyke, with a hardy line of firs and Caledonian pine to stop the wild wind, and of course the snow that came in with September's end; not a sign of brown peat was seen until it was vacated in April. My grand-dad looked after the garrons, those sturdy hill horses which carry the deer down the mountain. He was given this job because he had a Horseman's Grip, in other words no one knew the hill ponies better than him. He also provided beaters for shoots. This was when my father, his younger brother Wullie and two cousins came in handy. Granny made pot-scourers from heather roots to sell around the area. So you can see how important this place was to my father's family.

Most travelling folk had their favoured winter place, and it usually centred on an estate where work could be plentiful. Some however considered themselves to be sea folk and worked along the coastlines, fixing creels and whelk-gathering, to name two typical jobs.

So there they were, heading towards the campsite, a natural hamlet snuggling between two spurs of rolling hills. Suddenly Granny noticed a spiral of smoke coming from the exact spot. When they last spoke in the spring, the factor had promised them the site would be cleaned and ready for their arrival that autumn. So who had got there first?

'Away, you and Wullie, run down and peek at whoever has lit a fire in oor campsite, Charlie,' she said, adding, 'I expect it'll be the factor himself burning brushwood to clean the place for us coming.'

Grand-dad had tarried further back to adjust some loose strapping under the belly of his own old horse. They had been forced to abandon a fine cart the previous day because of twisted wheels, and all they possessed was either tied to the horse or back-packed. They were already two days late in arriving, and Grand-dad was worried his boys would be missed at the beating.

Daddy and Wullie removed their bundles and did as Granny asked, jumping and running through the coarse heather like two young deer. In no time they stood eyeing the campsite. There was indeed a fire, a big one. Four untidily erected tents cluttered the spot that their tents should soon be occupying. Matted-haired bairns ran back and forth, tearing at slices of braxy ham like young wolves. Two massive black pots filled with foul-smelling meat hung from iron chitties, cooking over the reekit fire. An elderly woman sat cross-legged, poking a blackened stick into the flames as she puffed on a pipe. A fine example of long life was this lady: she made Daddy think of a banshee resting before puffing life into a parcel of broom and scooting toward the day-moon peeping through a veil of clouds.

'Hello, laddies, whit dae ye want?' asked another toothless woman, with a face that seemed to have been moulded by a drunken goblin. Running her hand across her wet nose and dipping a bent spoon into the meat-pot she asked if they were hungry.

'Thank you mistress, but no; we was wondering why you stole big Wullie Riley's site.' Daddy pretended not be related to Wullie Riley, and asked if they knew of him?

'Aye,' growled a deep croaky voice from within one of the tents, a dark shadowy hole of green tarpaulin, 'we ken the Rileys, don't we?'

A chorus of roars and cackles, joined with coughs and splutters, answered my father.

'Noo git tae hell awa frae here, unless ye have drink and baccy,' ordered the croaky one.

'Oh shit,' exclaimed Wullie, 'wait until Mammy finds oot the wild MacSpits have stolen oor winter grun! She'll rip a pound o' flesh aff faither's back for sure.'

'Oh, Lord roast thon MacSpits,' Granny screamed, when her breathless sons told her who'd stolen the jewel in the crown of campsites. 'Yon bare-heided, rid-eyed yaps o' the Devil's ain wild folk ken fine that we winter there. Not an inch o' spare grun is there tae pitch another tent.' She turned to scan the hillside. 'You'd better go and see whit yer Faither has tae say.' She ranted on about the factor, and how it wasn't like him to let the site to anyone else. Daddy and Wullie, along with cousins Matthew and Thomas, ran back to tell him about the campsite being invaded and taken over by yookies (rats). Granny, when riled, had the devil of a tongue in her head, and rats was the mildest name she could muster to describe the undesirables down on 'her' land.

Poor Grand-dad, his back was burdened with a wheen of heavy gear, and the only thing that had been keeping him going was the thought of building a fire sheltered by the stane dyke, and a hot cup of sweet tea.

'You get doon among thon hantle, big Wullie,' she warned him, 'and fling yon buggers aff my winter grun. Bash them intae pulp if ye have tae, but I want them run aff afore nicht comes.'

Grand-dad shifted his bonnet and scratched his head, saying in answer to his wife's call for arms against the MacSpits, 'lassie, them craturs have every right tae settle where they want. Who am I to order them anywhere?'

'But I thought you and the factor had an agreement tae keep that place free fer us?'

'Well, something must have happened. What bothers me mair than the grun is all the work we usually get frae the estate. You ken fine, without it bellies will be hard-filled.'

Granny fell silent as Grand-dad laid aside his pack and set off to find the factor.

Meanwhile, with night rearing shadows, it was decided to find a dip in the glen and set up camp. Granny warned the boys not to go down among the squatters in case they were fuelled with drink. 'Whit Tam o' Shanter saw was nothing tae yon witches.'

They laughed—not Granny, though, the dour scowl was on her because she'd a mother's worry to contend with. Winter in those parts took old and young alike when it had the bite of a hard frost, especially those that had no good food in their bellies.

'Auntie, you sound like you have a grudge agin them?' asked

Matthew, amused by her temper. Such a wee creature, hardly five feet tall, but by the gods she had a rage in her towards those folks.

'I have nae grudge agin ony living soul, but thon hantle are soulless. Now away and fill the kettle at the burn, and make sure no tae fill it with heather seed, or else the grouse will go as hungry as us if we fail tae get work on this estate.'

Boys will be boys, they say, and my father's lot were no exception. It bothered them that these uncouth travellers, who had little respect for themselves, would have none for the ground which had always been theirs. Daddy knew every tree and bush. Granny had left her drying rope tied from one tree to the other to be there for her return. No doubt the squatters would have used it for securing their dirty tents. Wullie had more reason than the rest to feel aggrieved, because wee Florence, his beloved collie pup, was buried down there in the ground under those filthy drunkards.

Yes, the more they thought about it, the more determined they became—they had to go! Be moved on, shifted. But how?

Grand-dad arrived at the factor's house, much to the man's surprise. 'Riley, ma man,' he exclaimed, 'I was told you weren't coming this year.'

'Aye, for sure, sir, what else would I do over the winter? Who told you such a lie anyway?'

'Och, it was the MacSpits. They're doing the hill ponies and the beating. Granted I'd rather have yourself, but we shook on it, and you know me, I'm not a man to go back on my word. I let them stay on your spot.'

'Well, fine I ken, sir, because yon wee wife o' mine is daein loops at not getting herself intae the stane wall. What other kind o' work have you? I've four sturdy laddies can graft harder than any youngster if you'll give them a chance.'

'Sorry, Riley, but the only work I have is emptying and gutting the old shooting lodge. There's no payment, but you're welcome to any scrap metal you can shift.'

Grand-dad, with a heavy pair of shoulders on him, headed back with the news to Granny that other folks had stolen her site. Before he set off to meet the factor he was of the mind that the MacSpits deserved to stay, but not now—not after discovering they had lied, the bisoms.

When Daddy and the other lads heard this they set off downhill to challenge their rotten, lying enemy. Only boys, the four of them, but boys when angered can take on the best of men.

Chests puffed out, they strode down, and soon the smoke from wet green sticks met them on the old ground. There might have been a blood-bath, had it not been that the travellers from hell were all stone horned drunk. Drunk as cuddies, as my Granny was wont to say.

The boys lined up behind the dyke, eying the enemy, before deciding to warm themselves at a half-dead fire. A moor wind was picking up the reek and swirling it into their eyes. The sound of snores filled the bitter cool air and mingled together like an orchestra of locusts. Daddy shrugged his shoulders at the futility of the MacSpits and decided all-out war was not the answer, at least not while the ale had rendered them as helpless as starlings on a maggot-less tattie. No, some other tactics would have to be applied. Meanwhile they made a dart back to their own cold make-do campsite. Thomas, who was a master storyteller, would entertain amidst the shadows and heather winds until sleepiness sent them all to bed.

It might be the best point here to add the names of my father's other family members. His oldest sister was Jessie, Anna came next, then Lizzie; a lot of mouths to feed.

The giant structure of the shooting lodge designed to please Queen Victoria's eye loomed above high trees. Turreted granite walls built to withstand eastern Grampian winters were now considered useless and destined to be pulled down and rebuilt. Prince George and his spoilt brother Edward didn't like the way the lodge was designed, so on a whim decided it had to be changed. That's what a ghillie had told my Grand-dad, but the truth wasn't important. What was, however, was his task of gutting the place of anything that might make some money to feed his family.

Granny, with her home ground firmly in other hands, set about tearing an old blanket into strips. Jock's Road was a long trail through the mountains before descending to lower ground. They'd settled one winter at the Blackwater, several miles north of Blairgowrie; maybe if they hurried and the snow kept to the heights they might just make it. The torn blankets would provide the bairns with puttees to protect their ankles. Armies march for miles with cotton puttees wound around their exposed lower limbs; her breed would do it with puttees of wool.

Already a lone monarch of the glen was sniffing the air. Snow began to fly in on a brisk wind. Granny's wee hands worked faster. She had other worries though; a tiny baby moved inside her womb, ready to add to her already large family. 'Oh, forgive me, Lord, but if I'd the "evil eye", its nae guessing who'd be getting its stare this day.' She stood up and punched a cold air, giving the long ribbons of reek coming from the fires of her old campsite a hate-fuelled gaze.

The lodge wasn't built only for a few well-heeled gentry. There had to be accommodation for staff and guests alike: it featured sixteen good-sized rooms on three floors. Already Grand-dad was eyeing up some long velvet green curtains containing as much material as would clothe a regiment of Gurkhas. He'd put them to another use—blankets of velvet would warm even the dead. Granny needed something to cheer her up. 'Boys, help me get these down,' he asked, pointing to pelmets almost touching the ceiling.

Wullie and Mathew gathered some boards and built a kind of scaffolding, while something caught Daddy's eye elsewhere. He and Thomas had descended to the kitchen down a long stone spiral staircase with iron handrails.

'What dae ye think they were for?' Daddy asked his cousin. His eye followed a row of wires that were strung together, leading around the ceiling and joining a line of wee brass bells. Daddy's cousin had noticed that the wires went further than the kitchen. They followed them from room to room. Further investigation revealed that a single tassel, when pulled, tightened the wire and rang a bell. Each bell had a number corresponding to one of the rooms in the house, and whoever wanted a servant to appear would pull a tassel to ring one of the bells, so that a member of staff would know which room to go to.

Daddy was fondling the bells and smiling broadly. 'I think you and me should have a fag before we go upstairs,' he told Thomas, smiling from ear to ear. He lit a cigarette and eagerly puffed away on a full-strength Capstan.

'You've something going on in that head o' yours, Charlie Riley—what is it?'

'Come upstairs and I'll tell everybody.'

'Faither, there's a lot o' brass in the kitchen, can me and Thomas gather it up?'

Grand-dad wasn't keen. 'It's no stuck ontae the walls is it? I don't want you pulling breasts of chimneys doon and getting hurt.'

My father assured him, 'No, Da, it's only a row o' brass bells. I'll bag them up for you.' He called over to the other lads, 'Matthew, I'll need you to help, you too, Wullie.' They had their hands full, though. 'Just as soon as we dislodge yon pelmet and unhook the curtains from the metal rings,' Matthew said.

My father's eyes lit up: he liked the idea forming in his head, 'Metal rings, can we take them as well, Faither?'

'Aye, of course, the factor says to take whatever we want.'

This news made him do a wee leap in the air.

'What the hell's the leprechaun jig for, Charlie, have you forgotten Jock's Road faces us when we've gutted this place?'

'Oh, Jock's Road doesn't bother me, Da, because I have a plan.'

Grand-dad waved his hand in a dismissive gesture, and went outside to fill and smoke his pipe, leaving the boys to plan something daft, no doubt. Whatever it was didn't concern him in the least. It was only lads' capers; he had far more serious business to worry him.

'Listen now, boys,' said Daddy, gathering them in a circle. 'I need all the brass bells, plus wires and tassels, and those metal rings up there will come in handy. Get going now—gather the lot.'

Without a word the boys worked like Trojans, until every bell, plus metal rings and wires, were all tied up in a big jute sack.

'Tell us, Charlie, what you're planning,' asked his brother.

'All in good time, Wullie, first get soup and bread into yourselves, because it's going tae be a long night. Now, yon MacSpits will be ontae the moor beating, so while they're away, let us plan the end o' them.'

Granny instructed them to wind her home-made puttees around their ankles before setting off, and further warned them not to go near the wild folk. Daddy promised, and then turned to his mates. 'We'll need the bag-fu' o' bells, so carry it between you.'

Daddy was always a wee control-freak, but as a planner he was hotter than a July lizard basking on a stone. 'Mammy, us boys will not be hame for supper, so dinnae worry because it's a mission we're on, a secret yin.'

'A mission hoose ye'll be in if we don't get back down country, for this nippy breeze is full of snow,' she warned, tying the last leg tight with her home-made puttees.

When the MacSpits' campsite came into view, Daddy sat down under cover of unburnt clumps of heather, and told his fellow soldiers what was to be done.

'Now, boys, this is as long a shot as I've ever taken, but it just might work. Wullie, Matthew, go to the far end of the forest, take all the wiring, arrange it between as many trees as it will reach. Leave some back. Thomas, me and you will go ahent, slipping bells onto the wires. The metal rings we'll place on the ground in a long row, joined by the remaining wire. But whatever you do, make sure you don't accidentally ring the wee bells, that will come later. Have you got that clear?'

'Only thing I see clear is you've lost the heed. God sake, brither, whit stupid way o' daein is that?' said Wullie, shaking his head. But Daddy, who he looked up to, had a plan, so he followed his instructions, though still of the mind he'd gone loopy.

The lads worked stealthily among the bushes and branches, making certain each bell was hidden from any curious eye that may stray too far into the thicket. Daddy took a ball of string from his pocket and went back through the bell trees. 'I've tied a piece of this twine to each bell; now I'll leave it hanging free, and hope thon MacSpits don't find it.' Still not understanding, Thomas said, 'Cousin, would you tell us what difference these bells will make?'

'The difference will all depend on how good your storytelling is round thon campfire later on.' Thomas's bottom lip fell so far it could have swallowed his feet, but then he jumped and shouted, 'Away you go, boy, there's no way under a crescent moon dae I sit at the fire of thon MacSpits and tell tales!'

'So you want my poor mother and sisters tae trek the long miles ower Jock's Road, tae look in heavy snaw drifts for a campsite down by the Blackwater?'

'Never mind scraping ma soul, I want tae know what my stories will have tae dae with bells!'

Wullie's face broke into a broad smile. 'I ken whit you are doing, brither; you're putting the skitters intae the MacSpits, are ye no?'

Thomas went deathly pale. 'Do you mean I've tae tell them a fearty tale?'

'Yes, cousin, the scariest tale you've ever told. Every time you reach a right ghostly bit, give a wind whistle, like a kind of long low one. We'll be hidden in among the bushes, and when we hear your whistle we'll tug on the bells. Matthew will rattle the rings. As long as there's plenty peeve in your audience it will work.' He thought for a moment, then added, 'let's hope there is plenty peeve, because the Devil loves a frightened drunk, and I'm banking on it. Aye, and here's a toast tae the Devil, because by the time we've finished wi' them Macspits, he'll need tae widen hell!' They each held an invisible glass to the heavens. Daddy slapped Thomas's back, then added, 'I've seen collie dogs cowed under sheep's bellies after hearing you tell a story, lad, but the night I want to hear a kelpie gallop intae a loch wi' it's tail curled atween its shaking legs.'

'Cousin,' says he, 'I'll turn a black witch white!'

Thomas approached his quarry with shaking knees, 'Hello MacSpits, how are ye daein this fine night? Can I sit awhile at yer fire?'

Already clouds of layered grey and yellow floated in strips across the moon. Some gave an atmosphere of mystery, others heralded snow.

'Aye, boy, sit doon and gi'es yer crack.' A tall man crawled through an opening in his tent and pushed thick hairy arms into a torn jacket; rammed a hand inside his pocket, rummaged through the bits and pieces in there, then pulled out a hanky which had been wrapped around a clay pipe. He pushed the pipe into his mouth, then blew his nose on the hanky.

'Man, it's a cauld night for sure, laddie, kin ye hand me a lighted stick frae the fire.'

He sat down so near the fire Thomas thought his legs would burst into flames as he handed him the stick.

'Are you a kin tae big Wullie?' he asked, puffing away so much on the pipe his face disappeared into a white cloud. 'It's just that I'm sure you came by wi' thon Riley lads.'

'Na. My father is a spare ghillie helping oot on the estate. I'm just oot for a walk, saw the smoke frae yer fire and thought I'd come among ye.' Thomas wasn't the best liar, because his face usually beamed red when he told one, but the fire was making his face red already, so he'd escape detection. It worried him that this man was the only MacSpit to be seen. No wild women and brown whisky. What good would it do telling tales to one man, and he with no whiff of the cratur off him either? It was hardly likely that the bells plan would put the frighteners on him. Yet his orders had to be followed: after all, the troops were in place, with frozen hands poised to yank on those wee brass bells. He decided to start. But before he began, his companion, with the clouds of puff hiding his face, said, 'Ye ken, son, ye tell me ye're a ghillie's son, but ah see a tinker in ye.'

'No, mister, honest—I'm just a country yokel, with no such blood as yer ain.'

'Well, far be it frae me tae upset ye laddie, but ah think ye've been reared on lies. Have a word wi' yer mother, cause she'd ken the truth.' From under canvas came a wheen of giggles bursting into laughter, but Thomas would not be swayed from his purpose, or angered.

'Dae ye ken there was a terrible murder took place in this wood, mister?' he said with a quivering voice.

'Ye don't say?' The old man turned sullen-faced, and always wary of such tales, changed the subject back to Thomas's true identity, repeating his question.

'Aye, ah dae say, and according tae the estate workers, spilt blood got splattered for miles. Some say her head was wrenched frae her neck and flung among the bushes. The auld fat cook at my bothy telt me the lady still searches for it, and can be heard wailing and screaming—the heed that is.' He gave thought to what his imagination was conjuring up, and shivered. 'Why the hell am I feart? It's my ain story, but by God I'm good the night, pity there's only an audience o' one.'

His pipe-puffing friend lifted one hand in the air and said, 'stop right there, laddie, before another word. Aggie, Dill, Moo, Peerie, weans, laddies, come on oot o' yer kips and hear this laddie. Come and hear him telling ghost tales. Oh, he's guid, quick noo.' His left leg in a jig-like fashion kicked out at the nearest tent. 'Hurry, get yer claithes ontae yersels, or I'll lift yez in the air wi' ma tackety boots.'

Thomas, even in the poor light, managed to count twenty bodies crawling from beneath canvas covers. They jostled themselves close into his side, almost dislodging his seat from under him. Tiny eyes, big round eyes, bums shuffling from hip to hip warming each other, and even three dogs launched themselves at his feet, slavers from their jaws drooling onto his boots. Coughs and splutters aimed at the fire sent blue flames upwards like Guy Fawkes night. This told him that all the booze had been drained earlier in the day. He had an audience that Shakespeare would have died for—half drunk and half sober. This was better than he'd imagined: no, truth be told, he'd never had as eager an audience, and what an atmosphere.

'Listen now tae the whistling heather wind lifting branches with a slow motion; see the silver moon, bluish pale, the kind you'd see when death is searching. But not lifeless death, oh no: I speak o' the kind that slithers around bare necks of those sat huddled close in a lonely wood-end, with shadows flitting frae tree tae tree. We'll soon hear the voices, as they get nearer us in the woods: strange, cackling, deep-throated and waiting. Hold hands, because if they see one of you unprotected—' he drew this out in a voodoo kind of chant, then howled, 'hot breath, then ye're awa.'

'Oh, lord roast ye, laddie, I near shit maself.' It was the old woman he'd met earlier, who thankfully had been far too drunk to remember him. She yanked a blanket from off the shoulders of two youngsters, who in turn yanked it back. At that she lifted a stick from the fire, sending sparks in every direction, and brought it hard down onto their backs. 'Granny, fer fuck sake, half ma hair got burnt wi' ye there,' squealed the one nearest her.

'Well, get another cover, I'm listening tae the laddie's tale.'

'Dear me,' he thought, 'I haven't begun yet—what will happen when the bells start I shudder tae think.'

Soon, when all that could be heard was a far off hoolit twit-twitting out there in the night, he began again. Such was the atmosphere he could feel the excitement himself: he felt his lungs fill up in his own rib-cage as the haunting took life from his vivid imagination.

'Her lover, like herself, was of royal blood, but he had no claim to her. That belonged to Sir Boris Bogley. Her father, a greedy auld Duke, lost her tae him one night efter a card game.'

'Oh, the bastard, fancy selling yer ain lassie,' whispered a female voice.

'God bliss me, if some auld man wid gi'e me lowie fer you, I'd be a contented faither.'

'Who in their right mind wid gi'e lowie fer her? She's twa een that stare at her nose and different-sized feet,' mocked a male, who was obviously not in fear of losing his ears, because the female flew at them, tugging and screaming.

'Hey, that'll do! Now, carry on, laddie.' The old woman touched Thomas gently on the arm.

Before he continued, he thought on the others standing in the forest on guard, freezing, and decided to hurry his tale. 'Well, one night this secret lover that the woman had was overheard telling an Irish dragoon soldier he was going tae enjoy her maidenheid. Now, did this rat o' a soldier no' go and clype tae Sir Boris. Anger raging through him, he mounted his horse and set aboot scouring this wid in the hope o' catching them red-handed.' Thomas got slowly to his feet, the dogs' heads following his movements as he pointed to a nearby tree. Its branches were moving from side to side like giant arms. He lowered his voice and spoke with a toff's haughty tones, ' "I see you, and death will come to both of you for deceiving my honour." Boris lifted his great broadsword now into the night air, and chopped it into the young lover's neck. His head fell awkwardly down, eyes staring from their sockets into the terrified face of his lost love. Blood splattered over the lassie. She trembled, unable through shock to move. She looked into his face of the demon on horseback who'd killed him and swore he'd never rest. "For this night's action you'll find sleep impossible for evermore. I shall bring evil from hell to seek you out."

"You will have to go there with him, then," he laughed, and the sword fell for the second time. Her beautiful head with its deep auburn hair rolled under a yew tree and settled next to that of her lover.

Boris spurred his horse, laughing hysterically, and galloped away like a fiend.

An army of dragoons scoured the countryside, but neither he nor his horse were ever seen again.

Thomas straightened his spine, lifted an arm toward the night sky and gave a long, low whistle. Then, for every ear to hear, the bells began to ring. Jingle, jingle, tring-a-ling, came the sounds from somewhere deep in the forest.

'What the hell was that? Eh lad! That ringing, whit is it?'

'I fear it might be the demons from hell searching for Boris,' he spoke with a shivering sound, and continued. 'Ye see, after the murder it was thought he had gone abroad, but auld shrivelled wives say the water kelpie stole him. It's just a mystery, because naebody kens whit happened tae him after that.' Another low long whistle, and this time Daddy, Wullie and Matthew all pulled together. Screams and howls come from the frightened listeners. Then Daddy gave the metal rings a shake. A voice murmured, 'That sounds like chains! Oh Mammy, them devils and goblins are in the woods, they'll haunt the life oot o' us. I dinna like this place!'

'Me neither, Da,' called another one, adding that a shooter at the beating was called Boris, and adding that he'd not go back.

Thomas acted; this was exactly the response he needed. 'Aye, but no jist demons come in among these pairts. Oh no! If ye stare long enough intae the bushes, ye'll see the headless lassie. Hear her wailing. She holds her lover's head, rotted wi' maggots, flesh stripped aff it like streaky bacon, and she screams for the soul o' Boris.'

Suddenly the old woman rose to her feet in a trance-like state and called out to the night, 'Spirits, awa noo, fer we dinna ken onything aboot Boris, go away an no frighten ma family.'

Thomas put his arm around her, gave another long whistle and waited. This time the bells were louder, the sound of chains dragging ever nearer.

'That's enough fer me, come morning I'm off. I'll not sleep another minute in this place.'

'Aye, I dare say the winter kin get mighty cauld up here. We'll pack first thing.'

'Never mind the morning, I'm pitting ma stuff intae bags right this minute.'

Thomas listened with the greatest satisfaction as all the MacSpits worked themselves up into wrecks of fear and dread. His work completed, he slipped away under cover of darkness to join the lads, helping them to ring bells and pull chains until a hoody crow flew over heralding the first light of early morning.

Not wishing to interfere in the migration of the MacSpits, they went back by a long way round to tell Granny that her campsite awaited, and to inform Grand-dad that the estate would need his expertise and they'd have to do some beating.

It took a while to clean the site, since its past inhabitants had left in haste, but that chore was a welcome one. Thankfully, Granny's washing line was still in its place from the previous year. Grand-dad and the lads built the tent's rib-cage, tying it together with wire. Canvas was criss-crossed to keep out draughts, heavy stones placed to anchor the tent and prevent damage. First a bed of straw was strewn over the floor, followed by those green velvet curtains to provide a carpet fit for a Queen. The wee three-legged stove stood proud in the centre with its chimney expertly placed through the roof.

Thankfully the winter snows didn't amount to a great deal, nor did the demons creeping for souls reappear in the forest, but on Christmas Eve the lads tied all the rings and bells to the old yew tree, and Granny swore she heard a fluttering of wings during the night. 'Maybe you bairns should take a wee deek, ye never know what kind of miracles abound this time o' year.' When the family investigated, they found big fat stockings made from green velvet laying upon the frozen ground, filled with sweets and fruit.

'There's only one Angel living in these woods, Mammy,' said my father, giving her a Christmas cuddle.

The 'eat, drink and be merry, for tomorrow you could die o' fright' MacSpits were seldom met from that day. Yet when they thought about it afterwards, my Father's family couldn't help but feel sorry for them. They were simple-minded folks, but as Grand-dad told their relatives later, 'all's fair in love and whoever gets tae a campsite first. Just dinna listen tae a master storyteller in a cauld wood wi' a whistling wind!'

By the following early spring, as lambs were popping up in the lower fields, my Granny gave birth to another boy.

25

A STREET NAMED ADRIAN ROAD

I hope you enjoyed that tale. Hearing it was for me just an accepted part of my rich cultural heritage. Let's go back now to Glenrothes for a while, and see how we all got on living in Shirley's five-apartment council house, on a street named Adrian Road. Number 5.

To be honest, life went on at a snail's pace. Davie, Shirley and her man rushed around in the early morning trying to avoid each other, because, according to experts, that's the time of day when we are most short-tempered. I expertly prepared sandwich boxes with whatever appealed to their bellies, and was pleased as punch to see the back of them, the moaning lot.

Weekends could be fun, though. Davie and my brother-in-law would take themselves off to the dog-racing at Thornton, leaving Shirley, me, Johnnie and toddler Stephen along with Shirley's two, Christine and Hughie, to wander through the wooded areas between Leslie and Glenrothes. Thankfully, at that time the town hadn't expanded into what was a lovely natural wood of old trees and a meandering burn. It has today, though. We'd take a picnic box filled with sweeties and ginger [lemonade], tip-toe when a squirrel was sighted, run when we saw a young fallow deer. Johnnie desperately wanted to see a badger, and followed Hughie around because he knew where a den was. Christine, like her mother, had little interest in the natural world apart from wanting to put it into song. For instance, if a colourful jay bird flew among the branches, Shirley would sing: 'Hello, bonny tartan bird, skipping through the trees, noisy screeching tartan bird, are you full o' fleas? Blackbirds arenae pretty, but they sing a joyous tune, but you, my lovely feathered bird, like a witch whirling aroon.' That was my sister. Christine always tried to go one better, but each had their own gift of verse and music. That for me was a double joy, and still is.

Wednesdays, I always remember, were by far the worst days of the week. I think it was because, back then, the Glenrothes workforce got paid on a Thursday. Rent, bills and so on saw the bulk of the pay packet empty out on Fridays, and more was frittered away through the weekend. Monday left enough to feed families to Tuesday, but on Wednesday it was empty larders and walk to school and work. But that was in the beginning, before new factory units provided a whole new way of life for the lads who had gone down the mines and the lasses who had worked long hot hours in linoleum factories and paper mills. Things were to change when companies saw this new town as the gateway to an exciting technological age.

Factories producing electrical components sprung up everywhere. They offered jobs that required small skilful fingers—women's. Youngsters, who at one time left school and stepped straight into coal mines and linoleum factories, were now offered well-paid jobs in a clean and healthy environment. The new lifestyle meant that dreams could be realised like affording your own house and owning a car. Yes, the hunger on a Wednesday soon dispersed, as families saw that to own their homes with two cars was not so much a dream but now a reality.

So let's for a wee while go back to the lean, mean, hungry days when Glenrothes was on the dawn of change, and I'm away down to fill my son's pushchair with Monday morning's messages. With three adults working full-time, we managed to afford mince and tatties. Four pounds of minced beef meant shepherd's pie for Monday and meatballs in tomato sauce on Tuesday. I'd scrape enough together to fill sandwiches for the lunchboxes. A pot of soup made with left-over vegetables and flavoured with ham-bones would fill bellies until Thursday, when fish suppers would abound all around the town. That was my plan.

If I were older I'd have felt like Janet, the wee housekeeper of the Doctor Finlay television series. My purse would be gripped firmly in one hand while I manoeuvred the pram and two big wicker baskets ready to be filled with tatties, bread and that very important minced beef. There was no room for my weans, they were happy enough toddling on and chatting to a young policeman covering his beat.

The supermarket was fairly busy, with dozens of women doing the same as me, Monday shopping. As I made my way through the crowds of people, many with weans like mine, I heard a woman shout, 'if yer looking fer mince then there's nane, the butcher couldnae get it the day. I'm right sorry, ye ken, but there is plenty ham-bones tae feed the man soup.'

Everybody in that place must have had the exact same menu planned as me, because a surge of jostling females had emptied the butcher shelves of hambones before I could blink. When I had made my way through to scour the glass shelves in the hope that something would be there to feed my hungry bunch, I was delighted to hear an assistant shout that more mince had just come in, but only a small amount.

'Four pounds, please,' I said, shoving the right money to the assistant who took it and handed me my precious bundle. Suddenly, like a weasel diving onto the neck of a poor unsuspecting rabbit, two big-knuckled hands grabbed at my mince, which fell from my grasp in a heap on the floor, where an army of leather-shod feet crushed it flat. I grabbed my boys, thinking a mad person was loose on the public, holding them tightly by my shaking knees. It was the most awful sight that stood before me—a great fat beast with bullet eyes, fists on hips and wearing a ton of hair rollers screamed, 'Ma Bob wid kill the hale o' Glinrothes if he didnae get his mince and totties!'

'But surely you'd get some down the road at Tom Baird's?' An elderly woman, feet in fluffy pink baffies, minus her false teeth, repeated the question to Two-ton Tessie. By mentioning the butcher down the road, the older woman, I'm certain, saved my jaw from stotting off something hard. Although the butcher at the bottom of the road had occurred to me as well, I was struck dumb by this woman's temper and just stood stiff with fear.

I remembered when I was only fifteen during my short time as an employee of a paper mill, the women there could either be sweet gentle creatures or roaring gladiators who even cowed the men. But frightened as she'd made me, I couldn't help but feel as if I'd been robbed, and truth be told, Shirley, her man and Davie wouldn't be too chuffed.

Jess's father, pictured when he was serving King and Country
during the Second World War.

Jess's mother and father in 1942, at Pitlochry.

Jess's children—Barbara, Stephen and Johnnie.

Jess's husband, Dave.

Jess with Johnnie (left) and Stephen in 1983.

Jess today.

'Well, yon's a cow that died for nothing!' I muttered eventually, and gestured at the mess of mince on the floor and on shoes and boots which were tramping away to be cleaned outside. The more I looked at this waste of food and thought about how much it cost me, the angrier I became. 'Stupid bugger,' I dared to say as the heap of slavers and sharp eyes moved menacingly toward me. The hand, with its cardigan sleeve rolled up, rose in the air. I thought my brains were about to be battered out of my skull, and they certainly would have been had a young trainee manager not intervened with a timely worded warning: 'There's a polisman outside!'

The arm fell to her side, and the female from hell shifted faster than Roger Bannister running the mile. I asked the butcher's assistant if a refund was out of the question? Thankfully it was given, with an apology. With my money back, I bought tinned mince and loads of tatties and bread, enough to feed us for two days. I also managed some flour and margarine for baking.

I learned a lesson that day—if a mountain of anger approaches on a supermarket floor, pray a nice member of staff is willing to intervene. I later found out, to my utter dismay, the big lady lived three doors away around the corner from our house. Every time we met she growled that my end was coming, so to avoid her I began taking the longer route to the shops. In time when I accidentally met her, the threats stopped and her stare became less menacing.

Telling you this, the memory of a similar experience my dear mother went through comes to me. She was a mere sixteen years old at the time she took on the Crinnan women from Dalwhinnie.

26

IN DEFENCE OF THE PEARLS

I'll speak in my mother's voice.

'I'd been hawking three solid days in a row. Started at the Atholl Palace in Pitlochry, where I foretold a cook she'd find her lost engagement ring under a stone bench, and thank God she did, because she presented me with a basket of fine oatcakes amongst other braw eaties. I loved them crumbly biscuits that only Scottish cooks can conjure up. She was so grateful that I left that kitchen with two whole florins and a bottle of the finest malt. The four shilling was well needed, but not being one for whisky, it gave me pleasure to pour it into the burn at Killiecrankie. Daddy, you see, was all too fond of the awful stuff, and when on it could blacken my poor mother's eyes; he was just a demon with drink, my father. I remember shouting down intae the water, where I think a certain soldier leapt to his death in days gone by, "if ye're still doon there, man, here's a guid dram tae ye."

I gathered washing for a Blair Atholl woman who'd hurt her shoulder, and in gratitude she gave me a present of two tweed skirts. Said she'd a bairn growing in her bowdie, and the skirts would be too small when her belly swelt.

I made up quite a few miles heading over the pass, but by the gods it wisnae half cauld. I arrived at Dalwhinnie, and met up with my family in our usual campsite a half mile beyond the Distillery. Mother was rare pleased with the basket and clothes. Daddy, thanks be, didn't take any drink, and as was the case when he stayed off it, he was a really pleasant father. He'd got a job burning heather on the moor, which took from sun-up to its going down. There was no time for drinking, but he joked that on a down wind the smell of the "Angel's Share" wafting from the froth-topped alcohol fermentation vats satisfied him.

I was feet-tired after my long road journey on the old A9, and after chores called over to my mother, sat stirring broth in a big black pot cooking over a grand fire, "Mother, if you don't need me, can I curl ma toes in the burn?"

"Aye, lassie, away you go. I'm rare pleased with your hawking these days. There's a laddie waiting somewhere, and he'll treat you good, for there's golden threads in you, wee Jeannie, aye, and silver yins and a'."

I loved my mother's way with words, and did hope that soon I'd meet a fine young man willing to better my lot, as all travelling lassies did in those fanciful days.

Over by the ash and willow trees flowed our lifeline, a freshwater burn. It wound down through miles of heather moorland and rocky ravines. The burn, a gift from Mother Nature to all wandering people, provided liquid to quench the thirst, and water to wash everything, especially our birthday suits, and on that day for me, with sore and puffed feet, it was heaven itself.

May blossoms glided softly from wild hawthorn bushes, dropping on waiting bluebells that were throwing out scents to please a fairy queen. Broom thrust above drystane dykes like hundreds of tiny soldiers wearing yellow caps. Summer was just around the corner; I felt weightless and content. I think in my heavenlike state I fell asleep, because then some lads were wading down the burn, shouting excitedly among themselves. They were not much younger than I, about four in number, and I went to see what all the noise was about. They seemed so busy my appearance hardly raised an eyebrow. "Hello boys," I called, "what are you doing?"

"We're pearl fishing, look at the pile of shells."

I did indeed see the heaps of emptied mussel shells, which made me feel sick. "Why are you raping the bed of all those young shells, surely you can see there winna be ony in them. These older ones maybe, but not them." I pointed to some shells that had hardly been hardened, and gave the laddies a right roaring.

One jumped up and lifted his hand, but the others warned him not to hit a lassie. I said to forget the lassie bit, I'd take them all on, but they pushed me and laughed. Before I left, one called out that their womenfolk would meet me and batter the spit from me.

Hot, more under the collar than sun-warmed, I dashed over to our camp site.

"Mother," I spat the words, "is there other travellers near us? I've just had a run in wi' wild bisoms who were raping a mussel bed, ripping intae the poor shells and them no near any age."

Mother, who was busy cooking over the fire a mammoth pot of vegetable soup, said when she heard me ranting on about the laddies armed with pearl knives, "it's a family o' Crinnin folk". She seemed worried, and asked me if I'd annoyed them. I told her I couldn't give a pirate's curse for their well-being, it was the annihilation of the mussel bed that bothered me.

My brother Matthew, who'd been out on the moor burning heather with Daddy, arrived home tired and weary and said, "Jeannie, yon Crinnin lads will be spouting tae their mither and her sisters about you. Mother is worried they'll visit now with wild fighting talk."

His words sent a shiver into my wet feet. Every travelling family knows too well not to upset the Crinnin, especially the women. It doesn't take much to spur them into a fury, but look out when they are! They were three big brutes of females, famed for one way of fighting—head butting.

"Matthew, the lads were ripping every single shell apart, kenning fine if there were pearls in them they'd not be the size of a pin-head. It was the horrible way they laughed and threw the empty shells at each other. You ken me, brother, I cannae stand that type of thing."

"Oh aye, Jeannie," said Matthew, with as serious a look on his face as I'd seen, "but nevertheless, yon Crinnin dogs love a fight. Any excuse will dae, they need little wind in their sails. Mind, if stories are true, it's the bitches that dae the fighting."

My mother told Daddy about it as she poured him a deep bowl of soup, adding that if they came seeking to pagger, it was his wee Jeannie who'd take it.

Daddy sat down, took a slurp of his broth and said, "well, that's a different way o' daein right enough. Sorry, lassie," he stuffed a chunk of crusty bread into his mouth and continued, "I darenae stand by your side if women throws the glove."

"Well," said I, "then it's time I was away again."

Mother shook her head, handed me my share of steaming broth and said, "No, Jeannie, I'm not seeing you off again, lassie, it's no more than a half day since you came back. We'll all go. Tae hell with the Crinnin belles."

"Margaret, I've a whole month's work burning heather. If we move, then where else will I get work?" My father handed over his empty bowl for a refill, adding, "listen, if they come looking for tae pagger oor wee Jeannie, then I'll have tae show her how to handle her fists." He sat down his too hot soup and grabbed my hands. Like he was handling gold he ran his fingers over each knuckle, asked for more bread and said, "we'll get started right away, Jeannie. If yon wimmin mean tae pagger my lassie's bonny face, then she'll not be taking it easy-like."

I was shivering inside, thinking what state my face would be in after three mountains of madness threw iron skulls in its direction, but Daddy's words took away part of the fear. My daddy was, during his peak, a first-class street fighter. In fact he told everyone that's what attracted our mother to him, his hard knuckles and swervy moves were irresistible. She always laughed at this statement, and pooh-poohed it, saying it was the black hair, twinkling eyes and the way he made the keys dance on his wee melodeon.

With an eerie silence coming from the Crinnin who were camped a mere half mile into the neighbouring glen, Daddy took me onto a flat grassy patch to show me his moves. Like a bee he buzzed around me, jerking and jabbing in a ghost-fight fashion.

"Don't turn your back on me, I could take you down. Don't leave the chin exposed, keep it low. Here, watch me."

He pivoted, he ducked and he parried, kept moving, blocking an invisible blow, and catching his opponent's jabs with an aggression I'd never seen in my father. I'd seen him angered with drink, but not like that, now he was controlled. He was in his past again, master of the ring.

"Now, Jeannie, whatever you do don't get caught off balance, always keep up your guard. Watch their eyes, follow them at the same time, imagine you have more eyes than them, in the back of the head, at the side, keep watching. And no matter how close they get, never lean back, and slip your head away when reading their moves. Oh, and lassie, if you get tired, please don't drop these hands.

And for God's sake keep the temper under control—a mad dog is easy kicked!"

For the rest of the day I became a boxer. It was strange how much energy flowed through my arms as I followed his expert instructions. Later, as we walked back to our beds, I asked my father why he never kept up his boxing.

"See this scar under my chin?" he lifted his head and removed his muffler. I never knew it was there on his neck, a scar stretching across his throat.

"That was a big brute of an Irishman called Traveller Buff Scarlet. We met on a field behind a pub on Stirling's Drip Road. Said he was a flyweight, but every man on that day could see he was a lot heavier. Well, I held my ground and we battered it out, reaching nineteen rounds; longest I'd ever boxed. A fearsome bastard, yon Irishman. He hooked me with a one-two, and when I moved back a fish knife was flung at his feet by some snake relative. All's I mind was the heat of blood running over my chest. Thank God he missed ma main artery, or me and you widnae be having this conversation. Come tae think on, you widnae be born."

That night, as I lay under our canvas tent, it seemed not a bad idea; not being born, that is. What a long drawn out night it was. I listened at the chirr-chirring of a lone nightjar chasing moths. A hedgehog had found its mate and the two scraped away good style inches from where my head tried to sleep. Minutes seemed to have gone by when a solitary peewit jolted me from a dearly needed sleep with its pee-twit call. I'm sure nature's creatures had got wind of a certain battle due to take place next day, because to cap it all I heard what I'd never heard before, the "squawk, squawk" of two herons flying low over our tent. One, aye, but never two of the noisy bisoms.

Sleep came in drips and drabs, and that night it was for me a luxury I'd been unable to afford. The dawn came in with a chorus from a skylark and I was certain no matter how apt my father's wisdom had made my fists, without a good night's sleep I'd be easy meat.

An early morning plunge into the burn sent all sleepiness flying, as water sprayed over every inch of my young frame. If thon women were approaching then I'd meet them wide awake.

It was quiet, though, and I began to hope that my imagination had been working overtime. Perhaps the dear ladies had no intention of fighting battles for their horrible offspring. But as I washed porridge plates and filled our tea koocazie [kettle], a great screech of soprano voices sent pheasant and grouse to shelter on a cloud. Wood pigeons joined them.

"Hey you Power lot, whaur's the wee worm that chased oor weans frae the pearl burn?"

My fears were realised, and by golly in big time mode, because three of the largest females I'd ever seen stood like gladiators on the brow of the hill. Dressed in tweed skirts and heavy cotton blouses criss-crossed by paisley-patterned wraparound aprons, they were as mighty a gathering of Crinnin as I'd seen in many a long while. My poor mother, who I'd forgotten to say was heavily pregnant, called to them that it had been a storm in a tea-cup, and come away doon for a share of the tea. Glancing at me she whispered, "pick up yer bag, Jeannie, and run like hell. I packed it last night when you and your father were sparring."

Daddy, however, who was in the process of shaving, rubbed the soap from his chin and walked up to me. Not a single look did he afford the Crinnin, just walked on by and said, "Remember and keep the head, Jeannie. Don't let them rage ye, lassie."

I felt my belly shift to my throat, and smiled through a frozen grimace. "Faither, I think yon beasts will maul me tae bits. Maybe I'll keep ma head and run!"

"And spend the rest o' yer days in the knowledge you run frae a fight? Do this, lass, and you'll do it all the days of your life. I know that along with your golden threads there's a Highland bull in there. Now get facing them heathen bitches."

Daddy was rousing me to find a courage I still hadn't known, but he was right: if I let these women chase me away, then who next? Travellers can't afford to show fear. One day I'd have to defend a family against polis, factors, and farmers. If there was fear in me, now was the time to face it.

However, as the earth moved beneath my flayed feet, fear seemed to reach through me with tentacles of terror. Suddenly it all seemed too late, with me shaking to the bone, and three very angry ladies lined up to batter me senseless. It might seem strange, but they resembled three reddish-brown Highland coos. I felt that if I'd the use of a cartload of hay I'd have offered it to them. Daddy saw, though, that the uneven odds were not to his liking, even though I'd a wee bit of knowledge that these creatures did not possess.

"Listen now, girls, if you need to teach oor Jeannie a lesson, then do it one at a time. She's a skelf-like lassie, so what joy wid ye get from attacking her all at once? I think she'd remember a lesson if she got it in turn from each of ye." Daddy was offering them a form of fairness, but I wandered if that word had any meaning in their dumb lives. Without a word Maggie stepped to one side and Ella the other. I stood alone facing a scrum o' a beast called Jinty. Her forte, and was I about to experience it, was the "frontal butt". All the moves my father had taught me fell by the wayside, as Jinty lifted me into the air with a kick, and when the butt connected with my brow, down I went like a crumpled newspaper. My empty lungs desperately sucked for oxygen, as stars and bells filled my throbbing skull. The three witches slapped each other on the back as I lay there useless. Mother lunged forward, and would have taken them all on, had Daddy not hauled her back. "Leave her, Margaret," he whispered, "oor Jeannie's no finished yit, she's rising to her feet." My father smiled that twinkling-eye smile and exposed the scar beneath his muffler. "Give them what for, ma lassie," he whispered, "do it for me."

Jinty moved sideways and gestured to another clone to take over. I knew if this creature got the better of me I'd be mince, so before her heavy forearm left her side, my clenched fist with a power-packed punch went straight for her jaw. I balanced on my feet and went in with a right-left-right-left-right just like Daddy taught me. Whoosh, she spun around like a thronged hen, with eyes going everywhere, before tripping up on tied feet and hitting the deck. "Yes!" and "boy-o-boy, bring on the rest!" was all I remember screaming, before my father grabbed me and whispered, "Keep the heed. Ye mind I telt ye no tae loss the thinking."

Too late, me and the remaining Crinnin had scores to settle. "Come on then, Maggie, here I am, you tae, Ella. Aye, you might knock me intae the gutter, but I'll blacken an eye before ye drop me. Question is, which one o' you Pretty Pollys wants it?"

Ella shook the ground as she stomped over and stood glowering down at me. I almost swallowed my thrapple when she put a hand on my shoulder. "By the gods, lassie, what would other travellers say if they heard us Crinnins got paggered wi' a wee mort [girl] that stood the height o' a puddock's nose. Keep yer upper cuts and yer left hooks—we'll shake a brave hand."

Maggie and dizzy Jinty came over to me. I swear my knees and head didn't know what to do. Was this a tactical move—would I be flattened by three overweight females? No! They each hugged me close, apologising for the laddies who treated the pearl shells with disregard, saying I was right to row them. I wasn't half glad, though, to wave cheerio to the big Crinnin women, as they followed each other back to their campsite over the brow of the brae.

It might be a good time to tell you here, that although that incident was momentous to me, Mother started her labour within hours, which overshadowed all other events.

My two older sisters Winnie and Maggie were married at that time, and were travelling the road over into Tummel from Calvine. If they had been at my side then the odds would have been better divided, yet if they'd been there, maybe the Crinnin would have half-killed the three of us.

Sometimes what seems a foregone conclusion turns out differently —just as well, eh?'

Mammy had a wee glow to her face whenever she told us that tale, and laughed when we circled our fingers around her upper arm and said, 'Tarzan Mammy!'

27

A BRUSH WITH THE LAW

Back to Glenrothes, now, and here's a turning point in our lives that I'd rather not think about.

Davie had been pestering me for a while to go and visit his folks in Crieff. He believed, and rightly so, that my in-laws should see our boys. 'It's not fair, Jessie, my poor mother isnae getting any younger, she misses the bairns. I think we should go over first chance we get.'

I reminded him, 'It's not so much getting time, Davie, it's affording bus fares. Your job is fine, but I've to put every penny by for when we have our own home. Sorry, but we just can't spare the money.'

Shirley gave us a room to ourselves, but a blind man could see we were far too tight-packed and needed a home. I'd filled in the necessary forms for a council house, and was assured it wouldn't be long before one became available. New houses were sprouting in every spare acre, so we didn't have long to wait before the letter fell through Shirley's letterbox to say that a brand-new three-apartment semi-detached was to be our very own home; just fill in the acceptance slip and it was ours. What a lovely home it was. We all trekked down with the keys to view it, in an area skirting Glenrothes named Cadam. We began packing.

A week before we were dated to move, Davie came home from work happier than he'd ever been. I put it down to our new house. He picked me up, gave a great big hug and said, 'I think I'll take

Johnnie over to see my folks.' He looked at me with eyes that spoke volumes. I could see he was desperate to let them know about his good job and our new house, so I agreed. He said he'd saved a few pounds and would use this to pay for bus fares to Crieff. I handed him a fiver to buy some chocolates for his folks and wished him and our oldest boy a good time. Knowing how fussy Margaret could be about her son's appearance, I sewed two missing buttons onto his best shirt before ironing the arm and collar crease. 'Tell your folks when the house is in order they should come and visit.' I knew when Davie's mother saw what a lovely home her son and grandsons were living in, she'd be well pleased. It was no secret how worried she was at our moving away from Crieff in the first place, and that she thought her laddie couldn't settle anywhere else. Not like his wayfaring gadaboot of a wife. Just as he and Johnnie set off, I warned my husband not to go near a pub! He winked and said he'd not enough money to go anywhere, so it was silly of me to worry.

Anyway, it was quiet with my wee family halved, so for something to do on Sunday I plopped Stephen in his pushchair and went for a very long walk with Christine. It was late when we arrived back in Adrian Road. I noticed a car parked outside the door, but at first thought it was a mate of Shirley's husband. When we got inside, however, imagine my surprise to see my father-in-law Sandy and Davie's cousin, Brian.

'What's wrong?' I blurted out, fearing my husband had met with an accident or some disaster. 'Where's ma bairn? Oh my God, have they been in a crash?'

Brian, a quiet, gentle soul, said, 'dinnae be getting upset, they're baith fine.' He turned then to Sandy, and gestured that he should tell me why they were there without my husband and bairn. My gentle father-in-law sat me down and tickled Stephen under the chin, saying, 'silly carry on, lassie, and I'm no right sure o' the events, but David' (he always gave him his proper name) 'is in the jail at Perth—well, mair like the station cells.'

I jumped to my feet, shaking as my vivid imagination sent pictures through my head faster than Charlie Chaplin's running feet. 'Jail! Cells! Why? Tell me at once, Sandy, because when he left me all's he wanted was to see you and Mither Smith. He was as happy as a pig in swill, knowing it was a long while since you'd seen the bairn. What happened?'

'Well, lassie, seems he got intae a running battle wi' other lads. He was drunk, and you ken what they are a' like when the drink fuels them.'

'Aye, I dae, but he'd nae money for drink, and I well warned him no tae go near a pub.'

Brian interrupted, and said David was just a bystander, not getting involved, until a polisman came up behind him. 'Did Davie no' think it was a lad looking for a fight, and with that in mind skelped the polisman. But it's no' as bad as it sounds.'

None of my wild imaginings could compete with the actual events—my husband was in jail in Perth, awaiting a charge of 'police assault'! My God in heaven, how bad was that!

Shirley promised to watch Stephen to let me go and see Davie. He was to appear before the Sheriff first thing on Monday morning, which was next day. All of a sudden my nice little life seemed doomed, and the beating of my heart was all the journey to Crieff afforded me.

Margaret was quiet and distant throughout, but unable to keep silent she blamed me. 'Traveller people are too fond of living for the day, with no thought for tomorrow,' was her exclamation about her son's predicament. I raised my voice, and with the tension of the situation blamed her for mollycoddling him. We cried and apologised to each other, but she'd said it—that traveller stigma once again thrown in my face cut deep. I didn't think much of my husband that night, nor did I give any future thoughts to our marriage. All I wanted to do was get my sons, find an old blue Bedford bus, and take to the road. Perhaps this was an omen. Perhaps the ancient ones were warning me I should never have married a non-traveller, and maybe our life together would be blighted by mishaps. Oh yes, the imagination went into overdrive that night, I'll tell you. Of course I hardly slept, and next morning even after Margaret hugged me and said not to worry, my mind was in turmoil. I'd a husband who lied to me and was violent to a man of the law; he had to go, we must part.

Sandy and I went through early in the hope we'd be allowed a moment with Davie before his court appearance, but nothing doing. We had to take our position in the courthouse like all the other relatives of criminals there to face the Sheriff's wrath. After three bad lads had been tried and sentenced, he crept upstairs and gingerly stepped into the dock. Oh my good God, what a state he was in: a new growth of beard along with his longish tousled hair made him look more like Ned Kelly than my man. My first thought was, why had his captors not allowed him the luxury of a wash? His shirt was ripped at the shoulder, with not a single button left on the thing; and to think on how I cut those buttons off my own blouse to match the ones on his shirt. I tell you this, folks, if I had been that Sheriff, I'd have thrown not one book at him but a dozen.

One good thing in his favour was that he'd been appointed a young lawyer, and was he good! He convinced the Sheriff that leniency had to be shown because Davie had a job and was soon to move into a house. He emphasised the fact he'd never been in trouble before, well, not a violent kind, and that this incident, because of the darkness and chaos in the street, was indeed a case of self defence, Davie had not meant to harm anyone. He really felt remorse and was sorry for how things had turned out. The Sheriff believed that if a man hits a policeman then he should take a severe punishment, but in Davie's case he thought that it could have been mistaken identity. The fact that he had a job and was awaiting our new home went heavily in his favour. He was let off with a fine of twenty-five pounds. Sandy said he'd pay it, but imagine my astonishment when Davie paid it himself. Where did he get all that money from?

The bloody tax-man, that's who. It seemed my lying-faced creep of a man had not told me about a certain tax rebate. When I thought back to the night he came home from work smiling from ear to ear, and saying he should visit his folks, the money was safely in his back pocket all along.

You're wondering if I got shot of him, aren't you, my friends? No, of course I didn't, but I'll let you into a secret—he was a sorry lad, because I took the rest of the money off him, which was about half of the rebate, and bought myself a new coat. The boys got kitted out too. Davie—well, he did need a new shirt, so I bought him a cheap bri-nylon one, knowing how that crinkly material made him scratch. A woman scorned, as they say.

We did a powerful amount of talking about that incident, and one thing I discovered was that if we were to settle in Glenrothes he would be unhappy. So the keys to our so long awaited new home went back to the council offices, and we went back to Crieff. Somehow, although she would never say, my dear sister was more than happy to have her home all to herself once again. She wrote to me to say how quiet the place was and how she missed my cooking, but I still think she was happy that her life was a wee bit less crowded. Another letter followed to say she'd a run in with a certain big roller-haired wife while shopping down at the supermarket. Remember her? Shirley told me this individual tried to wrench a bag of tatties from her hand. Now, I ask you who in their right mind would dare take on my sister? Silly woman ended up having every one of those plastic rollers pulled from her head. Wish I'd seen that!

28

ON THE GALLOWS' HILL

Number 1 Gallowhill was our new home. There was a small row of houses, long since turned into flats, and we were in the first one. It was an area steeped in history. Where several roads met there was a place called the Chains, and in that place over a hundred years ago criminals hung from the gallows while cattle were driven by, filling the street with dung. The place was haunted by stories of drunken murders and whisky-fuelled drovers seeking red bisoms of prostitutes after they'd sold cattle at the Tryst, their ghosts still wandering in a shadowland of waste ground opposite our home. Lying below this grassy stretch was Crieff's graveyard. Dark marble statues towered on monuments above small cheap stones, but each carried the same bleak message—'we all go the same road.'

Back home for Davie was back to square one for me. I didn't like the place, not in the way I do now. As a child travelling in my bus, Crieff was a stop-off point before the 'berries'. We might pass through a winter or two there before gathering at the real travellers' meeting place, Blairgowrie, where the raspberries hung their ripened fruit onto long green bushes for us to work through a fun-filled summer.

Now July would come and I knew that the berries would not wait on me. I was stuck just like all the other flatties—static—imprisoned.

Although this upstairs flat was new to me, to Davie it was a home he had lived in many a time, because it was the home of his deceased grandparents, Sandy's parents. I never met this pair of grandfolks, but tales abound about how well-respected they were in Crieff.

James and Margaret were their names. His work was selling fruit around Crieff with a horse and cart, and wood-cutting. It was not that different from how my old relatives lived, just that they carted themselves from place to place, whereas he did the same with fruit. Old Maggie, his wife, was a stern body, so I'm led to believe, who seldom went further than her own front door. As I said, they had long since passed away when I came on the scene, but I'll tell you later that Maggie still crept about that house, and she seemed to have a thing about how I made the bed!

Davie soon got a job, and Margaret was as pleased as punch to have her little grandsons only ten minutes down the road. Things settled easily into the ways of scaldie folk, except for one tiny flaw— me—I wasn't one. I needed to get away, but after many an argument Davie knocked holes in my arguments for moving around the country and said I was being selfish. The boys needed stability, and anyway, how many times had we heard stories from travellers about the extermination of their kind from the roads of Scotland. I was aware of the situation when I lived in my bus, and matters had became worse. What was left for my kind? Where would we go? How could we make a living? Yes, I think it was round that time my mind told me that memories of the old ways was all I had, that I should just lump it and be content with my lot.

So, for the first time since I had my boys, I got a job. I was twenty-three years old. Yet I felt like an auld humpy-backit wife stuck hard in her routine. Davie would come in have his tea, we'd do the dishes and I'd go to work in an old folks home. At ten pm I came in, kissed the bairns goodnight and went to bed. Yes, a scaldie life was just grand—aye, right!

Well, there you have it. So why not fill that cup and come back with me to those happy old days when life was full and clocks had no faces. This story is from our days in the bus.

If that old mutt of yours needs a walk then take him, I'll wait until you come back. If you don't own a dog, then read on.

29

MY SILENT FRIEND

We'd not meant to drive so far down country, but as the weather had been diabolical in Perthshire and Argyll, my Daddy went to Galloway searching for better climes. We knew lots of travelling gypsies from that area, like the Marshalls, the Blythes, the Youngs and the Gordons. Daddy went searching for an old wartime mate of his. He was a real olden-style traveller who made horn spoons; his name was Billy Hearne. After we'd stopped on several fields cracking with other gypsies, the man's whereabouts were revealed to us by a big hairy blacksmith who had bought a smallholding for his wife and horses. He directed us to a place amid miles of sand dunes, where we discovered Daddy's old mate and his family.

Dina was one of his daughters, a ten-years-old deaf mute with three brothers and two sisters, who were brilliant fun. Me also being ten, I hit it off with Dina from the first moment we met. Her folks were old-fashioned tinkers who refused to modernise, and it was a joy to sit in their long tunnel-like tent with its rows of beds and a stove fixed in the centre. Within a night of our arrival, Dina's old granny, Billy's mother, a brilliant storyteller, had me glued to my seat with her tales. She told biggies about Hell's long-tails (rats) dragging a phantom bogey filled high with the souls of bad weans. She was amazing, because at first glance you saw this wrinkled old half-dead-looking body, but the minute she opened her mouth it was like listening to a young woman: terrific.

We couldn't pull our bus onto the sand, so were forced to leave it on hard ground and walk down to Billy's place. This was a nightmare, because the first night I was there I had listened to so many tales I had a bladder like a fish-bowl. Well, how could I be expected to squat down in ghostly sand dunes, with sea winds whistling like eerie elves from every angle? Dina had no fear, though. Because of her inability to hear and speak, she never heard a word of her Granny's ghost stories, although she made faces of staring eyes and covered her mouth when a creepy bit was was being told. I thought her antics were just from copying her siblings, but certain events would soon change my mind.

Billy had some farmwork to do, and as Daddy had been recovering from chest problems he was under doctor's orders to take things easy. I really mean Mammy's orders, because she was as near to a healer as he got. Anyway, he decided he'd go with Billy for the crack. Me and Dina wandered on behind our fathers, she hand-gesturing and me stumped at first as to what she was meaning. It didn't take me long, though, to make out what she meant, because her hand signals were very artistic. She followed with her eyes the wild creatures of the Galloway countryside, and made birds by joining both hands and fluttering her fingers. Rabbits were represented by a few hops and jumps.

As we trudged on and communicated in our own way over knolls and burns towards a low-lying farm surrounded by steadings, a sudden sound rent the air. The blast of a powerful horn reminded Billy of something he'd clean forgot—there was a hunt on that day. 'Nae point in heading through thon fields, the farmer will be sitting astride his cuddy tuggered up like a lighthouse beacon, red face tae go with his jacket. He'll not be needing me.' Billy reached into a torn waistcoat pocket, retrieved chewy baccy, popped some in his mouth, spat a brown spyuch onto a flat stone and turned to go back. Daddy refused the offer of a breath-choking chow and followed on. Laughing over at me, he said, 'Listen, Jessie, you keep a civil tongue in your head, my lass. This is hunt country, and I dinna want you screeching at the riders.'

I pretended not to listen, and knew if I saw one red jacket I'd fly into a rage.

His companion told him that Dina was the worst wean in all the world. He'd a red face and hard job explaining to a furious huntsman, who was missing a saddle and a whip, that she was a mute lassie.

Daddy asked how that came about. Billy said that his daughter had spurred a horse, and when the rider fell off she'd unsaddled the beast to prevent the rider returning to the hunt. When he lifted his whip to take it across her legs, she tore it from his hand and threw it into a fast-flowing burn.

'But what can ye dae at chastising a poor wean wha canna hear nor speak, aye, Charlie?'

'Aye, man, it must be sore tae live in a silent world, right enough.'

Billy then quelled the rage swelling in my heart at the thought of witnessing a fox hunt, when he said it was just a gathering of riders who met every so often to ride wild across the moors and low-lying fields. Then, far off, I heard their whistles and horns, and when on the horizon appeared a line of well-bred horses straddled with straight-backed riders, I had to admit they certainly looked a grand sight. I forgot for a moment that my friend couldn't hear, and said to her, 'Dina, dae ye hear the thumping o' yon horses' hooves?'

She smiled and nodded, and then it dawned on me: this fly wee bisom can read lips. Now, in a small way, I didn't feel so helpless towards her. I knew now if my explanations with hands and body movements failed, then I'd to face her and slowly mouth what I wanted to say. That, though, in itself was a mystery to me, because if she lived in a silent world from birth, then how would she know what words were, never mind their meaning? But this was only a momentary thought for me, because what was on my mind was the same thing that all ten-year-old weans have; all I wanted was to play and rout the place.

Dina didn't want to go back home; she needed to explore, to show me her countryside. It was her countryside, because although the Hearnes were travellers, they never moved any further north than this area. She pulled on her father's jacket, tugged at his sleeve, and made signs with fingers touching his lips and her own. I didn't understand, but her father did—she wanted to go wandering over the hillside and down the next valley. 'She has a favourite stream where she plays with otters. She must like you, lass, because not many folk get taken there. Sometimes when she goes missing for hours we know where to find her.'

Daddy wasn't keen to let me go far in a strange place. Like Mammy he knew how much I had the wander urge, so he told me to 'be home when your shadow grows longer'—in other words, by late afternoon. I'd had a bigger than usual plate of porridge that breakfast, so no doubt my belly would be happy enough missing lunch. Billy assured Daddy nothing would happen to me, because Dina knew the ways of the countryside; she also knew when to be home. Deaf or not, her backside would still feel a sharp wallop, just like her siblings, if she disobeyed the family rules. And as for roaming away from home, four hours was considered enough for any traveller bairn; after that whistles were blown and dogs were sent to search.

So, after waving goodbye to our fathers, we set off to explore Dina's stomping ground. The sun shone bright in the early summer sky, and the air was filled with the scent of every wild blossom one could hope to smell; and this sense to my mute companion was her finest. She held my hand as she stretched her neck upwards, then turned her tilted head in every direction. Like a hound she sniffed the fragrant air; then letting go my hand ran and ran around until dizzy, whereupon she fell upon the grass laughing silently. I joined her and began pointing at a few fluffy clouds that danced across the bright blue heavens; she in turn pointed to a lone buzzard. He must have thought we were tasty food, because in an instant he left his thermal to swoop down; once he distinguished our human forms he flew back up to his resting-place on the wind and ignored us.

We lay there for some time, me laughing loudly and she doing the same in her silence. Suddenly my friend's eyes narrowed; she sat up, then stood, stiffly turning her head from east to west, then from south to north. I was puzzled: it looked as if she were listening. Then, without warning, she lay down hard upon the ground, pressing the front of her body into the earth. She stared at me, and the look of terror on her face was indescribable. Quickly she jumped to her feet, gripped my hand and like a whippet tore across the braes, pulling me with her. My futile attempt to slow her down only had her leaving me trailing behind, as she skipped and almost flew across the hillside. She plunged down a steep embankment, only stopping when she came to a wide stream.

Without pausing for breath she waded into the water, and pulled her soaked body onto a small island in the middle of the stream. She began frantically running her fingers amidst tree roots, and then a smile spread across her wet face. She gestured that I should come over, and being the curious age I was, I didn't need asking twice.

Soon I was staring down at something my young eyes had never seen before—two tiny baby otters snuggled together in a nest of thick river grasses and broken twigs, built with the skill and care only a loving parent could provide. Dina didn't touch the little ones, yet she would not leave them. Rather to my annoyance on account of my wet clothing, she pulled me up to sit at the other side of the sightless water babies.

Dina sat down, making no movement apart from folding her arms over her knees, and darting those fast-moving steely blue eyes up and down stream. I could see she was expecting company, as her gaze moved from high ground to low, scanning every inch of the stream's embankment. She knew we were not alone, yet at that time I heard no sound. Suddenly something moved among the long grasses on the bank; she smiled and pointed. I looked in the direction of her finger, and was amazed to see two adult otters come swimming towards us. They swam past us, yet made no attempt to get us away from their offspring. Dina lowered her hands and fanned the baby otters. I think she was calming the parents in doing this. I felt they knew her—don't ask me why, because I have no explanation, just a gut feeling that my new friend was more known to the animals than me. I had seldom taken an interest in these semi-aquatic creatures, believing them to be vicious in the protection of their young, yet here we were sitting inches from them and no screeching or attack took place. One, which I thought must have been the father because of his size, nosed the air, then like a grey streak he dipped his head, rolled his eyes and dived.

The smaller otter followed him. I could only think that we should not have been there: they couldn't get to their young while we humans were holding them back. My face spoke what I thought; but Dina shook her head as if she were telling me I was wrong.

Then, as if from nowhere, a panting, snarling hound came bounding upstream, followed by several men. One had a long stick with which he was poking the water. He shouted to the other men that there were wee lassies on the island, meaning us. 'Wait back, lass,' he called to the dog, who was already heading in our direction, slavers dripping from loose jaws. I grew stiff with fear and grabbed Dina's arm. She, unlike me, didn't flinch, just gazed with a cold unmoving stare at the fierce animal which continued to ignore her master's command. Only a few feet from us, I could feel the hot breath of the beast's nostrils on my face. 'Lord help us, we'll be shredded, because that gadgie canna control his bitch,' I thought, as shivers ran the length of my spine. All of a sudden, just as my eyes tightened with a fear that sent my heart into my throat and blocked my screams, the man with the stick lunged forward, hitting the hound hard on the back. She yelped and drew back, shook her wet coat and bounded toward the bank to sit by her master's side.

'You bloody bairns had better no hing around this burn when the hounds hae a scent, awa hame with ye.'

I squeezed tight upon Dina's arm, which felt like hardened steel. She had not heard him, but by her stern face there could be no mistake, she knew exactly what he had said. She shook her head fast, then faster, flailing both arms in an erratic fashion that prompted one man to say, 'she's simple, better keep the dogs away. Anyway, if there's young 'uns we'll chase the otter away, and sure as fate they'll not come back.'

I wasn't quite sure what these wet-trousered men with their rolled up shirt-sleeves were doing there with their sticks and hounds. I didn't dare ask because I was so far away from my secure bus home and Dina from her tunnel tent; fear had entered my young body. This pool in the stream looked deep in parts, and these men had hungry, lantern-deeking jaws onto themselves.

'Yon otter is hiding up here in a holt. Come on, boys, the dogs will have him soon!'

'Bloody hell fires, the bastards are hunting the poor wee otter!' I shook with anger. I made to stand on my feet, but Dina yanked me down, pointing to the babies who were by now moving uncomfortably, probably needing fed. Dina covered them over with more damp grasses and they quietened. I could see now what her plan was. Obviously, being from these parts, she knew of the practice of otter-hunting. I didn't, and there was nothing worse than an ignorant body screaming the odds at folks she neither knew or understood.

So while the hounds took off after the male otter, who had left his dangerous hiding place and was tearing towards a wooded area, we sat protecting the young. Every now and then I saw my silver streak, with a big snarling hound inches from his low-lying tail, but each time he escaped. Further downstream I lost sight of him, and he disappeared from view in a patch of slimy thick stagnant water. All the while the dogs barked and howled, the men brandished sticks, shouted orders to go here and come there, growing hoarse now. I prayed to every god I hoped there might be, but to no avail. Suddenly, without seeing any evidence of a kill, I knew by the stillness that the brave water-coloured animal had lost his struggle for survival.

He had fought well, the little fellow, but when I saw his broken body held in the mouth of the very bitch who wanted to take a bite from us, I knew it was over. Poor otter, what a brave wee lad. In minutes the hounds and their masters were gone over the knowe's flank, whistling and chatting happily. Some women, who for their own reasons had held back, when the hunt was over joined the troop of men to examine the dead beast. To them this was just another otter, just another out-of-doors incident. But to me, albeit briefly, it was one of the saddest of days I'd ever witnessed.

I watched Dina's face, and of course she too was sad, but already she was pulling and tugging for me to leave the island. Dripping wet and more than a bit stiff, we made our way onto the mossy bank opposite, where thin willow branches were interspersed with silver birch. Dina tugged at my sleeve, pointing to the island from which we'd just come. I looked where she indicated, and suddenly the still water rippled as the mother otter, without doubt now broken-hearted, curled onto her young.

If she could speak, I knew she'd say how proud she was of her man, and how strong a husband he was. He gave his life by drawing the pack away from his tiny family, knowing his partner would continue to rear their young. And was it his last wish that when they, the hunters, came again next year, those fully grown otters would outrun their predators? Yes, I knew little of such matters, but as is the way with most travelling children, I had seen life as it is—in the raw!

Dina was smiling as we ran back home, because she'd thwarted the destruction of the two young otters. The sun's light was lengthening our shadows, and for sure we'd both be chastised for it, but hey, wasn't it worth it?

I never told my family about the hunters—I'd have suffered for it if I had. Our survival in those days depended on maintaining a healthy country attitude: don't interfere in our culture and we won't interfere in yours.

That night the old granny held us all spellbound with her ghost tales. To say I was frightened was an understatement. Rather than go for a pee I kept it in, resulting in a sore belly.

Dina's family just popped round the side of the tunnel tent, and it's as well the thunder and lightning storm that night that threw our imaginations into realms of terror was followed by a deluge, or the smell of hot urine would have made pigs retch.

Next day Dina and I went gathering nettles for old Granny Hearne's rheumatism. She needed new heads from fresh growing nettles to make a concoction which she swore blind made her lift her old legs like a spring lamb; without it she stiffened with hard knotted joints.

It was very early, about seven a.m., when my pal Dina appeared at the side window of the bus where my bed was. I peered out to see her all dressed and ready for the day. I wouldn't go anywhere without my breakfast, not even if Jesus himself had called for me! So, after a quick swallow of porridge and toast, my feet once more began a journey with the silent but masterful Dina. I can't tell you what so excited me about this wayward lassie: perhaps it was they way she seemed to be so wise about nature, even the human kind. Life with this wean was neither dull nor silent. I was becoming fond of her and knew that when the time came, our parting would be sore.

We'll sort that scene out when it breaks, but in the meantime—those nettles.

Granny Hearne had told me the previous night, before I scooted home in the moonlight with my hair on end after her final story about a fiendish brown puddock with one eye, that her old recipes were closely guarded secrets. If my mother wanted to know what the nettles were for, I had just to tell her, for soup. But of course my mother had her own carefully guarded recipes. The last thing she whispered to me as I walked off that morning was, 'there's only one cure for stiff joints, and that's to keep moving—walk plenty miles a day and you'll live supple. An auld auntie o' mine from Kintyre jumped intae her widden box when she died!' She added, 'but try and find out how auld Hearne makes her stuff, just in case ma bones should stiffen one day, Jessie.'

Travelling people set a great importance on every flower and herb growing wild, whether for eating, medicine or healing, and have gifted to each up and coming generation recipes that go back centuries. My own mother had, as a lassie, acquired her mother's herbal cures, but sad to say she used only a fraction of them, this being a result of the fifties wonder cure, Penicillin.

Dina knew exactly where nettles, with their young tasty heads, grew abundantly. As we trekked off, I hoped she didn't feel the urge to revisit the mother otter, because I was afraid of the huntsmen and their dogs, especially yon slavering bitch which I was later to see in a film about Sherlock Holmes called *Hound of the Baskervilles*. Well, it certainly seemed like the same beast! But as Dina ran ahead of me with the stamina of someone twice her age, it soon became clear we were headed in another direction entirely. We kept the shore to our right, and on the sandy ground to our left a bank of nettles and Michaelmas daisies, which had not yet come into flower, were growing tightly together like flowing green walls. If you don't mind, I'll skip quickly through the gathering of those waspish plants, because my skin still cringes when I think of the dozens of stings I got: my arms and legs were red and swollen.

Dina stuffed a big bag with the nettles, as large as we could carry. We picked the nettle tops, because that's the sweetest part of the weed. I grimaced and rubbed my hands over my itchy and uncomfortable arms and legs. (A stupid idiot you'll think me, lacking a spit of sense and heading off without covering my skin, but what wean thinks ahead?) Even Dina, who I thought would be well used to this method of harvesting, didn't escape the nips of nettles. She pointed over at the seashore, where there were some docken plants. I knew that if we rubbed them on our stings this would alleviate some of the pain, and in a flash we were ripping up the green fans and covering ourselves in their juices. My companion started off then towards the water, and it didn't take words to tell me that a good dook in the salty Atlantic would further help our aching skin.

Sanderlings rushed by on twinkling legs along the surf, slowing only to eat, as we raced through them to belly-flap into the foam. The salty water further stung my poor skin; I made to rush out, but Dina gestured me to stay. She rolled over and over, so I did it too, and honestly, I kid you not, those nettle stings began cooling down. I thought my body would be covered for days in pink calamine lotion, but thanks to my wee silent mate every red spot had gone.

We wandered home toward her tunnel-tent in the dunes with her granny's nettles, feeling recharged with new blood. I don't know if the stinging or the salty dip did it, but my flesh was tingling with newness. Yet it might have been that I'd not bathed for ages! Shameful, I know.

Granny Hearne washed the nettles, correcting me when I called them weeds, saying they were vegetables. What a let-down, when all she did was simply cut and boil them in salted water. I thought I was going to be initiated into an ancient weird spell—involving a black pot with frog's elbows and spider's webs thrown in to add to its healing power.

She then drained them and popped them back into a dry pot with butter and some cut mint.

'I'll give your mother a taste if she comes by,' said the old woman with a wink to her eye, as she handed me the drained liquor from the boiled nettles and added, 'drink that, Jessie, it'll clean any nettle poison from your blood.'

I was alarmed by this remark, but she said that sometimes allergies can be started if too much poison gets into good blood. I didn't fancy drinking nettle juice, but Dina halved it with me, swallowing it quickly, so I did the same.

That day when I arrived home, I was saddened to find my family packing away to head back on the road next day. Daddy planned to go up to Stirling. So that night I said my tearful farewell to Dina Hearne, a remarkable wee lassie who, thanks to my father's visit to his old friend, I now had the honour of calling my 'silent friend.'

30

STIRLING TALES

Stirling in the central belt was the place travellers called 'the nei-ther-here-nor-there town.' This was simply because it was as far north as it was south, and so folks couldn't make up their minds about the geography of the place. I heard tales that at one time it was submerged under the ocean, but I believed that was rubbish until I discovered a few facts for myself about Stirling. It was known as the royal seat of Robert the Bruce—the hero-king of Scotland made for this castle stronghold after defeating the English at neighbouring Bannockburn. There were strange secrets hidden beneath the thick marshland that covered the flat country around as far as the eye could see. Here two rivers, the Teith and the Forth, flow from east to west. Let's take a look at this place, and the travellers' folklore about it that was kept secret from the wider world. Three very old travellers who asked for anonymity gave these wonderful stories to me. Let me now share them with you. After all, according to one of my tale-givers, 'Stories of Scotland belong to the Scots and whoever else lives here.' So take these gifts, my friends, they are yours after all!

Neptune and Dunvegan

Once, in a time very long ago, when the world was more water than land, there was a beautiful island called Sphag. Neptune, the King of the Ocean, sometimes loved to get away from rocking wa-ters and stormy seas, where the sun boiled the water and made the earth sizzle under its heat. His favourite place was the small island of Sphag. The blue waters that surrounded this idyllic spot were seldom rough or stormy, and its inhabitants were a handful of giants who never interfered in each other's business.

Neptune was a bachelor king, and although a wife would have been a treat for him, a suitable female never seemed to catch his eye. Until one day, while he was swimming around the west coast, he heard a hypnotic sound. On investigation he discovered it was the beautiful singing of a mermaid. On further investigation, her captivating beauty revealed itself in splendour as she dived from a rock into the sea. At first all he could do was listen and watch this gorgeous creature as she flipped and dived and swam, with her silvery tail, in and out from the shoreline. Her long golden hair bobbed upon the tide as she swam, turning over and over and singing all the while.

Not wishing to disturb the mermaid, he sank deep into the sea, swimming around to the east coast where the water spirit Shanna lived. When he arrived at the home of this sea spirit, he told her of his love for the mermaid and asked what manner of gift would be suitable for her. The spirit thought for a moment, then said that a bed of rare mussel shells lay at the mouth of a gentle river, collecting pearls within themselves of an age-old beauty.

There were four beds of these, and when Neptune visited the place he decided that the fourth bed was the biggest. He instructed Shanna to name this river 'The Forth,' because of his choice of the fourth as the best bed. Such lovely pearls grew here that when strung into a necklace they would be a love token like no other. The mermaid would be His Majesty's for ever if she were presented with a gift of such wonder by his hand. That was settled then: the bed of mussels must be protected until they matured to perfection.

Next day, Neptune swam back into the west to find his beloved and tell her of his gift. First he introduced himself as Neptune, and she, he discovered, was the coy Dunvegan. When she saw him her heart skipped a beat—here, with promises of love and fine pearls, was the King of All the Seas. She thought him a fine lover, and soon they were to be seen sunning themselves together on the shores of that bonny little piece of land which was her home. He said that when they were together he felt like he was floating in the heavens, so they named their secret meeting place Skye.

However, somewhere in the north, a giant named Aberdeen had fallen in love himself, but the giantess he desired was not interested in him. She was known as Stirling, and had long since shown an interest in fine jewels. One day, when Aberdeen was striding across the land, he heard an elf singing a song: 'Listen to me now, a worthy snip of news, the king of mighty ocean has fallen mad in love, with a golden haired mermaid, with swishy tail of blues, he will shower her with pearls from a warm mussel glove'.

Aberdeen was intrigued, because it was always thought His Majesty would never wed, and never find a queen. It was further believed that there was no one good enough for him. He had to find out more. So he listened, pretending to be a sturdy oak tree, and stood for days holding his arms aloft. Eventually he overheard two tiny elves saying that Shanna was guarding the fourth mussel bed, because in its shells lay the most beautiful pearls in the entire world. His eyes lit up at the mention of precious gems. If he owned such wonders, surely Stirling would find him irresistible.

Now, no one had ever beaten Shanna in a fight, because she was a spirit creature, invisible except when the moon was full. Then, and only then, did she lose her powers and could be seen by all mortal eyes. Aberdeen knew this, so he waited until he saw the moon waxing. Each night it got bigger, and then on the night of the full moon he challenged her to fight. Shanna, it was later reported to the King, fought bravely, but she was no match for Aberdeen, who took the victorious spoils, those silver pearls.

Stirling was delighted when she received them, swearing at once she would wed her warrior.

It was a sad, sad day for Neptune, however, because when lovely Dunvegan heard the terrible news, she swam under her glorious island of Skye and was never seen again. Neptune's heart broke for his lost love. Such was his desire for revenge that he summoned the heavenly gods to make a decree that Aberdeen and Stirling be separated for their part in the destruction of such a perfect love.

Soon winds began to blow, fierce and terrible, until trees were wrenched from their roots and crashed to the ground in other faraway places. Awful lightning shrieked across the sky, forking from one corner of the universe to another. Neptune's fury would soon be released upon Sphag. 'Come to me,' he screamed at the ocean, 'now!' Drawn by the power of the god, the sea rose and rose until it reached the heavens; then, with a scoop of his mighty arm he withdrew all the dreadful weeds contained in the ocean and began piling them back towards the island of Sphag. Over and over again, day after day, he worked, drawing back the water and stuffing the seaweed in its place until there was not a drop of water left. Finally, exhausted, the mighty sea lord called for all ears to hear—'I have withdrawn my sea from you and left the weeds. Now you will not swim in my ocean, nor will you feed from her bounty!' Then, with a mighty swish of his swordlike green scaly tail he was gone, and would never visit Sphag again.

Nothing grew on the land of weeds, later to be known as mossland. It concealed, in its green and black depths, slimy creatures that would, on the darkest nights, crawl out of their murky mysterious filth to steal little animals and feed on them in their underworld. Nothing grew, no human lived on its surface; there was only the sound of a low wind to remind people living on higher ground that Sphag was a place not to venture into. The word for no man's land in those days was 'num'. The mass of packed weeds was therefore known as Sphagnum. Centuries later, because a proper seafood diet was no longer available to them, giants gradually shrunk until they reached no more than five or six feet tall. These people became known as the Scots, which means small; it was after them that the land of Scotland was named.

The elves, however, being renowned for their adaptability, found a way under the moss and built a world for themselves called Elfin, and it is to this world we now pay a visit.

Blun' Harry

From his first waking moment of life, Harry the fiddler was without sight; he couldn't tell you what colour were the water lilies that grew in flat circles around his low-roofed cottage, any more than he could describe the brightness of a yellow moon. Folks felt sorry for him, and neighbours would call with bread or some small token of their admiration of the best fiddle player that ever lived on the outskirts of the moss-lands. No one knew what age he was, but it was thought he had reached the age of seventy. His parents, who had died young, left Harry with nothing more than a tiny cottage and little else. Yet even without sight he could work and fend for himself.

His fondness for the fiddle and skill with it was inherited from his father, who in turn inherited his skill from his own father. So as far back as the poor folks of the bog could remember, music had been played and enjoyed in that area.

It was at weddings that his fine music was mostly employed; no payment ever crossed palms, because Harry always refused it, saying music is a gift and should be shared. Yet it was always at such happy events that his playing brought him sadness. He would never hold a lovely fresh bride in his arms or sleep with another under the roof of his small but cosy home. So many happy, unseen faces; he knew they must be happy, because did they not all laugh and sing, dancing around him in his world of darkness? Yet what of his loneliness? Why could he not join in the joy and fun? Poor, sad fiddler, though all thought him happy because of the uplifting music he played, the opposite was the case. So he'd sit in that darkness and pretend to all his friends and neighbours he was just as happy as they were for the newly-weds. The way he disguised his true feelings was to drink, and to drink more than was ever good for him—there was no moderation, just pour and swallow until natural thought had been dispersed and everything was given over to his wonderful music. Then, at the end of every wedding, he'd collapse into exhaustion, relying on some strong person to walk him home along the narrow causeway that wound its way through the treacherous moss and see him safely home.

One day a request for him to play came from the Laird, who lived in a grand house perched high upon a steep hill overlooking the moss-land. The invitation came by one of the Laird's horsemen, who read to Blun Harry its fancily worded request: 'On the 30th of October, Madam and Lord Kane have great pleasure in inviting you to play at the wedding of their daughter Annabelle to Kenneth Duncan.'

'You'll be expected around three o' clock in the afternoon, Blun' Harry,' said the horseman, who like every one else knew and respected the fiddler, adding, 'there will be fine food, and plenty mead, my lad, to wet the thrapple.'

Harry waved his hand in a half-hearted gesture. What did it matter to him if the wedding took place in rich hall or lowly barn, or if the drink were good or bad, so long as its effects were the same. When it came time for the wedding, an old neighbour woman who did more to help Harry than anyone else came by. 'I've brought a clean sark for you, man, and will give you a shave of those whiskers.'

Harry ran his hand over a rough chin and nodded. When she'd cleaned him up, she guided his feet along and off the causeway. 'Now, remember and tell them you need to be guided back over the causeway, because no doubt the drink will have your feet going a different direction from the head, so remember now, lad.'

The friendly horseman met and escorted him to the grand ball-room. When he walked inside, the first thing he noticed was the sound of voices, lots of them, laughing and chatting in a light-hearted manner. But it wasn't the voices that alerted him to what kind of room he was in, it was the way the sound carried from floor to ceiling. He'd never been in the house of the Laird before, and was glad he had come.

After the wedding, when the guests had eaten and finished with all the formalities relating to such occasions, it was Harry's time to entertain. Requests came thick and fast from all who'd heard him play, and soon the place was filled with dancing and wonderful music, which along with the fine wine lasted well into the night. One by one the guests headed to bed, leaving a few late revellers and Harry. For once, the wine which seemed to flow like a water fountain among the guests was not offered to him, but he didn't mind; the sound of his music travelling towards the roof and echoing in sweet notes from the walls soothed his spirits.

'Time to go home,' said a tired man-servant. 'Harry, lad, I'll put your fiddle into its case and some one will help you home.'

Well, there didn't seem to be any of the fine guests willing to escort the musician home, and soon he found himself pushing his weary feet blindly through heather roots and shrubs. On and on he went, until he no longer knew where he was or where he was going. The terrain beneath his feet was strange, and once or twice he called for assistance, but it was very late, long past the bedtime of decent folk. Then, just when he thought he'd never find the cause-way, his feet at last felt familiar ground. Edging his way inch by inch, he went on until the smell of wild garlic filled his nostrils; it grew abundantly behind his cottage.

Thinking he was safely home, he widened his stride; then without warning something wound around his ankles, causing him to fall backwards with a heavy thump. As he attempted to rise, it dawned on poor Harry that he'd slipped into the bog. All who fell into it knew its peril; the bog had a life of its own. He felt it sucking and pulling him down; it was futile to struggle, the great marsh had found another victim. Even if a kind neighbour had come to his assistance it would have proved an impossible task; once the bog has hold of a body it does not let go. He struggled all the same, and tried desperately to find a piece of root of an ancient tree to cling onto, but he'd fallen into a deep part; his life began to ebb away. As his weakened body gave way to its fate, he thought, 'well, at least my loneliness will end, and where I go all are like me—blind.'

Now, just as that last breath of life was rushing forth from his crushed lungs, something happened which made him think that he had already passed over into death's realms.

He found himself standing in a passageway; he could feel slimy, mossy walls and there was hardly any room to stand upright. He felt a sharp tug on his sodden jacket sleeve. He ran shaking fingers down to feel a tiny hand.

'Come on, Harry, the wedding feast can't begin until you've played alongside our piper.'

'I don't understand—am I dead or not? Is this the place where the passed over go?'

'Na, na, laddie, this is the world of Elfin; can't you tell by the size of me?'

'I am blind and can't see you. But one minute the bog had hold of me, the next I'm here in this slimy tunnel.'

'You are our guest. Listen now, Harry, the King's daughter had been planning her marriage for ages, and decided to have it today, but did the rich Annabelle not decide to have her wedding too!'

'What has that got to do with me?' asked Harry, still unsure if he was dead or not.

'She had to have a fiddler—not just any fiddler, she had chosen you, man. So we all thought it best to wait until that other wedding was finished, then to bring you down here into our underworld.'

'So it was one of you who tripped me up—but how did you manage to get me through the bog?'

'Never mind asking an elf his secrets, because we keeps them to ourselves. Now come, the food is served, the party awaits and our piper has been eager to play with you since he first heard you as a boy. I'll give you a clean-up first, though, because the moss sticks and hardens.' There was the swish and whoosh of a soft brush, and all the dirt was gone. Harry felt quite fresh, even although his fiddle arm had been played sore.

Harry was whisked along by the elf at such a speed he thought at first his feet weren't touching solid ground, and in no time he could hear loud laughter.

A door creaked open. 'Watch now, and don't hit your head off the ceiling beams,' said a sweet-sounding female, who held his hands and guided him in. A great wave of applause vibrated throughout the place. 'This is our King,' he heard the young woman say, 'and he wants you to begin playing.'

Harry felt a hand grab his; a stout little hand with podgy fingers. 'Hello, lad, it's so kind of you to join us; and on behalf of my family and subjects I invite you to take your place alongside our beloved piper.'

Harry was then led onto a stage where another elf spoke. 'I'm old Dougal, and I love to hear that fiddle of yours. Sometimes it gets lonely down here, being the only musician, so with His Majesty's permission I sometimes sneak onto the bog surface to listen. We all hear your playing and love you, man, so play for us now at the wedding.'

Harry put out his hand at the gentle request of the female elf, and she laid in it his instrument; it had been cleaned, for like him it had been swallowed by the moss and was filthy. Without knowing or reasoning why, his heart felt overjoyed here in this elfin world, and he slipped the fiddle into its usual comfortable position between his chin and neck, drew back the bow and played his instrument like it had never been played before. The piper filled his airbag and he too began playing. The harmony was brilliant; not a single foot wasn't tapping and beating upon the floor. Tiny elves were shrieking and whirling; Harry felt the breeze they created as they reeled and danced, it was wonderful.

When he rested, it was apparent that his female companion was by his side. She asked if he needed any drink, but they didn't have human alcoholic drinks only fruit juice. He accepted that, and as she poured it for him he became aware of her perfume. He touched her face, and felt the most soft skin he'd ever felt. 'What do you look like, little lady?' he enquired.

'I have curly black hair, we all do, my eyes are green and I am wearing a silken gown made with flower petals. Now my father, the piper, is summoning me to let you play; please go on.'

'She sounds so pretty,' he said to himself, 'I wish I could see her.' Then as if the female elf had read his thoughts, she stroked his forehead and ran her hand over his eyes, and the veil of blindness lifted in the most magical way. His head filled with lights of every colour, and then he saw her. Mira was a picture of loveliness. She gazed into his newly-sighted eyes, and as their eyes met it was love between them at once. The tiny elfin girl was in love with old Harry, the human fiddler.

'I cannot let you keep your sight, because it is not allowed,' she said sadly.

Harry stared at her, and then she faded, leaving him once again in his world of darkness.

He had been able to see for a single moment, and what a vision of beauty he had before him. But alas, it was over, so on and on he played with Dougal by his side, until, exhausted, he could play no more. The King, his daughter, her new husband and all the guests thanked him from their hearts as they set off to wherever they lived, leaving Harry with old Dougal and Mira.

'You can go back home now, man, and if my time is right your sun will be rising. Come on, we can't be seen, or your kind will start emptying our bog land searching for us.' Old Dougal had already opened the door for him. Mira slipped her tiny hand into his. It was warm: he closed his fingers upon it and felt a love he had never felt before in his lifetime. Then in a flash his little new found world was gone, and he found himself lying half in and half out of the bog, with his neighbour's dog licking his face.

'Look at the state of you, I warned about that rich wine at the Laird's house—shame on you!' His neighbour helped him to his feet, declaiming about the evils of drink as she guided him home.

If she only knew, he'd not touched a drop that night; and if he seemed intoxicated, then it was because of a moment's miracle when the little elfin girl gave him sight!

He never divulged that he'd been in the company of the elves, even although he so wished to share with his friends the beauty of Mira and the stirring tunes played on the smallest bagpipes in the entire world; instead he said nothing. Anyway, who would believe him?

From that day Harry refused all requests to play his fiddle at weddings. He became more and more reclusive, opting instead to sit by the edge of the bog, hoping for one sign of his tiny beloved presence. Sometimes a dragonfly would whirl around him, and he'd be heard asking the insect how were Mira and Dougal. This behaviour convinced his friends that, after being blind and living alone for so long, the old man had lost his mind.

Even the kind elderly lady hardly gave him a thought, and came to see him less and less. One day, however, her conscience bothered her about him, so she put some scones in a basket and tottered along to the low-roofed cottage on the edge of the bog. Finding the place empty, however, she began to think perhaps poor sad Harry had given up his lonely life, opting for a an early death within the bog. It made no difference how much she searched and called his name, her friend had simply disappeared.

She was old and tired, so for a moment sat down on a stool Harry kept on his porch, when something caught her eye—footprints: two sets that came all the way from the bog and up to the door of the cottage. She investigated at once, because they were the footprints of children; very small children. She followed them and found at the rear of the house that there were some more, but these were of normal size, presumably Harry's. As she went around the side of the house she could clearly see that those tiny footprints were joined by the large ones, then as if transformed by magic the bigger ones disappeared, and all the way back to the bog were three tiny sets of footprints. This was a complete mystery, and no matter how often she went over it in her head, she could find no explanation. All she knew was that Harry and his fiddle had gone, and they were never seen again!

The First Famous Labour Colony

So there you have the legend. Now I shall give you some facts relating to the mystery marshlands, that because of a lord's dream are to this day what we know as the central pastures of Scotland.

In the latter half of the eighteenth century a remarkable experiment was begun by a remarkable man on his land in the Vale of Menteith, the name given to the upper part of the Forth Valley. Seven years after the Carron Ironworks were established, Henry

Home, Lord Kames, dreamt about turning part of his land which was a barren moor into a fertile plain. He planned to populate land which was once an uninhabitable quaking bog with scores of happy families.

In 1766 Lord Kames, who had been improving his land in another district, succeeded through his wife to the estate of Blair Drummond, near Doune in Perthshire, part of which included the Carse land above the point where the Forth and Teith rivers joined. At that time most of the Carse land between Stirling and the Menteith Hills was covered by a dreary expanse of peat, moss and heather which stretched for twelve miles up the valley, and formed with its deep and treacherous pools an almost impassable morass from one to two miles broad. Known at different places as the Flanders, Cardross, Kincardine in Menteith or Blairdrummond Moss, it lay to a depth of from 6 to 12 feet over a plain of good fertile land, the surface of which was about 30 feet above the level of high tides. The underlying ground consisted of fine grey clay with beds of shells, but no stones of any size. He considered it a highly desirable matter to remove the peat and lay bare the good land below, but how to sweep off the barren covering and reclaim much of the ground in an economically viable way had not yet been discovered.

Lord Kames, although in his seventieth year, had a young heart and a strong mind, and at once set himself the task of tackling the problem. His plan required many years to complete, but he courageously set to work, and although he did not live to see the end of it, he laid a good foundation, and worked at it for the remaining sixteen years of his life. He died in 1782 at the advanced age of eighty-six, and his son and successor, George Home Drummond, carried on the work with even greater skill and energy, and introduced several improvements, which eventually brought about the final and complete success of the old man's great project.

When in the beginning Lord Kames had the idea of doing it, he approached the ruling fathers in Stirling who laughed at such a ridiculous project. To begin with, where were the skilled hands? Who knew anything about peat bogs?

Lord Kames had his answers ready: 'It's twenty years since the Jacobite uprising. The clan system has been broken up. Many of the poor clansmen have seen their homes burned and been chased from Scotland to make way for sheep. But you all know there are hundreds of them outlawed and hiding in the hills. They have the skills of working with peat. If pardons are given, I know we will see them looking for work.'

One councillor said that the Highland clansmen could only communicate in Gaelic, and anyway, there was not enough money to pay them even if the work was completed.

Lord Kames said if they gave the clansmen the pardons he was asking for, he would see to their wellbeing. So that was settled, permission was given and the destitute highlanders began the reclamation of Blair Drummond Moss. At long last they had work, a useful occupation for the strong and hardy men of the Highlands. It would prove a difficult task, and one for which they received no wage, but Lord Kames fed them and allowed many to lease the land. This proved a sound plan, because each section of the land being leased had to be cleared by its holder. There was no payment in money, but they were allowed to build small houses made of dried peat, and for a hard and successful year's work, they earned a pig or a cow or some fowl.

A channel was cut from north to south through the moss and down to the clay below. At the north end a stream of water that had been used to drive a mill was diverted into it, and was thus led for a distance of about a mile to the Forth. The men would throw the peat into the stream, and the water had a powerful enough current to carry it down to the river. The underlying clay of the canal bed was as slippery as soap, so the thick stream of water and peat was well lubricated as it moved slowly down to the river.

This act of clearing the central belt of her peat bogs began with the clearing of Blairdrummond Moss. The Highlanders called this the First Famous Old Labour Colony.

When they and their families began to populate the cleared moss grounds, they built schools and chapels and set priests and teachers to work teaching their children and keeping their Sabbaths holy. If one takes a stroll throughout the Carse of Stirling, it is interesting to note how many places have Gaelic names.

As mile upon mile of moss were cleared, secrets held within its boggy depths were revealed. Whalebones along with other aquatic skeletons proved that indeed the ocean had covered that area many thousands of years ago. Something else was discovered—hundreds of Roman artefacts, including swords, knives, shields and helmets, pots of clay and some remnants of jewellery, proving that the Romans had been there during their occupation.

Another thing that may be of interest to you was that up until the beginning of the twentieth century, tinker women used sphagnum moss for nappies; this antiseptic plant had so many antibiotic properties that babies never suffered sore bottoms. The using of cloth brought with it that plague of babies, nappy rash, but this was never Mother Nature's gift.

I hope you liked those wee snippets of moss stories. I think we'll head back to Crieff now, and see how this scaldie fared in our flat at the bottom of Gallowhill.

31

FAMILY LIFE

Travelling people hate to part with their weans, even for a visit to relatives, and I was no exception. If for one day my wee boys were not under my wing I was unable to get on with everyday routine for worrying about my children. Johnnie had reached the age I dreaded; he was going to school. When I think back to those years I can still see his wee face all lit up with excitement. He wore grey trousers, shirt and jersey, black shiny shoes, satchel over his shoulder, ready to face a bigger world than the tiny storytelling one I'd cocooned him in.

Stephen whinged that first Monday morning because he wanted to go with his brother, but when I promised him a lollipop he sat quiet and watched his big brother, all five years of him, leave to take his place on the first rung of society's ladder.

We left early to visit Davie's parents first, because Margaret needed to see the new schoolboy in his uniform. I remember the way she fussed over him before slipping a folded handkerchief into the breast pocket of his blazer. That made me blush red, because I should have remembered a hanky, but she smiled, obviously aware of my embarrassment, and said, 'that was his father's first hanky, I've kept it for his wee boy.'

I felt unwell that morning, and put it down to leaving my child in the hands of complete strangers, but when I saw those other mums, some crying their eyes out, I thought mothers are the same the world over, be they scaldies or travellers. Stephen got his lolly, and for a while we walked about Crieff chatting to folk. Crieff folks love to blether, and even today when you wander through the town you'll see them just standing about the place chatting away, forgetting the time, just enjoying a crack. Stephen and I had a coffee in Rugi's Café, which was a favourite spot for women taking a break from shopping before either heading downhill to collect school kids, or in the case of older women, going home. Crieff's High Street splits the town, with half uphill and the other down. So the folks going down needed a break before returning, and the ones climbing uphill needed refreshment when arriving.

When it was time to collect Johnnie, it couldn't come fast enough. My God, how I missed my wean, and him only out of my sight for three hours. Lining up with all the other mums at the school railings, I watched as one by one the little primary children filed out like soldiers. He saw us first and came running towards me, eyes filled with tears. 'Mammy, I done school and dinna like it, so I winna be going back!'

Well, as it happened he'd been in the middle of a lesson when the teacher gave a child a row. Her loud voice and stern face frightened him, so with half a tinker in his blood, he told the teacher she was a 'Banshee'. That resulted in him getting a row and being made to sit at the back of the classroom. I tell you it took some powerful amount of persuading to see my laddie don that uniform the next day and walk back to face the 'Banshee'.

My feeling unwell soon resolved itself in another pregnancy. I didn't know whether to laugh or cry, because after having Stephen the doctor warned my health might suffer if I became pregnant again, and he tried to convince me to have a sterilisation. However I wanted a girl, and if one didn't come, only then would I get the operation; one way or the other, I needed to try.

I kept on working as long as I could, and what with seeing to my husband and ever-growing laddies, plus a baby on the way, all thoughts of my past and the ancient history of my people was, like a family heirloom, folded and put away in a cold linen drawer. No more did I cling to the memory of my dear old bus, or those wild remote places I so cleaved to in the olden days. Gone were the berry fields o' Blair, and bracken-cutting in Inverary. Filed away in the further reaches of my mind were the bowed tents filled with dirty-faced weans laughing and dashing from yellow broom to knotty oak. The clan system maintaining ancient feuds, which had me loving some tribes and terrified of others, was just a lost memory. I was now the property of mainstream society. My life was insured through a red-faced collector for the Co-operative, who came every Friday at tea time. I was registered with the local health practice; even the mole on my back and the scar above my forehead was noted on a record held along with thousands of others in a doctor's surgery. Even my teeth were counted, and unwillingly filled each time I visited the dentist—and if I failed to go he warned me that rotting teeth would poison my blood. Well, if I had bettered myself then it certainly didn't feel like it; yet how easily one slips into the way of life that is dependent on others. I'd never wanted to be a link in that chain of settled, controlled members of society. I remember seeing a film about Dracula, and in a strange way I envied him because he changed at night into a bat and flew over cities and people. Lucky sod, was all I thought when I left the cinema.

I hated other people knowing my business, poking eyes and ears into my affairs. Yet everybody was centred in the same small community. However, I knew the importance of my past, at least what it meant to me, and I allowed the farmer to close the gate but not to lock it. One day, when my role as mother was no longer needed, this old cow would bolt through that gate and run free onto her familiar pastures.

A lovely, dark-haired, beautiful baby girl, born on 14 June 1972 when the summer was at its height, completed our family. Because of my contracted pelvis the sterilisation took place immediately after the caesarean birth. The pregnancy wasn't as simple an affair as the other two; sickness and painful backache plagued me for the whole nine months. My baby, who we named Barbara after my youngest sister, weighed only five pounds five ounces, but she was perfectly healthy. I could hardly believe how tiny she was. Davie was frightened to pick her up.

My stay in hospital could have been easier, though, had I not taken an infection. Let me tell you about it. I had been in for seven days when the nurse who removed my stitches thought two of them looked a bit red. She said that before going off duty she'd check my scar. I was to be going home next day. That evening, at visiting time, Mammy came in and said, 'what's the matter with you, lassie, your skin's yella!'

'Mammy, I'm fine, I got ma stitches out nae mair than four hours ago, see.' I pulled back the covers to let her examine the scar. 'That's alright, but I still think you're a funny colour.'

Well, the visiting hour passed, but my mother knew something wasn't right, and when she left me she headed off to speak to a nurse. When she voiced her concerns, staff assured her that I was fine. Mammy, however hard the staff tried to convince her, would not leave until a proper doctor listened to her woes. 'Doctor, I ken these things, now that wee lassie lying in thon bed has the poison in her. Please give her another check, because I'm never wrong.'

This kind doctor had Mammy brought a cup of tea and said he'd do a check on my blood himself, but it would take several hours for results. However my nurse, the one who had promised to look at my scar before she went off duty, was to change the ward's plans that night. She smiled and said as she lifted the thin piece of gauze from my scar, 'well, Jessie, I'm off duty now, but let's see this...' Whatever she planned to say never came from her lips, as immediately her fingers were covered in red and yellow gunge. Infected fluid oozed from my scar like a hot volcano as the stitched area split open. I don't remember much from then on, only my mother screaming—'I telt ye, now. Ma bairn, ma bairn!'

Well, as it turned out I did have blood poisoning, and did that not half put the dampeners on me getting home. Back into the theatre I went to have all the rotting tissue cut out, and then for another seven days I laid on my back while tons of antiseptic gauze was packed into the open wound. Before each meal I was given a great big injection of penicillin.

What concerned me more than anything else was my sons; I hadn't seen them for the whole time I spent in the Maternity ward, and boy did I miss my laddies. Davie's parents looked after them well enough. I remember when Margaret sent them to visit. She didn't come herself, as she hated hospitals, but Sandy brought my wee boys to see me. They weren't allowed in because I was in a room on my own due to infection. What a shock I got, because when they walked round to the French windows to look in, all I could see were two wee Lipton's orphans. Margaret had dressed them in belted tweed coats, and they'd had their hair cut in the shape of a bowl. If you have ever seen photos of war refugees, then that's what they were like.

I'd dressed my boys in trendy gear and let their hair grow long-ish; like wee hippies they were until my mother-in-law got her hands on them.

Still, that was the least of my problems. I had to be restitched, but that didn't bother me, it was getting the buggers out that worried me. Because of the severity of my failure to heal, massive deep tension sowing was done on my wee belly. I couldn't get a minute's peace from worrying about these new stitches rupturing again—would I never heal? This certainly became an obsession with me, so a bit of diversion therapy was applied by the staff. Every four hours my wound was cleaned and checked. On the seventh day a stern-faced nurse came in to do the duty. I'd never met her before, and wondered where the other nurses were. She didn't answer me, just got on with what she was doing. I tried several times to converse with this guffy-faced mort, but nothing doing. Still, I'm not one to give up, and told her that on the previous night I'd seen from my window a new father enter the main ward all the worst for drink, probably he'd be celebrating. Well, she sank me a look that would have scuttled the Bismarck and called me an interfering busybody, with nothing better to do than laugh at others' misfortunes. I can tell you here and now that nurse was lucky I didn't burst the nose on her flat face. I told her to clear off and send another more civil nurse. It was then she pulled off her rubber gloves and plumped the pillows behind me saying, 'you can get up now, lass.' I told her I could not move until the stitches were removed. Her answer was, 'what stitches?' That nurse had been sent to get my mind off the removal of those deep tension stitches, and by talking about the drunken father I had given her the chance to get my mind onto something else—hating her.

Well, from then on I never looked back. Me and Barbara, who'd put on a whole two pounds in weight since her birth, went home to the rest of our family. In a short while the boys had longish hair and were wearing flowery shirts and dungarees again. Margaret's war-time coats were passed on to a travelling woman, more than grateful for such warm garments, who came to my door doing a bit hawk-ing.

Within six months we had moved to Murrayfield Loan, a new block of flats. This place with its mod cons would see us through another eight years in Crieff, before we flitted to a more substantial house. But before we leave Gallowhill, let me tell you about Davie's crabbit old Granny.

I won't linger long over this, so here is all I know of her. I can't speak ill of anyone and don't intend to, but even although this wiry old lady had long since died, she left her presence in the house. It was nothing I could honestly put my finger on, but you know when something isn't right. In that house I had that feeling many a time.

A breath of air against my cheek as I'd pass by one particular place would bring me from a train of thought to see if I'd left a window open. Dishes arranged in a certain way would mysteriously be changed from one shelf to another. Lights were switched off when no one was in a room. These things are easily explained, I expect, but one thing I can swear on my heart was down to her was the way my bed-making wasn't to her satisfaction. I'd make the bed as usual in the same manner daily by tucking in the blankets and sheets, and leave the room, yet when I'd go back they were untucked. I always laid the top cover with a lacy bit to the bottom; she turned it to the top. This happened every day, until I made the bed the way she desired it to be made.

What I didn't know at the time was that both the bed and those covers were at one time hers! I thought they were part of the furnishings we had rented with the accommodation, and indeed they were, but after the Smiths died the new owner had inherited certain pieces that were theirs.

32

SPITTALY BANK

Ghosts are not a new topic in my stories. People have given me many tales, and whether or not I believe in their existence matters not, because a story is a story. This next wee present I received did not come from anybody specific, it was always there, inherited from the smouldering embers of countless camp fires. The teller always swore blind it was his mother who had told it to him, because had she not felt 'it' in the place described in the story.

Half drunk and melancholy, some quiet elderly gent who up until then had listened to other stories, would at the gloaming hour tell his version. And maybe down an old quarry road I'd wander up to yet another campfire and hear a different version of this tale. It was never far away from the tinkers—this tale of 'Spittaly Bank'.

About a hundred or so yards off the Kirkton to Lethendy road there's a snug spot known by locals in the Spittalfield area as 'Spittaly Bank', often frequented by travelling tinker families, mainly those from Perthshire like myself. This story relates to a couple named Maggie and Jocky Burke. It was between the war years that we go and find them in their wee flimsy tent beyond the road at the Spittaly Bank campsite. Jocky had been away to visit his parents at Burrie's Spoot near Coupar Angus, who were stricken with the flu. This was a campsite many folks stayed on during harvest time. Older travellers, unable to walk far, were allowed to live out their lives there if they wished, and if they were there, relatives worried less about their well-being. Not all farmers or landowners were so benevolent, but the man who owned Burrie's Spoot had a fondness for his lot of travellers. He had grown up with them and they were his friends. So while Jocky tended his sick parents, Maggie kept her campfire burning at Spittaly.

I will now take a back seat and hand you over to old Maggie.

'Weel, it wis roond aboot the time atween the wars, ma Jocky wis awa' doon at Burrie's takin care o' his old yins—the puir craturs were sair croupit. My Jocky had a haun on him wid soon pit them back on their feet; he kent a' the herby medicines. I didnae like bein on ma ain, but he'd left me plenty habin [food], so there wis naethin comin ower.

I'd pit a roarin fire on, cause man, wis it nae half a cauld nicht, when this gadjie cam' by ma bowdie barricade. He frickit the life frae me, cause he wis as high as the yew tree branches hingin above ma bowdie; near on seven feet he wis. I was afeard and thought, "God help us this nicht if this shan gadjie [strange man] tak's it intae his heed tae pagger [murder] me tae death." He niver said a word, an' sat doon at ma fire. He wis wearing a black cape, an' his big heid wis covered ower wi' a hood hiding his een frae me.

I pit some braxy ham ontae a lump o' breed an' offered it tae him, but wi' a brush o' yin finger he refused. I flung it tae ma auld jugal [dog], and Lord did it nae scoot aneath a hap, no' even gi'ing the ham a sniff. Ony ither time that habin wid have disappeared doon yon jugal's thrapple, but no' that nicht, the puir animal wis shakin inside its auld mangy skin. Noo, I didnae ken whit shanned ma jugal, but it bid under thon hap, shivering and cowed. Noo whit could I, a wee five-fit manishi [woman] dae if ma visitor should hae wild intent tae burn me and ma bowdie in the dark hours o' the nicht?

I thought the dug wis a fierce chat, but no nae mair. Then without a single wird, I felt a cauld shiver run up an' doon ma back as the gadjie made a breenge at me. I fell back and and squealed intae the nicht, "whit is it ye need frae me, ye big shan bastard?" I felt the grun and grabbed a bit firewid, jumpit tae ma feet and cam doon ontae his humpit back. He laughed like it wis a twig that hid battered him, but still no a wird.

I kent this gadjie wisnae at ma fire fer ma habin, he didnae eat the ham an' it wisnae a crack he wanted, fer no a word cam oot o' him. Only thing he wis there fer wis tae wait until I fell asleep, then he'd pagger me intae bits an' burn the auld bowdie. So I stood there in the licht o' me campfire, knuckled stick firmly in ma haund. I couldnae rin intae the dark nicht, he'd catch me fer sure; so I waited. The shan gadjie hung his heid, staring intae the flames. The reek frae the campfire curled intae grey ringles aboot his hooded heid.

My God, wis it nae a terror in yon silent dark nicht, but thank the Lord he didn't mak tae grab me agin. It wis a richt lang nicht, the worst yin I'd iver lived through, an I wisnae half gled whin I saw a glimmer o' licht push up abun the mountains. A cluckie doo flew inches frae the claws o' a big hungry hoolit watching it frae the yew tree abun ma heed. Then, as quick as he'd come, the creep stood up. I thocht, "if he's goin tae pagger me, he'll dae it noo." The panny wis starting tae bile in ma blaidder, cause I'd nae relieved maself a' nicht. The gadjie, still wi' his heid covered, pit a haun forward fer me tae shak it, the langest pointed fingers iver I'd seen on ony haun, but I kept tight haud o' me stick and widnae shak his haun. Then he grabbed the stick frae me and threw it intae the low burning embers o' ma fire. Then, slow, he took haud o' ma haun, and I tell ye this wi' ma haun on ma hert, his grip wis as cauld as ice. Then that panny that wis hissin in ma blaidder ran doon ma legs, cause the gadjie's feet that turned tae walk awa' wir hoofit, he hid the cloven feet o' the Hairy Man—the Deevil.

My Jocky's auld mither telt me, whin me an' him first gat merried, no' tae be alane, cause the forkit tail o' the Deevil wid seek a lane lassie oot an sit waitin on her soul. If she'd a weak bone in her body he'd seek it oot, an' awa' wi' her he'd gang. I niver waited tae git a bit habin tae brak' ma fast, cause me an' the auld jugal, we took aff tae meet up wi' Jocky at Burrie's Spoot. Oh, div I no half shiver whin I tell hantle o' that nicht.'

Maggie has long since departed from this earth, but no one would have forgotten the way she contorted her face and slanted those flashing blue eyes of hers when describing the appearance of that visitor. If he was a figment of her imagination, then she had a very good one.

Do you know, if I'd a shilling for every time I'd listened to past travellers tell a tale of him from the underworld I'd be rich, no doubt. This next tale, also well known among my people, is terrifying to a child, yet sad to an adult's ears. I heard it when my childlike mind believed every word, and to say it petrified me is an understatement. I've been unable until now to bring myself to tell this story, and it had to lie unspoken in my youthful memory; but now that I'm a mature manishi I'll share it with you.

33

THE GIFT

Though cold be the clay,
Where thou pillow'st thy head,
In the dark silent mansions of sorrow,
The spring shall return
To thy low narrow bed,
Like the beam of the
Day star tomorrow.

The above is a verse from a poem Burns wrote for a favourite child after she died. I thought in view of the following tale those tender words would touch all who have experienced that unique bond a parent has for their child, which goes beyond the boundaries of life and death.

A travelling tinker lassie by the name of Bella Johnstone, who was related to my father's side of the family, experienced an awful happening in Nether Kincairney near Clunie. And after it, witnesses swore that her bonny jet black hair went snow-white, and her only twenty-one.

She and her young man Donald had pitched their camp well into the wood at the end of a track that went past several wee cottages, now all derelict and dilapidated. It was at the beginning of the First World War. Tinker laddies were volunteering in their droves to take arms and fight for their country. Donald went along with his brothers, leaving pregnant Bella alone. She wasn't the only lassie left to fend for herself, though she was the only one camped in the forest, but she had a good strong back and busied herself gathering firewood and piling it up for the coming winter. She would earn her meat by hawking her baskets, and Donald had left her plenty of pails he had made, which she would sell to keep herself fed. For a few hours helping his wife in the dairy, a local farmer would supply all the milk, butter and cheeses she'd need. Tatties and turnips came from the farmer's wife, so Bella was fine on her own. This campsite was warm and sheltered, but something seemed to set her nerves on edge when she passed the ruined cottages. She felt it several times, a strange, cold feeling that seemed to find its way into her very bones. It got so intense that, rather than take the way along the track, she circled around it, going through a boggy field instead.

Donald had been home on leave with tales of death and lone pipers, leaving behind a melancholy lassie who was longing for the war to be over. However, much as she yearned for her soldier laddie, the baby moving vigorously in her womb was taking up more of her thoughts. This coming wee child would be their first baby, and she longed so much to see and count its tiny fingers. Whether it was a boy or girl didn't matter to her, as long as the bairn had healthy lungs.

Into her eighth month, and with news trickling home of the war's fiercest battles, her mind wandered away from her fears about the ghostly ruined cottages. Forgetting to circle round by the field, she found herself walking past them. 'Oh well,' she thought, averting her eyes from the blank-paned windows with their torn, shredded curtains. 'I'll hurry past and maybe I'll no' feel the icy cold.'

She pulled her shawl over her head and quickened her pace. No sooner had the edge of the shawl touched her forehead, when an almighty gust of bitter cold air blew hard against her face, turning her lips blue and bringing water to her eyes. It seemed as if something unseen was breathing on her. Then the wind came so hard it nearly blew her off her feet. Holding the shawl around her swollen womb, Bella lowered her head and tried to walk into it, but hard as she tried, she could not move her freezing limbs. It was like a raging storm, so fierce it became difficult to breathe; it was blowing her back towards the campsite. Now Bella was a strong young woman, and she began to feel anger at whatever phenomenon was obstructing her, and pushed all the harder against it. Suddenly she could hear thundering hooves coming up the old road, and at the sound she was lifted off her feet and thrown against the middle house. At that precise moment a rider straddling a massive black stallion raged past, shouting to her that his mount was out of control. Then, as clumps of earth ripped up by those racing hooves went flying everywhere, he was gone.

'My God, if I'd been in the way of that beast I'd be flat for sure!' She lay slightly stunned, then slowly rose onto wobbly, weak legs, in the knowledge that something unnatural, a powerful force, had saved her life—but why?

Unable to move very far, Bella went back to rest in the safety of her warm bowed tent. The pain in her back where she was thrown against the wall of the house was quite severe.

A voice came from outside; it was a man calling to her. 'Excuse me, but are you alright? My horse is a new purchase, and we're not used to each other yet. Please except my apologies, are you all right?'

Bella crept from her tent mouth to see a well-dressed young gentleman holding a riding hat in one hand, two gloves and a whip in the other, as the horse grazed quietly near by.

Just as Bella moved to stand up, a rush of the severest pain shot into her abdomen, and there could be only one reason; her labour had began. 'Oh lad,' she said, as she held out her arm for assistance, 'can you fetch a farm wife for me. Tell her Bella's pains have started.'

Nodding, with an embarrassed look on his face, the young man, now in control of his fiery horse, galloped away to fetch help.

It was just getting dark as Bella heard voices. Two lassies from the farm along with the young rider made a very welcome appearance at the tent. 'Hello, Bella, how far on are you?'

'I'm taking them every ten minutes, so it winna be long.' She thanked the rider for his help, and he wished her well before taking himself away down the track road. All night long her labour continued, and just as the first rays of a spring sun pushed over the horizon, a tiny cry echoed over the fields and surrounding countryside with the sound of new life. Bella and the absent Donald were parents to a bonny healthy boy.

In time when all the cleaning and assuring was over, the women left a happy Bella to care for her gift of life.

Tinker folks, it is well known, live close to Mother Nature, and unexplained events like the cold ghostly presence that had saved her from going under the hooves of the runaway horse were seldom questioned; instead they were put down to something that had happened in a time long ago, that wasn't the business of the living.

Bella in Donald's absence named their son Peter, because she thought he had the makings of a wee cock's curl on his thickish head of hair, the same as her late father by that name.

Within a week, with Peter rolled into a shawl around his mother's front, the pair set off to make their living. The track which ran round by the old cottages brought Bella back in front of them, and once more she stood curiously frightened. Her baby had kept both her mind and body occupied, allowing little time to think about the past weird experience. Yet whoever had saved her meant no harm, so she scolded herself, but still wondered if she should dare to walk on past. Taking the longer boggy route now that she had a baby presented her with more trouble than she needed, so with the thought that the ghost had saved her from the horse she stepped on past the houses with more confidence than before.

But mysteries have their own reasons, and just as before the icy wind rose and blew into her face. It stopped her, growing as fierce as the last encounter with each laboured step. This was much to her terror, for now she held a baby, and it was for his safety that she cried out, 'please stop it, whoever you are, and let us go in peace. I thought you saved me from the horse, but why do you haunt me and my tiny infant like this?' The wind grew stronger and colder, with an added ferocity that made Bella pray, 'Oh God, what is this thing that tears at my skin with its icy cold fingers? If it is in pain, then please release it from this earth.' At those heartfelt words the wind decreased to a slight breeze, yet the icy cold remained. Then something to her left caught her eye, and for a moment imagining there was someone else there, she called out, 'who are you?'

There was movement in the cottage nearest her: she saw the torn curtain being drawn aside, yet there was no hand to be seen. Then there was a creaking as the middle house door opened very slowly. Someone was trying to contact her, but oh, how terrified she felt. She wanted to run away, but her legs were still weak after the birth. Those shaking legs had a power of their own as she walked over to the door. 'Will you harm me and my baby?' she asked, although no-one could be seen. Standing inside the old ruin she began to wonder if perhaps Donald's absence was playing tricks with her mind. Her heartbeats grew louder in her chest, they beat with a deafening thump.

'Who are you? Do you want to tell me something?' Then came the most horrifying experience: it made her draw in her breath as if it were her last. Peter was taken from her bosom and laid gently on the broken wooden floor. Then it was as if two invisible hands lifted him, and he began to move back and forth; those invisible hands were gently rocking the infant, who still slept soundly. Powerless to control this supernatural experience, Bella was rooted to the spot, when a noise from outside made her turn. She heard horses, several of them, gathering speed. At the same time she heard a whip cracking the air, wheels whirring on the road, then cries from a coachman, 'Whoa, boys. Mind out, lassie, watch your bairn! Oh God, woman, he's been trampled!'

Instinctively Bella pulled open the door, but to her utter astonishment there was no sign of any coach, horses or coachman, only a cold breeze blowing through branches overhanging the ruins. She turned to gather up Peter, who had been laid softly on the floorboards. Bella held him tightly to her bosom, still unable to make any sense of the happenings. Then, just as she was about to leave, she noticed one of the floorboards had a thin sliver of cotton sticking out from under it. She leaned down and pulled at the piece of material. It was lodged between two of the boards, so she lifted one aside. Something was beneath the boards, and somehow she felt the answers to this mystery were in there. Peter, now wrapped inside his woollen shawl, was tied firmly to his mother's back as one by one the rotted floor boards came away in her hands. The sight that met her eyes spoke volumes as she made it out in the dim light. There were two skeletons: one adult, the other a tiny infant! Now she could piece together the story. After hearing the sound of the coach and horses and the cry from the coachman that they'd run down a baby, she realised that no-one had come to the aid of the dying child. Unable to cope with what had happened, the mother buried herself under the floorboards with her child.

Bella went for help, and soon a church minister was burying in the local graveyard a sad set of bones. From that day on, no icy wind or strange sounds were heard near those derelict cottages.

The war ran its course and brought Donald safely home. Bella had the farm folk pitch her tent nearer the farm now that she had a baby to look after, and she felt more secure. It was that experience that told Bella she was born with the 'Gift'. And the ghost with her child was not the last to communicate with her from the other side. Although according to her this was more of a curse than a gift, she accepted her lot and helped many miserable souls.

The 'Gift' comes upon a person at the seven stages of life. In other words it can be made manifest in people aged seven years old, or fourteen, or twenty-one and so on. Bella was twenty-one when that first visitation came to her.

34

MY TOP FLOOR HOME

Back to Crieff now, and I don't know about you, folks, but I think a cuppy just now would go well.

So, if you have yours, then here's how things progressed with my scaldie lifestyle.

The flats in Murrayfield Loan were a big block of human emotions. In other words, they were filled with young families; a heaving mass of same-age kids and hard-working parents. These flats were Crieff Council's first attempt to provide what cities in Scotland had been developing for years. As homes went, they had everything to offer a growing family unit—central heating, spacious living quarters, big roomy kitchens—but the Crieff folk never understood why flats had to be a necessary part of their landscape. There were plenty of green fields around with miles of space on which to build houses, so why build flats? No one was ever given an explanation, but I kinda liked my top floor home, and with other families beneath us we soon settled on good terms as neighbours should do.

Davie's parents lived a stone's throw away, and every morning as the kids set off for school, they'd conveniently pop into Granny and Grand-dad's for a sweetie.

Changes in my own family were taking place: firstly my parents had left Macduff. Sister Shirley had just separated from her man, and was the reason why Mammy and Daddy left their Morayshire home and settled in Glenrothes. This suited me, because with my parents living nearer Crieff I could visit them more often. It was round this time that I remember Daddy telling me he had decided to write a book about his life as a tinker laddie living on the road in Scotland.

He planned it to be autobiographical. He told me about a time when his family, being pearl fishers, travelled remote bridle paths, carrying all their belongings in a custom-built barrow which had a single wheel and extra long shafts. I was so excited that he'd planned this, and each time I went to visit he'd read me another piece. I knew from tales he'd shared about his early days that it would not be an easy book to write, and some times he was so down I could hardly get a word from him. He and Mammy existed on a bare state pension, yet he still managed to pay a typist. When it was finished he sent the whole manuscript to folklorist Hamish Henderson in Edinburgh, whom Daddy had met many years before. A letter duly arrived from Hamish stating he was looking forward to reading it over the festive period. Daddy's wonderful book was called *The White Nigger*.

Now this is where I come against a solid brick wall, because I don't know if Hamish liked or disliked the manuscript. I have no knowledge beyond that the document remained in Hamish's possession. Daddy never smiled much after that, nor did he ever mention his masterpiece.

Thirty years later, I am still searching for it, but it seems to have disappeared. Daddy died in 1982, and according to Roger Leitch who edited *The Book of Sandy Stewart*, his manuscript is mentioned in the said book, which was published in 1988. So at least it was still kicking around six years after Daddy died. Hamish died in 2002, making my search all the harder.

We travellers believe that if something is meant, then so be it. In other words, if *The White Nigger* is to be, then it will find me.

The flats were on four levels, and I remember one time when Davie had been overdoing New Year celebrations. Several of his mates, ones who came back to Crieff for a holiday at Hogmanay, called on him, and with my blessing he took himself off to the pub for a richt guid blether.

The bairns had been given bikes by Santa, and we spent all day cycling country roads until the poor things had frozen fingers and itchy bums. I'd borrowed an old bike of Sandy's, and, oh God, was I hippit! After tea, all I needed was a bath and my bed. Davie, being a guid bletherer, I knew would not be home until late, so I locked the door meaning to open it in time for his homecoming. But I didn't realise how sleepy I was; the bairns too were out of it. So when Davie began knocking, we all failed to hear him. Now, not one to be undone, the bold lad with more than a fair share of the booze in his belly, decided he would scramble over each balcony to reach his own. I kid you not, when I say that for a sober man this would have been a job for mountaineering equipment and abseiling gear, with experts on hand for guidance—but you know that old saying, 'when the drink's in, the wit's oot.'

I remember the shocked look on my neighbour's face, when she described the appearance of a man throwing his lanky legs over her railings and heaving upwards towards the next floor. She blamed too many Babychams on Hogmanay causing her to imagine things, and I failed to enlighten her. Not only that, my Spiderman was so drunk that he'd not a single memory of his escapade. It was our Johnnie, relieving himself at three am, who heard his Dad gently knocking on the verandah door to be let in. All I can remember was the freezing cold body that huddled into my back, swearing to every god on the entire planet that he'd never drink so much again. Aye, aye!

Bringing our family up in the flats was fun. It wasn't my idea of a home, but the people were great. In the summer when it was sunny and hot, all the mums would fill baskets with food and we'd sit and blether having a braw picnic. Whoever lived in the bottom flat fixed a hosepipe onto their bath tap, allowing the bairns to frolic in the water. They filled polythene bags, chucking them at each other in water fights, and when the council erected a swing park nearby the kids had added enjoyment.

Yes, as houses go I liked the flats, but with our growing family, two bedrooms weren't enough: we needed another room for our budding little female. In due course we left our flat and settled into a four-apartment house in Monteith Street. This spacious house was great (do you notice how my preoccupation with travelling the road is fading in favour of the scaldie life?) and soon, with Barbara in her fifth year, I watched my last bairn set off to school.

This house had what the others didn't—a cosy fireplace. At long last there was somewhere to gather my kids round and tell my resurrected stories. One cold winter's night, when a thick layer of snow covered the land for miles, I remember telling this story to my family. Even Davie gave me his ear.

The Precious Black Jewel

A long, long time ago, before cars or tellies or glass windows, the land was covered with lovely flowers. Lanard picked a bunch of sweet smelling red roses to present them, with his undying love, to Wisa. Pretty Wisa lived across the glen, and Lanard and his cousin Rigg had both fallen in love with her. She had a way with her though which wasn't so attractive in one so bonny—her greed for precious jewels.

One day, after years when both men had been vying for her affections, they were summoned to her house. 'Boys,' she told them with a flirtatious flutter of her long silk eyelashes, 'if you love me, now is the time to bring me what I desire more than any other thing on earth. It is a jewel; one so sparkling, so big, so immensely beautiful, that I will not be able to refuse my hand to whoever brings it to me. She writhed around them like a serpent circling its prey, stroking their muscled arms with her long fair hair.

'I shall dig for gold and bring you a mountain of it, my sweet,' said Rigg excitedly; her perfume lingering in his nostrils.

Lanard knelt on one knee, took hold of her hand and said, 'I don't know where to find jewels to match your beauty, my love, all I have is these two strong arms and a heart filled with undying love and devotion.'

'That is as it may be, but I shall marry whoever brings me the most precious of gems.'

With a last flutter of eyelashes she closed the door on them, and promised not to speak to either until they'd fulfilled her dearest wish.

Rigg sneered at his cousin, saying he was only wasting his time, because he had no knowledge of jewels and it would be he, Rigg, who would marry Wisa.

Poor Lanard, those words rang so true. All his life what he had cared about was what the earth gave in way of food to sustain its people, and not useless commodities like gems, which were just simple stones as far as he was concerned. They couldn't help the sick or feed the poor and hungry. Yet how much he loved the only precious gem that meant anything to him—Wisa.

Rigg searched high and low, covering hundreds of miles and taking little sleep, digging and gouging the earth whenever he saw anything sparkle in the sunlight. Weeks passed, when one day, while resting under a shady willow tree, he overheard a conversation between two merchants. These overweight men of substance were, according to their serious discussion, carrying a treasure to some rich man who lived several miles further up that road. Rigg's eyes widened at the thought of what the silver boxes hanging either side of the mule held, and the more he thought about it, the more he felt that he was getting nearer to claiming Wisa over his cousin.

'Good day, my fine fellows,' he said, smiling, 'can I be of any assistance to you?'

The merchants, weary and thirsty after their long journey, were more than glad of an offer of help, for it was obvious they were lost. 'Could you be so kind as to point the way to Lord so and so's castle? We seem to have taken a wrong turning.'

'This is a coincidence, my friends, because I too am going to see his Lordship.'

So, with a fox-like cunning, Rigg then proceeded to take the pair of tired men with their fine cargo to a quiet spot, where he duly robbed them. The way home was full of imaginings of what Wisa would say at the wonderful present he was bringing to her.

Lanard would never have robbed anyone, in fact he probably would have taken the merchants to their destination without expecting payment. But having searched everywhere for a sparkling gem without success, poor sad Lanard rested under the branches of an oak tree. It was very hot, and in his tired state he fell asleep. He slept for only a little while, however, because something pushed against his back, a movement from the tree behind him. He rose, and saw to his utter amazement a tiny hand opening a door in the tree's trunk. Then, without a word, the smallest man he'd ever seen darted out and lifted some twigs before darting back. 'Wait a moment, sir,' said Lanard, 'pray tell me who you are. I don't know if I'm dreaming or not.'

The tiny creature laid his twigs down and stared at Lanard for a while, before saying, 'I'm one of the little elves who take care of the earth's crust. Who are you, and why do you look so heavy laden?'

Lanard told his companion everything about Wisa's conditions

212

for marriage and how futile his situation was, because he knew nothing about precious gems.

The elf sat down, scratched his head and tugged upon his red beard, then said, 'I will give you the most precious gem in the entire world. Unlike other stones it is a life-saver.'

The tiny creature promised he'd go and bring this stone if Lanard would be patient and wait. After what seemed an eternity, the elf returned holding a small cloth bag drawn tight by a cord. He open it, pushed his hand inside and brought out a horrible-looking black stone. Lanard's heart sank. What would Wisa do when she saw such an object?

The elf watched him and read his thoughts. 'Listen to me, son, I have never told a lie in my life, so when I say this is the world's most precious stone, I mean it. Now take it, give it to your love, and tell her what I have said. If she does not love you, then she'll reject it, but if she does then you'll have a good wife.'

Lanard, full of new vigour, set off to present his love with this gift. When he got to her house he met his cousin, laden down with his illegal offering.

Wisa opened her door, her eyes feasting on the silver boxes. 'Ooh, what have you got, Rigg?'

'For you, my dear, not one, but two caskets filled with every kind of jewel in the world. See.' He opened the lids to reveal piles of the most exquisite gems, gold, diamonds, emeralds and rubies, everything to adorn a handsome lady.

Lanard watched as she ran the gems between her fingers, giggling with excitement. She turned and stared down at the greyish cloth bag hanging limp at his side and said, 'Well, what have you brought me—hurry, open it.'

Rigg folded his arms and sniggered while Lanard clumsily unwound the cord, pulled open the bag and took out the black stone. 'Here,' he said.

'What kind of insult is this? I ask for gems, you bring me a filthy dirty stone, and your cousin presents me with more than a princess would possess. You won't be given the chance to insult me again.' With that she turned to Rigg and led him inside, slamming her door in Lanard's face.

This was terrible. How long had he dreamed of caring for the beautiful Wisa, his beloved. There was, and never would be, any other for him, yet how stupid of him to trust an elf, a horrible weasel-faced man of lies. He'd allowed himself to be tricked. Filled with these thoughts, Lanard ran and ran until he knew or cared not where he was. At last, exhausted, he lay down and fell into a slumber, muttering to himself, 'I wish to sleep forever, and never to walk this earth again, in the knowledge that my love is joined to another!'

What he failed to notice was that he'd stopped at exactly the same spot beneath the branches of the oak tree where he'd encountered the little man, who just happened to hear Lanard's heartfelt wish.

So with a wave of his hand, night came upon the land and with it the first winter. Up until then it had always been summer, with sunshine and rain, but it was never cold. So when this spell was cast upon the land, no one knew what to do, it was a nightmare. Flowers withered and died, trees shed their vivid green leaves, and fruit lay on the ground and was covered with snow. Old people died of cold. Rigg and Wisa hid behind their doors, shivering under all their bedcovers. Their useless gems secured in boxes offered no comfort or warmth. The tiny man took care of Lanard, who slept through all this, by covering him over with piles of fallen leaves. Then one dark and foggy day he sprinkled magic dust over those closed eyes and whispered, 'Time now, son.'

Lanard opened his eyes and stretched his stiff bones. He sat up and wondered what manner of place he'd slept in. 'Where am I?' he called aloud, 'is anyone about?'

'You have been asleep lad,' said the elf, 'for a long time; ten years to be precise.'

His awakening did not eradicate the memory of losing his love and the reason for it. He grabbed the little man and said, 'You tricked me, how could you be so cruel as to lie to me?' He felt the freezing cold air rushing around him, and added to his questioning, 'Why has the land turned so cold? Is this another of your wicked tricks?'

'I do not lie, nor do I create evil. Now remember when I told you the black stone was the most precious of all stones, that stone your greedy love refused? Now, do you still have it?'

He felt the bag tied to his belt and took out the stone. 'Here it is, but I think you owe me an explanation.'

'Come with me, young man. It is time to give your world its other sun.'

He watched in amazement as the tree trunk opened to reveal a concealed passageway, along which he followed his companion. At its end was a cave with black walls, where hundreds of tiny people were working away with axes cutting out stones. 'These are our gems, now watch.' The elf took some twigs, laid them in a pile, then put a handful of the stones on top. He put two twigs together with a smaller one between and rubbed hard. Lanard thought it was another feat of magic when he saw smoke appear, then fire. It was the first time he'd ever witnessed this flaming stuff, but it warmed him and he stopped shivering.

'This will save the people of your world until the sun shines again. Take a big basketful. Now go and bring heat to your freezing world.'

He went first to Rigg and Wisa. 'I have brought you back the black stone: now will you accept it?'

When they saw how it worked and warmed them they were repentant. Rigg confessed to his crime of theft, and Wisa swore never again to put a finger on worthless gems.

The elf instructed Lanard how to dig the black stone from the earth, and soon every house had a plentiful supply to use for heating and to help them survive the annual winter.

The stone was later given the name of coal.

Coal is precious indeed, but even although my new home had its fireplace we opted for gas. I managed many a tale around that warm coal-effect gas fire on the coldest nights, when the weather kept my growing brood indoors.

35

YELLOW IN THE BROOM

I want to go back now to my own childhood, to a time when we were living in our bus. Daddy was away at Kinloch Rannach getting rid of a farmer's vermin. Mammy, I and my sisters were to face several nights alone. Travelling women don't like the night, especially when the campsite is surrounded by thick broom. Come with me, folks, and I'll tell you about one such night.

We were at Braidhaugh in Crieff, down by the low Comrie road. I may have been only nine at the time, but every single moment of that night I can remember vividly. As I said, Daddy had plenty of fields to clear of moles and rabbits. It didn't make sense driving from Crieff to Rannoch each day, so he took a bothy for the duration. It was early spring and the clocks still had their winter faces on them, but it was a rare opportunity for Mammy to get spring-cleaning our bus home. Hearing a grand wind getting up in the night, she rose early that morning and took down her winter curtains for laundering. 'Lassies,' she announced to all her brood—Mona, Chrissie, Shirley, Janey, Mary, Renie, Babsy and me, 'we've a guid going wind blowing the day, so I want all the curtains washed and out on the rope. And this bus needs a guid clean, so there's plenty tae dae.' She looked at me and said with a pointed finger, 'You, ma lass, can never mind trailing through the broom or skimming stanes at the river. I want those hands daeing woman's work now, dae ye hear me?'

'Aye, Mammy, but can I go and rake the midden later on?'

'You bide away frae the coup! My God, I canna take ye ony place but folks wonder if I batter ye, wi' the cuts and bruises ye get raking among splinter wood and broken bottles.'

'No use bothering her this day,' I thought, because the rest of my sisters threatened to chuck me in the River Earn if I shirked my duties.

By midday each one of those heavy tartan curtains was blowing briskly from a rope tied between two beech trees. Shirley had climbed to quite a height, and after we'd pegged all the curtains on, she tightened the rope to raise it so that the washing would get a braw blaw. Chrissie sponged the windows and Shirley polished them up. Mona went through all the dishes and discarded any chipped cups or cracked plates. We were never allowed to eat or drink from chipped or cracked dishes, for fear of harboured germs. Later on, with all our chores completed, we giggled and laughed, eating beef and mustard sandwiches while Mammy began putting up the light-weight summer curtains which she'd made that winter from blue and white gingham material. She'd enough left over for tie-backs; man, how bonny they were, she could fairly work a needle, my Mammy. If she saw a hole in a sock or elbow, it got darned with a weave of the prettiest pattern. No hem or cuff was left to tatter if she spotted it. Sometimes she'd attack a garment with her needle and by the time she was finished there wasn't a single thread that had been original. Just a great wee seamstress, was my Ma.

It was late in the day when Mammy let out a scream, 'Bloody blue bleezes, it's pourin doon!' We all dropped what we were doing to see that indeed the blue sky which dominated the morning had given way to heavy grey clouds, dropping buckets and soaking the curtains which had probably been bone dry. 'Och, I wanted them in and folded before tea-time—now I'll have to leave them out all night.' She wasn't pleased, but much to her relief however the clouds soon dispersed and the wind got up again. 'They might dry before then, though,' she said as we settled back, all doing our own thing.

I might tell you now, folks, that because of the earliness of the season there were no other travellers on the site, only us. As I mentioned in my other books, this site was once a P.O.W. camp. German and Italian prisoners had been held there during the war. The Nissan huts were dismantled, leaving concrete bases which made grand solid stances for caravans and our bus. Tents fared best, because they stayed dry when the weather was bad. For years the site was also used by Boy Scouts, who came annually to do their dib-dibbing.

We thought when we heard a service bus stopping at the road end and the sound of lots of male voices that the Scouts had come early that year. I wandered up to have a nosey. It certainly wasn't boys, in fact it was loads of men. I ran back to tell my sisters, who never failed to check out any talent that came into their vicinity. Shirley and Janey ran out to see about twenty Teddy Boys, decked out in their drainpipe trousers, knee-length jackets, beetle-crusher shoes and pipe-cleaner ties. They all had those classic sideburns and the slicked-back hair styles which were known as D.A.s (from duck's arse).

The moment they saw my pretty sisters they started wolf-whistling and calling them over to join them, but Mammy could whistle with more power than a group of mere wolves.

'You stupid buggers, Daddy's away and we're alone. Those laddies nae doubt will fill themselves wi' peeve. By the way, I canna see a single yin that's younger than twenty one. They're big men, far too auld for you, so bide here and no' go near them.'

Our mother's tone and instructions were meant for my four older sisters. I was far too young to bother about men—it was the midden-raking that I missed that day, and I wouldn't have minded skimming flat stones down at the river.

So that was that, back to quiet reading in the safety of the bus. We watched those Teddy Boys erecting tents and wee haps in the broom, which prompted Mammy to call them stupid scaldies. Every traveller knows that the broom is filled with insects of every description, most enjoying tasty flesh—especially the human kind. She smiled, thinking of them trying to sleep, then said, 'even if they dinnae get bit, they'll surely find a branch or twa either up their nose or their arse.'

We laughed so loud we failed to hear a knocking at the door, 'Missus, kin ye dae us a favour?' It was three of the men, one holding a knife like one that Davy Crockett might have used to skin a buffalo when out on the wild frontier.

Mona opened the door and asked what they wanted.

'We was wandering if we could use they tartan rags scattered around your bus, we need something to sleep on the night!'

Mammy ran outside and was horrified to see her lovely freshly laundered curtains thrown over the broom, and when she saw that knife it didn't take much to know who had cut the rope.

'You shit-pots, just wait until my man and sons come home, they'll knock the living daylights oot o' ye.'

'Never mind waiting on Daddy and pretending you have sons, Mammy, I'll sort them oot,' Shirley breenged at them with arms outstretched, took two off balance and put an upper-cut under the third. 'You reekit faces think you can come here and wreck ma Mammy's washing, well, think again.' By now her eyes were out on stalks as venomous curses flew from her mouth. Mona and Chrissie intervened, dragging her off them. The cowards got to their feet and ran off, saying it would be a long night. We watched as they joined their mates who were heading along the Comrie road, no doubt for a night in the nearest pub.

Suddenly something dawned on us—we were under threat. How often had danger come from strangers? More times than was comfortable to mention, but before Daddy was always with us. If the danger was menacing he just positioned himself behind the steering wheel and left, going to a safer place where there was no threat; but now he wasn't with us. Mammy, only five feet tall, had the full weight of responsibility on her narrow shoulders. Oh yes, her older girls were strong and with weapons could hold their own against the best of men, but not against drunk men. This frightening problem was taxing to say the least.

'What time does a pub chuck oot?' she asked. Her girls never went near pubs, but at least if she had an idea when they'd be back we could all be in bed, lights out and with doors and windows locked.

'Ten, most drunks are seen swaying hame after then,' Chrissie told her.

So after we'd gathered in the dirtied curtains, we quickly took some supper and then went to bed. I say bed in the singular, because all eight of us were piled onto Mammy's courie-doon at the rear of the bus. My younger sisters began to whinge, even although we pretended there was nothing wrong, so Mammy told stories and the girls sung ballads. I can still recall how nervous Chrissie's voice sounded as she sang 'Fair Rosie Ann'.

Shirley was in the middle of 'Flooers o' the Forest' when there was a deafening thud against the side of the bus, which stunned us into a shivering silence. Waiting through the next minutes, I can only describe them as some of the most terrifying in my life, it was awful. I thought I had swallowed my tongue, such was the thump in my throat, so God knows what my younger sisters, who were eight, six and four, went through. They sat staring like a bagful of kittens about to be drowned, with round innocent eyes. Shirley, fiery warrior that she was, was also afraid, but we all knew that in her case it was the dark that caused her fear, and not what lingered in its shadows. She began mumbling; Mammy touched her arm and said she had to be strong.

Mona said we should have escaped while the louts were away, but Janey said if we'd left our home it would have been torched. 'I'll sneak oot,' whispered Shirley, 'and slit each and every one o' them reekit buggers' throats.'

This remark, gruesome though it was, made us start giggling at the thought it conjured up—our sister wriggling about through the broom with a dagger clenched between teeth covered in blood and booze—a top soldier of the SAS or an ancient warrior queen.

Mammy brought us back to reality. 'Listen, Boudi-bloody-cea, so far all we've heard is some daft drunk thumping the bus. The rest o' the fear is coming frae inside this bus. Now calm doon and listen.' Our mother had spoken; Shirley sat down, slipping her hands under her shaking knees.

It may have been a minute or an hour later when cries came from the broom, drawn out as if the Teddy Boys were imitating ghost calls. 'O-o-ohh see them in the broom, the lights are coming tae get ye, watch how the lights glo-o-ow.'

We peered out of slits in the curtains to see, to our utter terror, yellow eyes staring at us. Some turned to orange, others to deep red. What was out there hiding in the broom? Were they vampires who had heard Daddy was at Kinloch Rannoch, and thought with him away we'd be easy meat?

Mammy, more concerned about our safety than our sanity, took control. 'Now, I smoke fags and I know what they look like in the dark—the same as yon ghost eyes. Don't be feared. As long as we're in here they can't get at us. Now take the seat cushions, pile them against the door and windows. Chrissie, put the carpet runner over the windscreen; if they throw stones that will stop glass hitting us.' Mammy then took a paper bag from her handbag where it lay hidden under her bed, and gave us each a peppermint. For ages the only sound to be heard was us sooking nervously on those sweeties, then Renie and Babsy began snoring, having fallen asleep, exhausted. Mona covered their shoulders with a blanket, saying their prayers for them.

Shirley asked for another sookie and said, 'if the Teddy Boys get in, yon two wee yins will be nane the wiser, the poor wee craturs are done in.'

Outside the yellow lights still shone from the broom; we could plainly see them, but there was no attempt to attack our bus despite our fears. Shirley was still ranting about taking them on single-handed, when suddenly a piercing noise rent the dark night.

'Help! For God sake, ye daft bugger! Look whit's ye've done. Get water, hurry, and get water!'

Cushions went in every direction as we clambered over each other, pulling back the curtains to see what commotion was taking place. We could hardly believe the scene—the broom was alight, it was on fire; great spirals of flames mingled with choking reek and millions of sparks. There were screams from the men darting back and forth, flames scooting from their bums as they rushed down to where they hoped they'd find the river. The threat was over: we knew that by the time those menacing Teddy Boys sorted themselves out it would be morning. So to bed we went, not the least bit afraid. In the morning there was no sign of our night tormentors. All that was left were a few empty beer bottles and several scorched broom tops.

There was no time to gloat—Mammy had a wheen of tartan curtains needing to be rewashed, but she did relent and I was allowed to visit and rake my midden. Do you know what I found? A big suede size ten beetle-crusher! Aye, only the one. Later I filled it with sand and sank it in the Earn, and as far as I know it's still there on the river's bottom.

36

JIP

I will stop now and take my dogs for a walk. Remember Brigadoon, my monster yellow Labrador with a bottomless pit for a stomach, and wee broon Jake, my twelve-year-old mongrel?

I've always loved mongrel dogs; they seem less inclined to catch diseases that thoroughbreds are prone to. Worms are got rid of by chewing grass and discarded sheep wool. Ticks don't pose problems, and if they smell a heaty bitch off they go. If they manage to find their way back, well, that's fine, but if not, then get another one. No, mongrels are, like the mangy mutt in 'Lady and the Tramp' their own masters. Take a wee while out from your day and journey back with me to the flats, because it was here I got conned into giving Jip a home.

Davie's Uncle Jimmy seldom visited us. For one thing, the stairs up to our flat were far too numerous, and for another, Jimmy only had time for cutting trees and horses. But I am not speaking here about nice old Uncle Jimmy—no, it was the tiny white puppy he brought upstairs with him, and deliberately failed to take away. I must say it had the most beautiful, cute face in the entire world, according to Johnnie and Stephen, who took it into their room to play with while I made Jimmy some tea. After he had finished it, he said he had a lot of work to do somewhere, and off he went. It took a minute to sink in that the ball of fluff my boys were frolicking with on their beds had been forgotten. I called out to Jimmy, but he didn't seem bothered, so I called again, 'Uncle, you forgot the wee dug!'

With a wave of his hand he set off down the road in his truck. Now do you ever get the feeling that you're being conned? Yes, and so did I that day. The kids were over the moon with the dog, but I knew it was cruel keeping one in a flat. 'No, that pup is going to Uncle Jimmy,' I sternly told the boys, who replied, 'Oh Mum, why? He's nae bother, we'll walk him.'

'Oh, nae doubt when he's a puppy you'll even take turns letting him share your beds, but what happens when he's older, a big dog? And that's another thing, we don't even know how much growth's in him. No, the jugal goes back, that's an end to the matter.'

The wee white ball of fluff moved his round head from side to side, and I could feel my icy heart melt. However, I had to be assertive. If I gave in now while the boys were nine and ten, what would I be like later on when they towered over me, telling me, their mother, what to do? No, I was the boss, and when I said no dog, I meant no dog!

Teatime brought the true head of the house home. I gave him that 'you better speak to your kids about a certain animal' look, as I pointed to what was belly-up at his feet.

'Hello Daddy,' they said, clambering over him with pleading eyes and whining voices, 'can we keep the dog?'

'Ye wee bisoms, I thought I said no! Now get your hands washed for tea, and if I hear another word there's a box of raspberry ice-cream staying in the fridge.'

The boys at that moment would have forfeited ice cream for the rest of their lives if I had relented.

Davie, who I must admit looked a little guilty about his Uncle's visit and the left-over dog, said, 'Jess, my wee darling, I forgot to tell you that I got the pup last time I went down to Nottingham with Uncle Jimmy.' He'd done a job woodcutting a week or two back, and at that stage the pups were too young to remove from their mother. 'Uncle Jimmy promised to bring the one I chose up with him when he came back. I was going to tell you, but I didn't think he'd bring it here until I had spoken to him. Sorry.'

'Oh well, that makes everything hunky-dory! I have a jugal plus three weans in a top-floor flat—great!' For the rest of the day I was the bogey man; avoided like a plague. However, you all know me and my mongrels, and that night before sleeping as I listened to my kids playing with the pup, I kind of decided to keep it. Next morning a tray was brought into my bedroom with a cup of hot water that slightly resembled tea, and burnt toast. I shall never forget them standing there at the foot of bed—Johnnie with a pair of pyjamas far too small for him, Stephen clutching his favourite toy, a big yellow tonka truck, and Barbara squeezing the breath from the pup. They had discussed its name while preparing my breakfast, and to this day I have no idea how or why they decided on the name Jip.

'Well, good morning Jip with snowy coat and black eyes—welcome to the Smith household. I hope your stay with us will be a dog's life.' What else could I say under such lovable pressure? He became the fourth member of our family, and the best pal of every bairn who lived in the flats. Thankfully he never grew so big as to be a problem.

Each morning before breakfast, and, I may proudly say, without protest, the boys took turns walking him. Barbara was still too young to do it, and I far too busy. I had a part-time job with Morrison's Academy, a big private boarding school in the upper area of Crieff. I was allowed to take Barbara with me until she was old enough for nursery school, which was a great help. I cleaned in Knox House, a girls' boarding-house, and since it was a school, during holidays I was able to be at home for my ever-dependent, growing family. Davie had a succession of jobs, sometimes on building sites, but when a position came up as a wood-cutter on Drummond Estate, owned by Lady Willoughby de Eresby, he jumped at the chance.

It was about Jip's ninth month when he let us know he'd a love for chasing rabbits. We had been for a drive down along the Broich Road. Davie suggested taking a walk to the river through farmer Simpson's fields. Well, the first rabbit he saw, he took after it like a hare—what a stride on him. The lads, along with their father, whooped and shouted, while Barbara and I, who had no stomach for such wildness, went down to the river to watch some mallards and visiting goosanders swimming quietly in and out of the bullrushes.

Jip the wonder dog hadn't caught his prey, but according to my menfolk he gave it a run for its life. However, although the dog seemed to have calmed down after his chase, he was still riled, and as Davie picked up speed on our road home, did Jip not spy a bunny on the verge. Before I could do a thing, he dived out of the half-open car window, hitting the gravel on the road with devastating results—half the skin on his jaw was hanging off, one eye-ball hanging by a thread. The vet's bill was so big I had to write and ask the electricity board if they'd allow me to pay the next year's account by instalments. In addition to the cost, it took a lot of nursing before Jip was fully recovered, and he had the scars to show for it.

At that time a beast with short stumpy legs and a long powerful spine was terrorising all the dogs in Crieff; he went by the outrageous name of Ganga. Many times he went for Jip, but our lad could run faster than him, apart from once when the beast gave him a terrible hammering. He tore lumps off him. We tried our best to keep the dogs apart, but one day, with his battle scars still hurting, Jip took off. I still remember neighbours screaming that Jip and Ganga were into each other for the kill. I half expected to be black-bagging our dog, and he appeared at the door with blood dripping from his white coat, but it wasn't his blood, it was Ganga's. From then on there never was another fight between the pair, just a growl and a snap.

Well, he grew through his first years, like any playful young dog, along with all the local youngsters. Whenever the lads, of whom there may have been around ten, ranging in age from nine to thirteen, took to exploring fields and hillocks around Crieff, Jip went along for adventure. They taught him to hunt rabbits, and by goodness could he chase the poor wee bunnies (so my boys excitedly informed me) from bush to burrows. He wasn't a killer, though, and I mind a time when Stephen came home, cheeks reddened, hair all over the place, bursting to tell me about his wonderful dog.

'Mum, honest, see that dug, he's the greatest wee thing. Dae you know whit he done the day?'

'Tell me, son, before these stovies go stone cold.'

'He wis chasing a rabbit, right, and me and my pal could hardly keep up wi' him, 'cause he wis going sae fast in an aroond the burrows.'

'Stephen, son, what burrows?'

'The ones roond the back o the Knock.'

Now, folks, the back of the Knock happens to be three miles from the flats, and I had told Stephen many times that was too far away. What if something went wrong? I scolded him, but in his eagerness to tell me about Jip he ignored the fact that I might ground him for disobeying me.

'Listen, Mum, this will please you. We lost sight o' the dug, right, and searched and better searched, but couldnae find him. I wis panic-struck, Mum, honest, 'cause I mind you telt us o' your wee foxy Tiny, and him getting stuck doon a burrow, and Grand-dad digging him oot, and him near deid whin he wis fund.' My son took in a great big breath, and went on 'I thought Jip might be deid, when all o' a sudden we hears this squealing, a rabbit squeal. So we ran ower tae where it wis, and ye ken this, Mum, that dug had caught a baby rabbit, but instead o' biting it and shaking it and killing it, he held it doon wi' his paw. Mum, he didnae have the heart tae kill a wee yin. Now, Mum, whit dae ye think o' that?'

I thought if my son didn't eat his stovies he'd die of hunger, and told him so. After he'd sufficiently filled his belly I told him that no dog would kill baby animals, because there was no point. No eating in them, son, I told him to his disappointment. Better to come back when the prey has grown.

Next day, while they were up Callum's Hill, another beauty spot by Crieff, the same thing happened, and when Stephen came home he was adamant that Jip did not kill baby rabbits because he hadn't the heart to. So I let him believe what he wanted to. He has always been an animal-lover, has our Stephen, but I remember a time he got it wrong.

We'll leave the Flats now and go back to Monteith Street to continue. I was coming home from work one day, when a massive black crow fell at my feet. The poor bird had obviously been stunned by flying into telephone cables above. I could see it was still breath-ing, and thought if I put it in a safe place it would recover and then fly away. So when I got home I duly laid it between two lilac trees in my garden. Stephen, on his way home from school, saw the bird in the process of stretching its wings. Now I'd reared my children never to let an animal suffer—if you think it's in serious pain then put it out of its misery. So on seeing this crow, he thought it was dying, lifted a garden gnome and killed the poor bird stone dead. I hadn't the heart to tell him the bird was recovering, and would probably have flown off.

Something that Mother Nature insists on, is 'multiplying', and always at the back of my mind was the question, when would Jip take off after that smell? Wee Tiny did it; many was the time Daddy left him to find us, rather than us trailing the streets in search of him.

He was usually sat waiting at some poor body's door for a poke at the bitch inside. So, being close to nature myself, I waited. And just as I thought, after his fourth year, the bisom's senses kicked in and he was off. My kids were beside themselves with worry, wondering if he'd been kidnapped or murdered. It didn't matter how many times I told them he would be trailing a bitch, and when he was finished he'd come home. When he did come home after his first conquest, he was bedraggled and slept for hours curled up behind the settee, avoiding my very angry foot.

It became so common, this trailing, that our boys forgot about Jip, taking their mother's attitude, which was that if he comes home, good and well, and if not, that's the way it goes. However, may I say my tinker attitude to dogs wasn't acceptable in mainstream society. It was annoying to have a pesky dog hanging around one's house. People with bitches in heat were followed by these droves of sex-starved dogs warring with each other for a sniff at their pooch, and who could blame them for objecting. Tinkers just allowed nature to take its course, and either sold pups or drowned them; there wasn't a problem. With me being a thoroughbred tinker, that's all I knew.

I can hardly bring myself to share this next escapade from Jip's life with you, but my sons insist that I do.

Lizzie lived somewhere in Crieff, with her beautiful toffee-brown boxer bitch, and boy what a cracker! Everybody spoke about this creature; dog lovers said there had never been such a gorgeous boxer bitch, and that she should be proudly shown in kennel clubs etc. Her owner mentioned that when the time was right she was going to have her sired with a boxer having a pedigree the length of a policeman's leg. One day I met a lady whilst out shopping who asked me if my dog had been sniffing about Lizzie's bitch, because there was a dog pestering her, which coincidentally was white, and if Lizzie caught this dog she said she'd shoot the devil. It seems the poor woman had every right to be annoyed, because one day, rather than leave her boxer who was coming on heat at home, she'd taken her to Perth in the car. There were several dogs of different breeds hanging around the house, so rather than have her and her neighbour's gardens trampled by slavering dogs she thought it best to keep the bitch with her. Now the distance between Crieff and Perth is seventeen miles; it's a busy road, but it does have a speed limit of fifty miles per hour. Lizzie saw something in her rear window as she made to overtake a tractor—a white dog running behind her car. She began increasing her speed, trying to shake off the animal, but it too increased its speed. Becoming more and more incensed, she pushed her foot hard on the accelerator, watching her pursuer in her rear-view mirror. At last he gave in and stopped, but that may have been because of the flashing blue lights of a police car overtaking him on the A85, on their way to apprehend a speeding motorist.

Lizzie was seeking revenge and when I opened my door to the wide-eyed, pale-faced lady, she pushed by me and gave Jip a right wallop with her umbrella. It was funny, yes, but not to that poor mongrel. From then on I walked him on a lead.

Here's another strange incident relating to our jugal.

My young sister Babsy had been visiting one night. She had her pet with her, a pedigree bitch called Goldie, a pretty-faced spaniel. Babsy warned us the dog was coming on heat, and maybe it would be better if we locked Jip in another room just in case. Well, she arrived earlier than planned, and before Jip could be put out of the way he was faced with the bitch. I was horrified, and had visions of throwing buckets of water over them to separate them, but the strangest thing happened, Jip looped his tail between his legs and began to shake, and when the wee dog sniffed him he shot under the kitchen table. Next day Babsy phoned to tell us her lovely dog had died. The vet's examination showed a large tumour.

That was another thing that made me question whether Jip was a dog, or a man whose seeds had got misplaced while Mother Nature was having an off day.

I had been baking cakes and sweet-making for a church fete. At night I heaped bags of tablet, individually tied into quarter-pounds, on a tray. I'd wrapped cakes with cling film. In the morning I boxed everything and transported it to my car, but when I did a final count it was obvious one bag of tablet and a cake had gone missing. I blamed the family, who swore blind they hadn't touched them. Days later, when I cleaned out Jip's basket, there hidden under his cushion was one quarter-pound of softened tablet and a flattened sponge cake, both still wrapped.

The last incident I'll share with you is when he came home after trailing for a week. I heard the bark and opened the door, to find he'd brought his bitch home. She was the scraggiest looking jugal ever I set eyes on, talk about a tramp; what a mangy cratur. I shooed her away, but each time I did so, he whined to get out after her, so eventually I opened the door and watched him go. It was strange that at the turning in the road he lingered, but only for a moment and then was gone. His eyes seemed to say thanks, Jess, but I'll away now.

And that was the last time I ever saw our Jip. Well, from then on we searched and searched, days followed days, but not one sighting of our bold lad did we see. We took turns following in his usual footsteps, but there was no trace. Did a gamekeeper shoot him? Did a dog warden pack him off to a dogs' home? Or did he decide himself it was time to move? Did the bitch belong to tinkers who offered him a home also? Yes, I think that might have made sense. I remember seeing a caravan out the Gilmerton way, and when I went searching for Jip they had gone.

Jip just vanished into thin air. He was six years old. Each one of us missed him in our own way, and the pain of not knowing was at times unbearable. Sometimes with the passing of time I get ideas in my head that he came with the blessings of my ancient ancestors to say, 'Look, this is how us tinkers have finished up, vanishing from our favourite haunts like a trailing dog. One day we are a healthy, happy clan, the next we are gone, no more!'

I began this book with my son crying real tears for us, the tinkers, and I shall it end it in the same way, with me shedding tears for my long-gone culture. A culture that by now you'll know has had me making a fool of my people in one chapter and then praising them the next. Like all societies we have our good and bad, our wise and mad, our sad and happy. There are class distinctions among my people as there are in all races. To quote my father: 'when people are low, they search for someone lower to make them feel better about themselves.'

Tinker, Traveller, Gypsy, we are all the same. Rome invaded and brought their slaves with them. When they came north they met more solid resistance from the Pictish warriors. Common sense suggests that a greater armoury was required, and so the early metal workers came to Scotland.

In the south of Britain, the Romans' Egyptian slaves worked with horses, leather, basket weaving, and clay. Rome withdrew and left the slaves, who I believe were at that time drawn from bedouin tribes—wanderers of the desert. They were dark-skinned people forced upon the Britain of two thousand years ago. Some called them Romanies after their masters, who incidentally marked them with ear-rings.

But generally they were looked upon as foreigners, belonging to the underclass of slaves of the Romans, those evil conquerors. This was senseless, because by the time Rome left it had been in occupation for hundreds of years. Still, long ago time changed little. You accepted Rome's calendar, its days of the week, months etc. Also its power as a mighty army, but you never offered a hand of acceptance to those wanderers who had been brought here against their will and who had spread throughout a hostile world, long, long ago. But blood mingles and intertwines. When you feel strong, that's the Viking in you. When wise, that's the Jew. When you yearn for the sun, that's the African in you. When you look in the mirror and a twinkle in your eye meets your gaze, that's the Gypsy winking back.

So if any of the tales and incidents scattered through these pages make you cry, then let them be tears of joy, because we are not gone; we are sitting beside you on a bus or a train. We lie in hospital beds and are healed by the same doctors who treat everyone. The earth will claim our limbs, and when we have climbed our mountain we will stand naked in the sun alongside you. As my sister Shirley wrote, 'Ye cannae sleep us away, we'll aye be there in the morning.'

For too long Scotland's Tinkers, Travellers and Gypsies have stood holding out a hand of friendship; please accept this offering and let us be one nation. After all, we are a mere five million in population, dwindling daily. Let's be fellow Scots and give our country a future where there are no differences, no racism, and no divides.

My friends, we have come yet again to the end of our journey, but this time I don't want to say, 'The End'. Instead I'll just part from your faithful companionship with the words, 'keep that kettle on the boil...'

abun—above
ahent—behind
ba' heid—bald person
baffies—bedroom slippers
bairnies—small children
bawbees—coins
bide—stay
birl—whirl around
bisom—rascally person
bool-moothed—posh-talking
bowdie—belly, womb, *also* shelter
braw—fine, excellent
braxy meat—meat which is dried, salted, stretched and cut into strips
braxy water—peaty water
breeks—trousers
breenge—rush, lunge
brock—cast-off wool from sheep
but-and-ben—two-roomed cottage
chat—small person
chitties—tripod
cluckie doo—woodpigeon
cornkister—bothy song
coup—rubbish dump
couthie—friendly, pleasant
cratur—creature
craw—crow
cromachs—sticks, shepherds' crooks

croupit—suffering from respiratory infection
cuddie—young fish
cuddy—horse, pony
deek—look
div—do
docken—dock (plant)
dook—dip, dive
dreich—damp, dismal
dukkering—fortune-telling
een—eyes
een-gouged—with eyes put out
face like fizz—an expression of great displeasure
fauld—sheep fold
fit—what
fly—cunning
frickit—scared
fu'—drunk
gadaboot—wandering person
gadgie—man, particularly a non-gypsy
gloamin—twilight
gourie—woman
guffy-faced—with a fat, flabby face, staring uncouthly
haar—coastal mist
habin—food
hantel—group of people
hingin'—hanging
hippit—stiff
holt—otter's lair

homer—casual job done for a friend
hoofit—hoofed
hoolit—owl
horn-moich—totally mad
jugal—dog
keeking—peering, peeking
kelpie, water kelpie—monster living in water which transforms itself into a horse to entice its victims
kye—cattle
leein—lying
loup—leap
lowy—money
manged—asked
manishi—woman
maun hae—must have
midden—rubbish-dump
moich—mad
mort—woman, girl
muckle—big
pagger—fight, hit
panny—urine
peeve—alcoholic drink
pirn—bobbin
plaidies—tartan capes
puddock—frog or toad
quine—young woman
ragie—silly, stupid
sark—shirt
scud—blow
shan—strange
skelf-like—slight, thin as a shaving
skelp—hit, beat
skitters—nervousness inducing diarrhoea

spirtle stick—stick for stirring food in a pot
spunk—spark
stappit—jammed
stookied—plastered
stotting—bouncing
swelt—swollen
tackety boots—hob-nailed boots
thrapple—throat
thronged hen—throttled hen
toories—caps
tushni—pieces of hand-made lace
wallies—false teeth
waur—worse
weans—children
whaur—where
wheen—large number, amount
yaps—individuals with too much to say for themselves
yookies—rats